DIRECTORY
OF LITERARY
MAGAZINES
1995–96

DIRECTORY OF LITERARY MAGAZINES 1995–96

Prepared in Cooperation with the
Council of Literary Magazines and Presses

Moyer Bell : Wakefield, Rhode Island & London

Published by Moyer Bell

**LIBRARY OF CONGRESS
CATALOGING-IN-PUBLICATION DATA**

Directory of literary magazines / prepared with the Council of Literary Magazines and Presses—1984—New York: The Council c1984–

v.;22cm

Annual.
Continues: CLMP literary magazine directory
ISSN 0884-6006 = Directory of literary magazines

1. Literature—Periodicals—Bibliography. 2. American periodicals—Directories. 3. Little magazines—United States—Directories. I. Council of Literary Magazines and Presses (U.S.)

Z6513.C37   85-648720
PN2   AACR 2 MARC-S

ISBN 1-55921-134-2 Pb

Printed in the United States of America
Distributed in North America by Publishers Group West, P.O. Box 8843, Emeryville, CA 94662, 800-788-3123 (in California 510-658-3453), and in Europe by Gazelle Book Services Ltd., Falcon House, Queen Square, Lancaster LA1 1RN England.

The little magazine is something I have always fostered, for without it, I myself would have been early silenced. To me it is one magazine, not several. . . . When it is in any way successful it is because it fills a need in someone's mind to keep going. When it dies, someone else takes it up in some other part of the country—quite by accident—out of a desire to get the writing down on paper.

—William Carlos Williams*

The *Directory of Literary Magazines* is compiled as a guide to the changing world of literary magazines of which Williams speaks. The literary magazine is a particularly American tradition that has provided early publishing opportunities for many of our important writers—including T.S. Eliot, E.L. Doctorow, Elizabeth Bishop, Ernest Hemingway, Ralph Ellison, Robert Lowell, Katherine Anne Porter, Raymond Carver, Richard Wright, Ezra Pound, Maxine Hong Kingston and Amiri Baraka. Through the medium of literary magazines, writers see their art in print and are given a permanent place in our culture. At the same time, readers are given an opportunity to discover new voices and talents and to experience a wide range of serious literature which is excluded from or underrepresented in the commercial marketplace.

This year's *Directory* includes nearly 600 magazines from the United States, Canada and Europe. Entries are designed to include information asked for by **readers, writers, librarians, publishers**, and others.

Entries include:

- descriptions of each magazine in the editor's own words in order to clarify for prospective **writers** the magazine's editorial directions and interests. Writers are strongly urged to research magazines before submitting work by using these entries, and most importantly, by purchasing and supporting the magazines that interest them;

---

* *The Autobiography of William Carlos Williams*, © 1951 William Carlos Williams. Reprinted by permission of New Directions Publishing Corporation.

- listings of types of material published by each magazine, subscription rates, ISSN numbers for use by **librarians** in selecting additions to their collections, and distributors for use by **bookstores** interested in increasing their magazine sections;

- advertising information for **publishers'** use, including ad rates and sizes as a complement to the activities of CLMP's Ad Program which offers advertising space in specially designed packages of literary magazines to interested publishers. For more information on ad rates and CLMP's advertising services to publishers, please contact CLMP.

The Council of Literary Magazines and Presses (CLMP) is dedicated to serving and supporting alternative publishing in the United States. As a membership service and advocacy organization, it works on behalf of literary magazines and small presses to strengthen the field from within, promote its many and varied accomplishments to the public, and provide an ongoing forum for the discussion of issues relevant to the greater literary community.

CLMP provides an array of programs and services to its member magazines and presses. The organization has also taken a leading role in field development, activities which benefit the entire field of literature (writers, readers, publishers, librarians, booksellers, literary centers), of which its members are a vital part. This work involves creating and implementing mechanisms for emerging publishers to learn from established ones; for literary publishers to collaborate with literary presenters; for the media, funders and other groups to be better informed about literary publishing and its role in America's cultural life; for research and data collection about the field to be undertaken and the results made public; for ensuring that literature has a place at the table where the politics of cultural policy are debated and decided; and ultimately for facilitating the flow of literature from the hands of writers into the hands of readers in America.

If you would like to receive further information about CLMP or becoming a member, please write us at 154 Christopher Street, Suite 3C, New York, NY 10014-2839.

DIRECTORY OF LITERARY MAGAZINES

We hope you are well-served by this edition of the *Directory of Literary Magazines*. CLMP would like to thank the staff at Moyer Bell for their dedication to this project. CLMP would also like to thank the National Endowment for the Arts and the New York State Council on the Arts for their general support, and the Andrew W. Mellon Foundation and the Lila Wallace-Reader's Digest Fund for their generous program support.

DIRECTORY OF LITERARY MAGAZINES 1995–96

KEY

NAME OF MAGAZINE
Editor(s)
Address
Telephone number

Material published
Magazine description
Recent contributors
Unsolicited Manuscripts Received/Published per Year
Reading Period
Payment to contributors
Reporting time
Copyright
First year of publication; frequency; circulation
Subscription rate; single copy price; discount for resale
Number of pages; size of magazine
Advertising rates and sizes
International Standard Serial Number
Distributors

Abbreviations

ea—each
ind—individual
inst—institutional
irreg—irregular
pp—pages
var—varies
v—volume
yr—year

All entries contain the fullest information available at date of *Directory* publication.

Index by State (see p. 284)

A

ABACUS

Peter Ganick

181 Edgemont Ave.

Elmwood, CT 06110

(203) 233-2023

Poetry.

A 12 to 20 page, newsletter format, single-author-per-issue periodical devoted to experimental and language poetry.

Clark Coolidge, Jackson Mac Low, Carla Harryman, Laura Moriarty, Joan Retallack, Leslie Scalapino.

Unsolicited Manuscripts Received/ Published per Year: 100/8.

Payment: 10 copies.

Reporting Time: variable.

Copyright held by author.

No ads

ISSN: 0886-4047

SPD, Small Press Traffic

ABIKO QUARTERLY

Laurel Sicks, Managing Editor & Publisher; Dr. Hamada, Director; Jesse Glass, Poetry Editor; D.C. Palter, Fiction Editor

8-1-8 Namiki

Abiko, Chiba 270-11 JAPAN

0471-84-7904

James Joyce Finnegans Wake papers, poetry, fiction.

AQ is primarily a James Joyce Finnegans Wake study journal, with poetry and fiction. Presently we allot ⅓ of the magazine to each category.

Burton Raffel, Skip Fox, Leo Connellan, Cid Corman.

Unsolicited Manuscripts Received/ Published per Year: varies—most mss. from contests/300 pages.

Reading Period: Sept.–Dec. 31.

Payment: 1 copy/poets, 1 /fiction; $1,000 prize money.

Reporting Time: 2 weeks.
1988; 2/year; 600
$50/4 issues; $15/ea
250 pp; B-5
Ad Rates: $200/page; $100/½
page/; $50/¼; $500/back cover
Japan Publications Trading Co.
Ltd.

Copyright held by Abraxas Press,
Inc.; reverts to author upon publication.
1968; irregular; 500
$16/4 issues; $4/ea; 40%
80 pp; 6 x 9
Ad Rates: $60/page (5 x 8);
$35/½ page (5 x 3½)
ISSN: 0361-1663

ABRAXAS

Ingrid Swanberg, Warren Woessner
2518 Gregory St.
Madison, WI 53711
(608) 238-0175
Poetry, criticism, essays, reviews,
translations, photographs,
graphics/artwork, "found" cultural artifacts. No unsolicited
manuscripts, except as announced.
Contemporary poetry: (non-
academic). Emphasis on
the lyric and experimental. Unusual graphics and "found" poems. Interested in poetry in
translation and Native American
poetry. Criticism and essays on
the contemporary scene.
César Vallejo, Ivan Argüelles,
Próspero Saíz, Andrei Codrescu,
Andrea Moorhead.
Unsolicited Manuscripts Received/
Published per Year: 3,000/20.
Payment: in copies.
Reporting Time: varies per project.

ACM (Another Chicago Maga-
zine)

Barry Silesky
3709 N. Kenmore
Chicago, IL 60613
(312) 248-7665
Poetry, fiction, reviews, essays,
interviews.
Literary, contemporary, non-
regional, socio-political outlook.
S.L. Wisenberg, Pablo Antonio
Cuadra, Ariel Dorfman, Maxine
Chernoff, Lore Segal, Sterling
Plumpp.
Reading Period: year–round.
Unsolicited Manuscripts Received/
Published per Year: 7,500/65.
Payment: $5–$25.
Reporting Time: 8 weeks.
Copyright held by magazine; re-
verts to author upon publication.
1977; 2/yr; 750
$15/ind, $15/inst; $8/ea; 40%
220 pp; 5½ x 8½
Ad Rates: $150/page (5 x 8);
$75/½ page (5 x 3⅞)

ISSN: 0272-4359
Ingram

AEGEAN REVIEW

Dino Siotis
220 West 19th St., 2A
New York, NY 10011
Modern Greek literature in translation. Works inspired by Greece by American authors.
Fiction, essays, interviews, poetry, art and photography.
Jorge Luis Borges, Lawrence Durrell, Truman Capote, Yannis Ritsos, Alice Bloom.
Payment: $25–$50.
Reporting Time: 6 weeks.
1985; 2/yr; 4,000
$10/yr ind, $18/yr inst; $5/ea; 40%
80 pp; 7½ x 10
Ad Rates: $265/page
ISSN: 0891-7213
DeBoer

AERIAL

Rod Smith
P.O. Box 25642
Washington, D.C. 20007
(202) 244-6258, 965-5200
Poetry, fiction, criticism, essays, reviews, translations, photos, graphics.
AERIAL 6/7 is devoted to John Cage & others. AERIAL #8 is a special issue on Barrett Watten. AERIAL #9 will be a special issue on Bruce Andrews.
Jessica Grim, Rachel Blau DuPlessis, Lyn Hejinian, Bob Perelman, Ron Silliman.
Unsolicited Manuscripts Received/Published per Year: 3,000/25–35.
Payment: copies.
Copyright held by magazine; we reserve the right to reprint accepted materials in anthology or other form. All other rights revert to author.
1985; irregular; 1,000
$20/2 issues; $35/3 issues inst; $7.50/ea; 6/7 $15; 40%
approx. 200 pp; 6 x 9; 6/7, 8½ x 10
Ad Rates: Contact CLMP for information.
Ubiquity, SPD, Desert Moon, Inland

AFRICAN AMERICAN REVIEW

Joe Weixlmann
Department of English
Indiana State University
Terre Haute, IN 47809
(812) 237-2968
Poetry, fiction, criticism, reviews, interviews, photographs, graphics/artwork.
Essays on African American litera-

ture, theater, film, art, music, dance, and culture; interviews; poems; fiction; book reviews; and graphics on black themes.

Amiri Baraka, Gwendolyn Brooks, Ishmael Reed, Houston A. Baker, Jr., Rita Dove, Henry Louis Gates, Jr.

Unsolicited Manuscripts Received/ Published per Year: 450/50.

Payment: depends on grants.

Reporting Time: 3 months.

Copyright held by author.

1967; 4/yr; 4,037

$24/yr ind, $48/yr inst; $10/ea; 40%

176 pp; 7 x 10

$200/page (5 x 8½); $120/½ page (5 x 4¼)

ISSN: 1062-4783

THE AFRO-HISPANIC REVIEW

Marvin Lewis & Edward Mullen

Department of Romance Languages

U Missouri: 143 Arts & Science Building

Columbia, MO 65211

(314) 882-2030

Scholarly articles, translations of Afro-Hispanic texts.

A bilingual journal of Afro-Hispanic literature and culture, publishing literary criticism, book reviews, translations, creative writing, and relevant developments in the field. Jointly published by the Department of Romance Languages and the Black Studies Program of the University of Missouri-Columbia.

William W. Megenney, E. Valerie Smith, Jerry Williams, Guillermo Bowie, Miriam DeCosta-Willis.

Unsolicited Manuscripts Received/ Published per Year: 44/15.

Payment: none.

Reporting Time: 3 months.

Copyright held by University of Missouri.

1982; 2/yr; 500

$20/yr inst; $5/ea; $1 off inst. rate

8½ x 11

No ads

ISSN: 0278-8969

Faxon, Ebsco

AGADA

Reuven Goldfarb

2020 Essex St.

Berkeley, CA 94703

(510) 848-0965

Poetry, fiction, midrash, memoir, essay, translation, and graphic.

AGADA has a specifically Jewish orientation and emphasis along with a universalist perspective and publishes work touching on traditional Jewish themes and contemporary concerns. It seeks to share the insights, memories, and vision of creative Jewish people with people everywhere. Thomas Friedmann, Yael Mesinai, Robert Stern, Shulamith Surhamer, Roger White. Unsolicited Manuscripts Received/ Published per Year: 160/20. Payment: in copies. Reporting Time: 2–3 months. Copyright reverts to author. 1981; 1yr; 1,000 $12/2 issues; $6.50/ea; 40% 64 pp; 7 x 10 ISSN: 0740-2392

AGNI

Boston University Creative Writing Program
Askold Melnyczuk, Editor
236 Bay State Rd
Boston, MA 02215

Poetry, fiction, artwork, essays.
AGNI publishes poetry and fiction, translations, commissioned essays and reviews. Our special interests are new and underappreciated writers.
Thom Gunn, Ai, Patricia Traxler, Donald Hall, John Updike, Ha Jin, Martin Espada, Robert Pinsky, Seamus Heaney, Tom Sleigh, Derek Walcott.
Reading Period: Oct. 1–April 30th.
Unsolicited Manuscripts Received/

Published per Year: 2,000/50.
Payment: $10/page up to $150.
Reporting Time: 4 months.
Copyright held by **AGNI**; reverts to author upon publication.
1972; 2/yr; 1,500
$12/yr; $7/ea; 40%
250–320 pp; 5½ x 8½
Ad Rates: $200/page (4½ x 7); $125/½ page (4½ x 3½)
ISSN: 0191-3352
DeBoer

ALABAMA LITERARY REVIEW

Theron Montgomery and Jim Davis
253 Smith Hall
Troy State University
Troy, AL 36082
(205) 670-3307
(205) 670-3519 (Fax)

Fiction, poetry, essays, photography, and short drama.
A state literary medium for local as well as national artists; supported by National Endowment for the Arts.
Eve Shelnutt, Paul Grant, Joe Colicchio, Elizabeth Dodd, F.R. Lewis, Paul Ruffin, A. Nanette Mansey, W.D. Gilardetti, Susan M. Gilbert.
Unsolicited Manuscripts Received/ Published per Year: 3,000/36.
Payment: In copies.

Reporting Time: 2 months (except
August).
1987; 2/yr; 850+
$10/yr; $4.50/ea; 40%
100 pp; 9 x 6
Ad Rates: swap equal ad or $25/8
x 5 page
ISSN: 0890-1554

Reporting Time: 3–16 weeks.
Copyright held by University of
Alaska Anchorage.
1981; 2/yr; 1,600
$8/yr ind, $10/yr inst; $5/ea; 50%
192 pp; 6 x 9
ISSN: 0737-268X
DeBoer, Fine Print

ALASKA QUARTERLY REVIEW

Ronald Spatz, Executive Editor
University of Alaska Anchorage
College of Arts & Sciences
3211 Providence Drive
Anchorage, AK 99508
(907) 786-4775 (Phone/Fax)
Fiction, poetry, short plays, cre-
ative nonfiction.
A journal devoted to contemporary
literature.
Stuart Dybek, Jerome Charyn,
Tracy Kidder, Arthur Danto,
Patricia Hampl, Susan Minot,
Alison Baker, Steve Stern, Ray-
mond Federman, Grace Paley,
Amy Hempel, Rosellen Brown,
Tobias Wolff, Jane Smiley.
Unsolicited Manuscripts Received/
Published per Year: 2,000 fic-
tion, 400 poetry, 100 other/30
fiction, 20 poetry.
Reading Period: Sept.–May 10.
Payment: in copies; other payment
depends on grants.

ALBATROSS

Richard Smyth, Richard Brobst
Box 7787
North Port, FL 34287-0787
Poetry, interviews,
graphics/artwork.
Since we see the albatross as a
metaphor for an environment
that must survive, we are primarily interested in
ecological/environmental/nature
themes, written in a narrative
style; however, this is not to say
that we do not consider other
themes and forms.
Walter Griffin, Daniel Comiskey,
Stephen Meats, Duane Locke,
Peter Meinke.
Unsolicited Manuscripts Received
/Published per Year: 300-
400/15-20.
Payment: in contributor's copies.
1986; 2/yr; 500
$5/yr ind/inst; $3/ea; 40%
32–44 pp; 5½ x 8
ISSN: 0887-4239

ALDEBARAN LITERARY MAGAZINE

Quantella Owens
Roger Williams University
1 Old Ferry Rd.
Bristol, RI 02809
(401) 253-1040

Fiction and poetry in all styles and genres.

We are an eclectic magazine that publishes both fiction and poetry in all forms, styles and topics. We accept submissions from amateurs and established writers.

Unsolicited Manuscripts Received/ Published per Year: varies per year/50-100.

Payment: 2 free copies of issue published in.

Reporting Time: 6–12 weeks normally.

Copyright reverts to authors upon publication.

1971; A or S-A; 250–300
$5/ea; $4/past issues
50–100 pp; 6 x 9 or 5½ x 8½.

Ad Rates: write to us for information.

AMBERGRIS

Mark Kissling
P.O. Box 29919
Cincinnati, OH 45229

Fiction, essays, graphics/artwork.

AMBERGRIS is dedicated to quality art and literature, and to fostering the emerging author and artist. AMBERGRIS gives special, but not exclusive consideration to works by Ohio writers and artists, and to works with Midwestern themes in general.

William Allen, Nicole Cooley, Mona Simpson.

Unsolicited Manuscripts Received/ Published per Year: 800-1000/8-10.

Reading Period: Aug.–April.

Payment: $5/published page; $50 maximum. Plus two contributor copies.

Reporting Time: 3 months for 1st round; up to 1 year for final decisions.

Copyright held by magazine; reverts to author upon publication.

1987; 1/yr; 800
$4.95/ea; 40%
160 pp; 5½ x 8½
ISSN: 1044-2006

AMELIA

Frederick A. Raborg, Jr.
329 "E" St.
Bakersfield, CA 93304
(805) 323-4064

Fiction, poetry, plays, graphics/ artwork, criticism, reviews, essays, photographs, translation.

AMELIA is a reader's magazine, intended to be enjoyed over a period of time, offering a unique blend of the traditional with the contemporary in virtually every printed art form by both "name" and unknown writers and artists of superior talents. Contributors from its pages have been included in Pushcart Prizes, The Artist Market and other prestigious reprint anthologies.
Pattiann Rogers, David Ray, Lawrence P. Spingarn, Larry Rubin, Stuart Friebert, Merrill Joan Gerber, Maxine Kumin, Matt Mulhern, Thomas F. Wilson.
Unsolicited Manuscripts Received/ Published per Year: 30,000/800+.
Payment: poetry/$2–$25; fiction/$10–$35; non-fiction/$10/1,000 words; artwork/$5–$50.
Reporting Time: 2 weeks–3 months.
Copyright held by magazine; reverts to author upon publication.
1984; 4/yr; 1,750
$25/yr ind, $25/yr inst; $7.95/ea; 40%
156 pp; 5½ x 8½
Ad Rates: $250/page (4½ x 7½); $140/½ page (4½ x 3¾); $80/¼ page (4½ x 1¾)

Rates for recognized literary magazines only. Others request rate card.
ISSN: 0743-2755

AMERICAN BOOK REVIEW
Ronald Sukenick, Rochelle Ratner, John Tytell, Editors; Don Laing, Managing Editor
English Department Publications Center
Campus Box 494
University of Colorado
Boulder, CO 80309-0494
(303) 492-8947
Criticism, essays, reviews.
AMERICAN BOOK REVIEW is offered as a guide to current books of literary interest published by the small, large, university, regional, third world, women's and other presses. It is edited and produced by writers for writers and the general public.
Hayden Carruth, Robert Creeley, Diane Wakoski, Marge Piercy, Joe McElroy, Kirkpatrick Sale, Ihab Hassan, Ishmael Reed.
Unsolicited Manuscripts Received/ Published per Year: 100/15–25.
Payment: $50 per review.
Reporting Time: 2 weeks to 2 months.
Copyright held by **ABR**; reverts to author upon publication.

1977; 6/yr; 12,000
$24/yr ind, $30/yr inst; $4/ea;
40%
32 pp; 10 x 14
Ad Rates: $425/page (10 x 14);
$260/½ page (5 x 14); $150/¼
page (5 x 7); $100/½ col (2¼ x
6¾); $60/¼ col (2¼ x 3¾);
discounts available.
Ingram, Interstate, Armadillo, LS,
Ubiquity

THE AMERICAN POETRY REVIEW

Stephen Berg, David Bonanno,
Arthur Vogelsang
1721 Walnut St.
Philadelphia, PA 19103
(215) 496-0439
Poetry, translation, criticism, re-
views, interviews, essays.
Lucille Clifton, Sam Hamill,
W.S. Merwin, Jane Miller,
Carolyn Forche.
Unsolicited Manuscripts Received/
Published per Year: 8,400/60.
Payment: $2.00/line for poetry;
$120/page for prose.
Reporting Time: 10 weeks.
Copyright held by World Poetry,
Inc.; reverts to author upon pub-
lication.
1972; 6/yr; 20,000
$15/yr ind, $15/yr inst; $3.25/ea;
50%
52 pp; 9¾ x 13¾

Ad Rates: $790/page (9¾ x 13¾);
$480/½ page (9¾ x 6¾);
$260/¼ page (4¾ x 6¾)
ISSN: 0360-3709
Eastern News

THE AMERICAN VOICE

Frederick Smock
332 W. Broadway, Suite 1215
Louisville, KY 40202
(502) 562-0045
Fiction, poetry, essays, criticism,
photographs.
THE AMERICAN VOICE pub-
lishes daring new writers and
the more radical work of estab-
lished writers. Feminist, multi-
cultural pan-American.
Isabel Allende, Maya Angelou,
Chaim Potok, Minnie Bruce
Pratt, Suzanne Gardinier.
Unsolicited Manuscripts Received/
Published per Year: 5,000/60.
Payment: varies.
Reporting Time: 4–5 weeks.
Copyright: first rights held by
magazine; reverts to author
upon publication.
1985; 3/yr; 1,500
$15/yr ind; $5/ea; 40%
130 pp
Ad Rates: swaps/$100 per page.
ISSN: 0884-4536
DeBoer.

THE AMERICAS REVIEW
(formerly **REVISTA CHICANO-RIQUEÑA**)
Lauro Flores, Evangelina Vigil-Piñon
Arte Publico Press
University of Houston
Houston, TX 77204-2090
(713) 743-2841
(800) 633-ARTE (Orders only)

Poetry, fiction, criticism, review, interviews, photographs, graphics/artwork.

THE AMERICAS REVIEW, A Review of Hispanic Literature and Art of the USA, is the oldest (20 years) and most prestigious U.S. Hispanic literary magazine. It publishes works by outstanding Hispanic writers and artists of the USA, as well as works by new and emerging writers and artists. Analysis, interviews, commentary and reviews of U.S. Hispanic works and writers.

Alba Ambert, Roberto Fernández, Virgil Suárez, Floyd Salas, Tato Laviera.

Unsolicited Manuscripts Received/Published per Year: 200/30-35.

Payment: varies.

Reporting Time: 3–4 months.

Copyright held by Arte Publico Press.

1972; 3/yr (2 + double issue); 3,000

$15/yr ind, $20/yr inst; $5/ea ($10/double issue); 40%

128 pp; 224 pp double issue; 5½ x 8½

Ad Rates: $200/page (5 x 8); $125/½ page (4 x 5); $75/¼ page (2½ x 4)

ISSN: 0360-7860

Ebsco, Ubiquity, Homing Pigeon, Armadillo

ANEMONE
Nanette Morin, Editor; Bill Griffin, Art Editor
Box 369
Chester, VT 05143

Poetry, reviews, interviews, translations, photographs, graphics/artwork, paintings.

ANEMONE is a quarterly literary arts journal publishing the expressive voice of the people. Our purpose is to help bring the spirit of man closer to his true self through art. We look for work that is different, always looking for the new voice. **ANEMONE** encourages "political" and "social" poetry.

Robert Chute, Arthur Winfield Knight, Teresa Volta, Sesshu Foster, John Oliver Simon.

Unsolicited Manuscripts Received/Published per Year: 1,600/240.

Payment: 1 year's subscription and 5 gifts.

Reporting Time: variable.

Copyright held by Anemone Press
Inc.; permission given to publish with mention.
1984; 4/yr; 3,000
$10/yr ind, $10/yr inst; $2.50/ea;
40%
32 pp; 10 x 15
Ad Rates: $200/page (10 x 15);
$100/½ page (10 x 7 or 5 x
15); $50/¼ page (5 x 7)
ISSN: 8756-7709

ANTERIOR FICTION QUAR-TERLY

Tom Bergeron
993 Allspice Ave.
Fenton, MO 63026-4901
(314) 343-1761
Short stories.
Fiction quarterly.
Lois Hayn, Rob Staggenborg,
Thomas Lynn, Salvatore Amico
Buttaci, Marian Ford Park.
Unsolicited Manuscripts Received/
Published per Year: 75/25
Reading Period: year round.
Payment: 1st place each issue
$25.00.
Reporting Time: within 2 weeks.
Copyright held by author.
1993; 4/yr; 50
$15.00/yr
20 pp; 8½ x 11
No ads
ISSN 1074-2042
Anterior Bitewing

ANTERIOR MONTHLY RE-VIEW

Tom Bergeron
993 Allspice Ave.
Fenton, MO 63026-4901
(314) 343-1761
Essays, 1st person, nostalgia.
Non-fiction monthly.
Pat Ide, J. Alvin Speers, Vivian
Bogardus, Virginia Caldwell
Gomez, Marian Ford Park.
Unsolicited Manuscripts Received/
Published per Year: 200/100
Reading Period: year round.
Payment: $5.00 to $25.00 on ac-
ceptance.
Reporting Time: within 2 weeks.
Copyright held by author.
1993; 12/yr; 50
$25.00/yr
20 pp; 8½ x 11
No ads
ISSN 1074-2034
Anerior Bitewing

ANTERIOR POETRY MONTHLY

Tom Bergeron
993 Allspice Ave.
Fenton, MO 63026-4901
(314) 343-1761
Poetry.
Poetry monthly.
Katherine Brooks, Marian Ford
Park, C. David Hay, Ruth
McDaniel.

Unsolicited Manuscripts Received/
Published per Year: 500/250
Reading Period: year round.
Payment: 1st, 2nd, 3rd, 4th, $25,
$15, $10, $5.
Reporting Time: within 2 weeks.
Copyright held by author.
1993; 12/yr; 200
$20.00/yr
20 pp
No ads
ISSN 1074-2026
Anterior Bitewing

ANTIETAM REVIEW
Ann B. Knox, Crystal Brown, &
Susanne Kass
7 W. Franklin St.
Hagerstown, MD 21740
(301) 791-3132
Poetry, fiction, photographs.
The **ANTIETAM REVIEW** is a
literary magazine for fiction
writers, poets and photographers
who are natives or residents of
Delaware, Maryland, Pennsylvania, Virginia, West Virginia, and
the District of Columbia. We
look for strong literary and artistic quality rather than local
interest. Guidelines available
with SASE.
Wayne Karlin, Joyce Kornblatt,
Amy Clampitt, Diane Wolk-
stein, Dick Scanlan, Ellyn
Bache.

Unsolicited Manuscripts Received/
Published per Year: 450–500
fiction, 1,500 poems/8-10 fiction, 18-22 poems.
Reading Period: Sept—Feb. 1.
Payment: $100 for fiction; $25 for
poems.
Reporting Time: 6 weeks–4
months depending on pub. date.
Copyright held by Washington
County Arts Council; reverts to
author upon publication.
1984; 1 or 2/yr; 1,600
$5.25/yr; $5.25/ea; 20%
60 pp; 8½ x 11
No ads

ANTIGONISH REVIEW
George Sanderson
P.O. Box 5000
St. Francis Xavier University
Antigonish, Nova Scotia B2G
2W5
CANADA
(902) 867-3962
Poetry, fiction, reviews, articles.
Literary quarterly; new and estab-
lished writers; short fiction; re-
views and light critical articles.
Michael Hulse, Sr. Bernetta
Quinn, Achy Obejas, Louis
Dudek, Omar Pound.
Reading Period: year–round.
Unsolicited Manuscripts Received/
Published per Year: 1,300-
1,500/200.

Payment: copies.

Reporting Time: poetry, 2 months; fiction, 4 months.

Copyright retained by author.

1970; 4/yr; 900

$20/yr; $7/ea; 20%

150 pp; 6 x 9

ISSN: 0003-5661

Canadian Magazine Publishers Association

ANTIOCH REVIEW

Robert S. Fogarty

P.O. Box 148

Yellow Springs, OH 45387

Poetry, fiction, criticism, essays, reviews.

ANTIOCH REVIEW is an independent quarterly of critical and creative thought which prints articles of interest to both the liberal scholar and the educated layman. Authors of articles on the arts, politics, social and cultural problems as well as short fiction and poetry find a friendly reception regardless of formal reputation.

Emile Capouya, Raymond Carver, Perri Klass, Gordon Lish, Joyce Carol Oates.

Unsolicited Manuscripts Received/ Published per Year: 3,200/25–30.

Reading Period: year–round, except poetry; (Sept.–May 14.)

Payment: $10/published page.

Reporting Time: 3–6 weeks.

Copyright reverts to author upon publication.

1941; 4/yr; 4,500

$30/yr ind; $42/yr inst; $6/sample

160 pp; 6 x 9

Ad Rates: $250/page (4½ x 7⅞); $150/½ page; $100/¼ page

ISSN: 0003-5769

Eastern News

ANTIPODES

Marian Arkin, Robert Ross

190 Sixth Ave.

Brooklyn, NY 11217

(718) 482-5680 or (718) 789-5826

Fiction, reviews, criticism, essays, poetry, interviews, photographs, graphics/artwork.

Focus is on Australian literature.

Thomas Keneally, A.D. Hope, Judith Wright, Thea Astley, Olga Masters.

Unsolicited Manuscripts Received/ Published per Year: 300/50.

Payment: in copies.

1987; 2/yr; 600

$20/yr ind, $35/yr inst; overseas $27/yr ind, $42/yr inst;

60–75 pp; 8½ x 11

Ad Rates: $300/page (7½ x 10); $175/½ page (7½ x 5 or 3½ x 10); $100/¼ page (7½ x 2½ or 3½ x 5)

APALACHEE QUARTERLY

Barbara Hamby, Lara Moody, Kim
MacQueen, Mary Jane Ryals,
Monifa Love
P.O. Box 20106
Tallahassee, FL 32316
Poetry, fiction, reviews, transla-
tion, photographs, essays,
graphics/artwork.
We are interested in well-crafted,
modern fiction and poetry. Sty-
listic innovation is encouraged.
Peter Meinke, Alfred Corn, Janet
Burroway, Steven Barthelme,
David Kirby.
Unsolicited Manuscripts Received/
Published per Year:
1,000/70–100.
Reading Period: Sept.–May.
Payment: in copies and money
when grants permit.
Reporting Time: 12 weeks.
Copyright reverts to author upon
publication.
1971; 3/yr; 500
$15/yr; $5 ea
100–200 pp; 6 x 9
Ad Rates: $50/page

APPEARANCES

Robert Witz, Joe Lewis, Bill Mut-
ter
165 West 26th St.
New York, NY 10001
(212) 675-3026
Poetry, fiction, interviews, photographs, graphics/artwork.
APPEARANCES. Literature, art,
civilization. New talent. The
works. Why wait.
Ron Kolm, j-poet, Nathaniel Bur-
kins, Max Blagg, Jack Wark,
Rodolpho Torres.
Unsolicited Manuscripts Received/
Published per Year: 150/3 or 4
to 10.
Payment: occasional.
Copyright held by magazine; reverts to author upon publication.
1976; 2/yr; 900
$15/3 issues; $5/ea; 40%
76 pp; 8½ x 11
Ad Rates: $180/page (7½ x 10);
$110/½ page (7 x 5½); $80/¼
page (3½ x 5)

ARACHNE

Susan L. Leach
162 Sturges St.
Jamestown, NY 14701
(716) 488-2601
Poetry, fiction.
ARACHNE is a small press dedicated to publishing well written
poetry with a largely, but not
exclusively, rural theme. We are
interested in new poets and in
poets who have been writing
but have not been largely published. We publish 4 contributors' issues yearly.
Gary Fincke, Penny Kemp, Nor-

bert Krapf, Walt Franklin, Wallace Whatley.
Unsolicited Manuscripts Received/ Published per Year: 1,000/85.
Payment: in copies.
Reporting Time: 1 week–2 months.
1980; 4/yr; 250
$18/yr ind, $20/yr inst; $5/ea; 40%
28 pp; 5¼ x 8¼

ARARAT
Leo Hamalian
585 Saddle River Rd.
Saddle Brook, NJ 07662
(201) 797-7600
Fiction, poetry, expository prose.
Publishes material relevant to Armenian culture or history; quality fiction and poetry.
Laura Kalpakian, Edward Alexander, James Hatch, David Kherdian, Ronald Suny, David Ignatius, Diana Der Hovanessian.
Unsolicited Manuscripts Received/ Published per Year: 70/10-15.
Payment: $50-$200
Reporting Time: 6 weeks.
Copyright reverts to author.
1960; 4/yr; 1500
$24/yr; $7/ea
72 pp; 9 x 11
Ad Rates: back inside cover
ISSN: 003-7583

ARDEN
Scott P. Burke
P.O. Box 41008
Philadelphia, PA 19127
Fiction, poetry, essays, reviews.
THE ARDEN publishes a wide range of material by new and established writers.
Lyn Lifshin, Lisa Dierbeck, Duane Locke, Tommaso.
Payment: 1 copy.
Reporting Time: 2–3 months.
Copyright held by magazine; reverts to author upon publication.
1992; 2/yr; 200
$12/yr; $6/ea
90–130 pp; 5 x 11
No ads
ISSN: 1069-0816

ARSHILE: A Magazine of the Arts
Mark Salerno
P.O. Box 3749
Los Angeles, CA 90078
Poetry, fiction, essay, art.
The bulk goes to (1) poetry; (2) fiction; (3) essays on art; (4) color covers. Inside black & white reproductions. Mix of established artists with up-and-coming.
Notley, Corbett, Sorrentino, Bronk, Creeley, Ashton.
Reading Period: November & May.

Payment: copies.
Reporting Time: 3 months.
Copyright reverts to author upon publication.
1993; 2/yr; 1,000
$18/yr; $10/ea
172 pp; 5½ x 11½
Ad Rates: $250/page (4 x 7)
ISSN: 1066-8721
DeBoer, Fine Print, Armadillo, BookPeople.

ARTFUL DODGE

Daniel Bourne
Department of English
The College of Wooster
Wooster, OH 44691
(216) 262-8353

Poetry, fiction, translation, graphics, reviews.

ARTFUL DODGE is open not just to American work combining the human and the aesthetic, but also to translation, especially from Eastern Europe and the Third World. We also have an ongoing section on American poets who translate, featuring the poet's own work and his or her adaptations of work going on in landscapes other than English.

Stuart Dybek, Naomi Shihab Nye, Jorge Luis Borges, Julia Kasdorf, Charles Simic, Jim Daniels, William Stafford, Zbigniew Herbert.
Unsolicited Manuscripts Received/ Published per Year: 2,500/60
Reading Period: year–round.
Payment: in copies, plus $5 honorarium, as funding allows.
Reporting Time: 1–4 months.
Copyright reverts to author.
1979; 2/yr; 1,000
$10/yr; $5/ea
150-200 pp; 6 x 9
ISSN: 0196-691X
DeBoer

ASCENT

Audrey Curley
P.O. Box 967
Urbana, IL 61801
Fiction, poetry.
Eclectic.
Stuart Friebert, G.E. Murray, Thomas Reiter, Marjorie Stelmach, Kathleen Wakefield.
Unsolicited Manuscripts Received/ Published per Year: 1,050/40.
Reading Period: year–round.
Payment: 3 copies.
Reporting Time: 1 week–2 months.
Copyright held by magazine; reverts to author upon publication.
1975; 3/yr; 750
$3/yr; $3/ea; 40%
64 pp; 6 x 9
ISSN: 0098-9363

ASIAN PACIFIC AMERICAN JOURNAL

Asian American Writers' Workshop; Curtis Chin, Managing Editor; Julie Koo, Soo Mee Kwon, Co-Editors
296 Elizabeth St., 2R
New York, NY 10012
(212) 228-6718

Poetry, fiction, essays.

The **APA JOURNAL** publishes prose and poetry that show the richness and variousness of Asian American and Pacific Islander Literature and experience. As a branch of the Asian American Writers Workshop, we seek to create a vibrant network that connects writers and readers of Asian American literature. We encourage both emerging and established writers.

Koon Woon, Justin Chin, Zamora Linmark, Susan Ito, Cathy Song, Russell Leong, Kimiko Hahn, Zamora Linmark, Yoji Yamaguchi, Katherine Min.

Payment: 2 complimentary issues upon publication, discounts on other copies.

Reporting Time: 2–3 months.

Copyright reverts to author upon publication.

1992; 2/yr; 1,500

$20/yr, $30/2yr $12/ea; 40%

150 pp; 5⅜ x 8⅜

Ad Rates: $150/page (4¼ x 7¼); $80/½ page (4¼ x 3⅜); $50/¼ page (2 x 3½)

Inland, Fine Print, SPD, Armadillo, DeBoer

ATOM MIND (Mother Road Publications)

Gregory Smith
P.O. Box 22068
Albuquerque, NM 87154

Poetry, short fiction, essays, artwork, photographs.

ATOM MIND, originally published in 1968–70, is a throwback to Jack Kerouac and the Beats, Steinbeck, Faulkner and Hemingway, a reflection of the original voices in American literature.

Charles Plymell, Charles Bukowski, Adrian C. Louis.

Unsolicited Manuscripts Received/Published per Year: 1,000+/120

Reading Period: year–round.

Payment: copies, occasional small cash payments.

Reporting Time: 2–4 weeks.

Copyright held by Mother Road Publications, with all rights reverting to authors.

1993; 4/yr; 800+

$16/yr; $5/ea; 40%

94 pp; 8½ x 11

Ad Rates: $80/page; $50/½ page; $30/¼ page

ISSN: 0004-704X

AURA LITERARY/ARTS REVIEW

Steve Mullen
P.O. Box 76
University Center UAB
Birmingham, AL 35294–1150
(205) 934-3354
Poetry, fiction, interviews, essay
Contemporary poetry and prose.
Experimental, traditional or
genre. Looking for work that
distinguishes itself from the
crowd yet remains successful.
Interested in artwork and docu-
mentary photography.
Payment: 2 copies.
Reporting Time: 3 months.
Copyright reverts to author.
1974; 2/yr; 500
$6/yr; $3/ea
120 pp; 6 x 9
ISSN: 0889-7433

A/B: AUTO/BIOGRAPHY STUDIES

Rebecca Hogan
English Department
University of Wisconsin
Whitewater, WI 53190
and/or
Timothy Dow Adams
English Department
University of West Virginia
Morgantown, WV 26506
Criticism, reviews, bibliographical
and newsletter information.
Purpose of magazine is to publish
essays—literary and
critical—about autobiography
and biography. Emphasis of
recent issues has been on special topics: women's autobiography, Mexican, therapeutic
(forthcoming), European, etc.
The journal serves also as a
clearinghouse for information
about convention panels, members' interests, etc.
Lynn Bloom, Janet Verner Gunn,
Richard D. Woods, G. Thomas
Couser, Silonie Smith.
Payment: none.
Copyright held by author.
1985; 4/yr; 200
$15/yr ind, $45/yr inst
70 pp; 7 x 8½
Ad Rates: $150/page (7 x 8½);
$75/½ page (7 x 4¼); $40/¼
page (3½ x 4¼)

AVEC

Cydney Chadwick
P.O. Box 1059
Penngrove, CA 94951
(707) 769-0880 Fax
Contemporary poetry, prose, &
translations.
Innovative, challenging work from
established and emerging writers. AVEC is particularly interested in translations of recent

French writing and the Russian avant–garde.

Norma Cole, Michael Davidson, Laura Moriarty, Jackson Mac Low, Michael Palmer, Claude Royet-Journoud, Leslie Scala-pino, Aleksei Parshchikov, Elizabeth Willis.

Unsolicited Manuscripts are only read in June & December: 1,000+/2 or 3.

Reporting Time: 8 weeks.

Copyright reverts to author upon publication.

1988; 2/yr

$12/yr; $8.00/ea; 40%

180 pp

Ad Rates: $200/page (7½ x 10); $100/½ page (7½ x 4¾) $75/¼ page (3¼ x 4¾)

ISSN: 0899-3750

Inland, BookPeople, SPD, Spectacular Diseases (UK)

AZOREAN EXPRESS

Art Coelho

P.O. Box 249

Timber, MT 59011

Southern Appalachian Mountains, Okie, American West, Hobo, Rural, Working Class, American Indian and Central California.

There's a focus on themes where people work with their hands; there's a celebration of life like in the poems of Sandburg and the stories of London and Gerald Haslam.

Badger Stone, C.L. Rawlins, Ann Fox Chandonnet.

Unsolicited Manuscripts Received/ Published per Year: 500/35.

Payment: in copies.

Reporting Time: 1 week.

1985; 1/yr; 500

$6.75 (post paid); 30%

80 pp; 5 ½ x 8 ½

B

B CITY

Connie Deanovich
517 North Fourth St.
DeKalb, IL 60115
(815) 758-4633
Poetry: Issue 9: Ron Silliman,
  Gloria Frym, Cydney Chadwick,
  Michael Friedman, others.
Special issues: 8–sestinas, 10th
  anniversary issues 1995.
Unsolicited Manuscripts Received/
  Published per Year: 700/2%.
Reading Period: Query.
Payment: copies.
$5/yr ind, $6/yr inst; $5/ea; 40%

THE BAFFLER

Thomas Frank
P.O. Box 378293
Chicago, IL 60637
(312) 538-3812

Essays, stories, poetry.
THE BAFFLER publishes essays,
criticism, and literature that de-
rive from its unique interpretation
of 20th century culture. The
American Mercury of the '90s.
Thomas Frank, Steve Albini, Jan-
ice Edius, Owen Hatteras.
Unsolicited Manuscripts Received/
  Published per Year: 200/5.
Reading Period: year–round.
Reporting Time: 5 months.
Copyright retained by magazine.
1988; 2/yr; 3500
$8/yr, $5/ea; 40%
136 pp, 6 x 9
Ad Rates: $175/page (6 x 8½);
  $90/½ page (6 x 4)
ISSN: 1059-9789
Ubiquity, Speedinpex, Fine Print,
  Desert Moon, Small Changes,
  Dormouse

BAKUNIN

Jordan Jones
P.O. Box 1853

Simi Valley, CA 93062-1853

Poetry, fiction, essays, reviews, artwork, drama.

BAKUNIN, a magazine for the dead Russian anarchist in all of us, seeks well-crafted and challenging writing and artwork, especially of sexual and social critique.

William Stafford, Sandra McPherson, Benjamin Saltman, Dorianne Laux, Stephen Dixon.

Unsolicited Manuscripts Received/ Published per Year: 1,000/60.

Payment: 2 copies.

Reporting Time: 2 weeks – 12 weeks.

Copyright reverts to author on publication.

1990; 1/yr; 1000

$10/yr, $12/yr foreign, $20/yr inst.; $10/ea; 40%

200 pp, 6 x 9

Ad Rates: $100/page; $50/½ page

ISSN: 1052-3154

Ubiquity, Fine Print, Armadillo

BALL MAGAZINE

Douglas M. Kimball, Editor; Jen Jarrell, Poetry Editor; Collin Coggins, Music Editor

Box 775

Northampton, MA 01061-0775

(413) 634-5687

Reviews (music, art, lit, sci-fi), fiction, nonfiction.

BALL MAGAZINE publishes all work of quality received biannually. Our format and content evolve according to what is received.

Des Lewis, Byron Coley, Matt Ernst, Lenora Rogers.

Unsolicited Manuscripts Received/ Published per Year: 500/50+.

Reading Period: year–round.

Payment: copies.

Reporting Time: 2 weeks – 2 months.

Copyright: magazine holds first rights.

1993; 2/yr; 2,000

$8/yr, $4.95/ea; 40%

80 pp, 8½ x 11

Ad Rates: $100/page; $60/½ page; $35/¼ page; $20/⅛ page; $12/classifieds

Fine Print

BAMBOO RIDGE: The Hawaii Writers' Quarterly

Eric Chock and Darrell Lum

P.O. Box 61781

Honolulu, HI 96839-1781

Poetry, fiction.

BAMBOO RIDGE has special interest in literature reflecting the multi-ethnic cultures and peoples of the Hawaiian Islands.

Juliet Kono, Wing Tek Lum, Gary Pak, Marie Hara, Frederick B. Wichman, Sylvia Watanabe,

Rodney Morales, Cathy Song, Lois-Ann Yamanaka.
Unsolicited Manuscripts Received/ Published per Year: 500-700/60-80
Payment: $25/poem; $50/short story; plus 2 copies and 1 year subscription.
Reporting Time: 3–6 months.
Copyright held by Bamboo Ridge Press; reverts to author upon publication.
1978; 4/yr; 1,000
$16/yr; $5/sample copy; 40%
120 pp; 6 x 9
Ad Rates: $120/page (5¼ x 8¼)
ISSN: 0733-0308
SPD

THE BEACON

Varies from year to year
The Beacon, SWOCC
1988 Newmark
Coos Bay, OR 97420-2956
888-2525 ext. 335

Short stories, poetry, plays, essays, line drawings and black and white photograph.
Magazine varies each year.
Public and students, local submissions only.
Unsolicited Manuscripts Received/ Published per year: varies/varies.
$4/ea
Page number and size of magazine varies with editor.

BEAT SCENE

Kevin Ring
27 Court Leet
Binley Woods
Coventry, England CV32JQ
(020) 354-3604

Beat influenced interviews, reviews, features.
SOS America onwards. Heavy emphasis on Beat generation writers such as Jack Kerouac, William Burroughs, Charles Bukowski. Interviews, features, and information magazine. Full colour covers/glossy pages.
Charles Bukowski, Allen Ginsberg, William Burroughs, Gary Snyder.
Copyright with contributors
1988; 4/yr; 8,000
$35 for 5 issues; $8/ea; all payments must be in actual US dollars—no checks please.
44 pp.
Ad Rates: $150/page; $75/½ page; $40/¼ page
Caroline International, Beat Scene

BELLES LETTRES: A Review of Books by Women

Janet Mullaney
11151 Captain's Walk Ct.
North Potomac, MD 20878
(301) 294-0278 Fax (301) 294-0023
Reviews, criticism, essays, inter-

views, personal essays, photographs, graphics/artwork.

BELLES LETTRES reviews literature by women in all genres. Our purpose is to promote and celebrate writing by women and to inform and entertain. Interviews, rediscoveries, retrospectives, theme reviews, and publishing news are regularly featured. Queries from writers are welcome.

Jewelle Gomez, Cheryl Clarke, Lynne Sharon Schwartz, Carole Maso, Deirdre Bair, Faye Moskowitz.

Unsolicited Manuscripts Received/Published per Year: 300/10.

Payment: in subscriptions, copies & honorarium, depending on grant funding.

Copyright held by magazine; reverts to author upon publication.

1985; 3/yr; 8,000

$21/yr ind, $40/yr inst; $7/ea; 40%

96 pp; 8½ x 11

Ad Rates: $500/page (7½ x 10); $500/back page (7¼ x 8½ or 8½ 7¼);

$400/⅔ page (4¾ x 10 or 7½ x 6½); $300/½ page (3½ x 10 or 7½ x 5); $200/¼ page (3½ x 5 or 7½ x 2½); $100/⅛ page (2.25 x 3.25 or 3.25 x 2.25)

ISSN: 0084-2957

Ubiquity, Small Changes, Inland, IPD, Fine Print, Anderson News

THE BELLINGHAM REVIEW

Knute Skinner, Editor

The Signpost Press Inc.

1007 Queen St.

Bellingham, WA 98226

(206) 734-9781

Poetry, fiction, reviews, plays, photographs, graphics/artwork. The focus is primarily on poetry, fiction and drama.

Leigh Mcdiarmid, Marg Wright, Peter Wild, Laure-Anne Besselaar, John Liddy.

Reading Period: Sept.–Mar. 1.

Payment: 1 year subscription.

Reporting Time: 2–3 months.

Copyright reverts to author upon publication.

1977; 2/yr; 800

$5/yr, $5.50 if agencied; $2.50/ea; 40% on 5 or more

60 pp; 5½ x 8½

Exchange ads only

ISSN: 0734-2934

BELLOWING ARK

Robert R. Ward

P.O. Box 45637

Seattle, WA 98145

(206) 545-8302

Poetry, fiction, essays, graphics/artwork, novel serializations, short autobiography, plays.

We feature work in the American Romantic tradition, i.e. editorial content is concerned with universal truths and the idea of transcending individual limitation. Content of a work is the primary consideration; form is a distant second, leading to a wryly eclectic mix, we are currently serializing our fifth novel.

Peter Russell, Susan McCaslin, Irene Culver, Muriel Karr, Harold Witt, Natalie Reciputi, Ray Mizer, Paula Milligan.

Unsolicited Manuscripts Received/ Published per Year: 4,000+/200+.

Reading Period: year–round.

Payment: 2 copies upon publication.

Copyright held by **BELLOWING ARK**; reverts to author upon request.

1984; 6/yr; 800

$15/yr ind, $15/yr inst; $3/ea; 40%; comp to libraries on request

32 pp; 11 x 16

Ad Rates: only in special circumstances.

ISSN: 0887-4115

Ubiquity, Faxon, Popular Subscription Service

THE BELOIT POETRY
JOURNAL

Marion K. Stocking
Box 154, RFD 2
Ellsworth, ME 04605

(207) 667-5598

Poetry, reviews.

We publish the best poems we receive without bias as to length, form, subject, or tradition. We especially hope to discover new voices. Occasional chapbooks; recently Afro-American, American Indian, and new Chinese poetry.

Susan Tichy, Sherman Alexie, Alice Jones, Brooks Haxton, Lola Haskins.

Unsolicited Manuscripts Received/ Published per Year: 11,000 poems (3,000 envelopes)/80 poems.

Reading Period: year–round.

Payment: 3 copies.

Reporting Time: immediately— four months.

Copyright held by magazine; reverts to author upon publication.

1950; 4/yr; 1,800

$12/yr ind, $18/yr inst; $4/ea; 20%

48 pp; 5½ x 8½

No ads

ISSN: 0005-8661

DeBoer, Fine Print, Maine Writer's and Publisher's Alliance, Ubiquity

THE BERKELEY POETRY
REVIEW

Rotating Editors
200 MLK Student Union Bldg.

University of California at Berkeley
Berkeley, CA 94720

Poetry, translation, interviews, photographs, graphics/artwork.

THE BERKELEY POETRY REVIEW is a long-standing literary journal that publishes primarily poetry. Poets should submit 4 poems maximum; we are always on the lookout for emerging writers.

Victor Hernandez Cruz, Thom Gunn, Heather McHugh, Robert Hass, Lyn Hejinian, Ishmael Reed.

Unsolicited Manuscripts Received/Published per Year: 4,000/100.

Reading Period: not in summer.

Payment: 1 copy upon publication.

Copyright held by author.

1973; 1–2/yr; 500–1,000

$10/yr ind, $12/yr inst; $10/ea; 40%

100 pp; 5 x 8

Ad Rates: $55/page (4 x 7); $30/½ page (2½ x 3½)

THE BILINGUAL REVIEW/LA REVISTA BILINGÜE

Gary D. Keller
Hispanic Research Center
Arizona State University
Box 872702
Tempe, AZ 85287-2702

(602) 965-3867

Poetry, fiction, criticism, reviews, scholarly articles.

Devoted to the linguistics and literature of bilingualism, primarily Spanish/English, in the United States. We publish creative literature by and/or about United States Hispanics, literary criticism and reviews of United States Hispanic literature. We do not publish translations.

David Rice, Judith Ortiz Cofer, Nash Candelaria, Connie Porter.

Unsolicited Manuscripts Received/Published per Year: 400/35.

Payment: in copies.

Reporting Time: 30 days.

Copyright held by magazine.

1974; 3/yr; 2,000

$18/yr ind; $30/yr inst; sample copies: $6 ind, $10 inst

96 pp; 7 x 10

Ad Rates: $200/page (5½ x 8½); $125/½ page (5½ x 4)

ISSN: 0094-5366

BLACK BEAR REVIEW

Ave Jeanne & Ron Zettlemoyer
1916 Lincoln St.
Croydon, PA 19021

Poetry, reviews, graphics, market listings, ads.

BLACK BEAR REVIEW is an international literary/fine arts magazine published twice a year. We welcome poetry that shows: knowledge of the craft, depth, and potency. Submissions should reflect a social awareness and concern. First Rights. Chapbooks considered.

A.D. Winans, Elliot Richman, Andrew Gettler, Joe Napora, Steve Levi.

Unsolicited Manuscripts Received/ Published per Year: 3,500/100.

Reading Period: year–round.

Payment: in copy.

Copyright held by magazine; reverts to author upon publication.

1984; 2/yr; 600

$10/yr ind, $12/yr inst; $5/ea; 40%

64 pp; 5½ x 8

ISSN: 8756-0666

BLACK ICE

Ronald Sukenick and Mark Amerika, Publishers

English Dept. Publications Center

Campus Box 494

Boulder, CO 80309-0494

(303) 492-8947

Fiction.

BLACK ICE publishes only fiction, with emphasis on non-traditional fiction. We intend to take risks with the fiction we publish and encourage writers to do the same.

Steve Katz, Erik Belgum, Thomas

Glynn, Harold Jaffe, Cris Mazza.

Unsolicited Manuscripts Received/ Published per Year: 350/15–20.

Payment: 2 contributors copies.

Copyright held by magazine; reverts to author upon publication.

1984; 1–2/yr; 800

$7/ea; 40%

100 pp; 5½ x 8½

Ad Rates: $150/page (5 x 8)

ISSN: 1047-515X

BLACK JACK/VALLEY GRAPEVINE

Art Coelho

P.O. Box 249

Big Timber, MT 59011

Poetry, fiction, photographs, graphics/artwork; mostly poetry and short stories.

BLACK JACK's focus is on rural America, regional writing; interests are on the the Dustbowl; Okie migration; southern Appalachia; Hoboes; American Indians; the West; American farmer and rancher. **VALLEY GRAPEVINE** focuses on anything in the San Joaquin and Sacramento Valley in Central California.

Bill Rintoul, Gerry Haslam, Wilma McDaniel, Dorothy Rose, Frank Cross.

Payment: in copies.

Reporting Time: 1 week.
Copyright held by Seven Buffa-
loes Press; reverts to author
upon publication.
1973; 1/yr; 750
$10/yr; $6.75/ea (post paid);
20%–40%
85 pp; 5¼ x 8¼

BLACK RIVER REVIEW

Deborah Glaefke Gilbert, Kaye
Coller, Editors
855 Mildred Ave.
Lorain, OH 44052-1213
(216) 244-9654 aa 1250 @
freenet.lorain.oberlin.edv.

Poetry, fiction, critical essay, book
review, b & w Art.

BRR presents contemporary writing of diverse styles and genres
aimed toward a broad audience.
We print work that exhibits
originality, craftsmanship, vivid
style, by writers both well-
known and as-yet-to-be-
discovered. More detailed
guidelines are available for
SASE. Please, no children's,
young adult, or women's magazine fiction.
B. Z Niditch, Sandra Nelson,
Ioanna-Veronika Warwick, L. E.
McCullogh, Paul Weinman,
David Mouat, Alysice K. Har-
pootean.
Unsolicited Manuscripts Received/

Published per Year: 1,000+/65+.
Reading Period: Jan.–May. Those
received any other time are returned unread. No response
without SASE.
Payment: in copies.
Reporting Time: 2 weeks–6
months.
Copyright reverts to author upon
publication.
1985; 1/yr; 400
$4/ea
60 pp; 8½ x 11
Ad Rates: query

THE BLACK SCHOLAR

Robert Chrisman, Editor-in-Chief:
Robert L. Allen, Senior Editor
P.O. Box 2869
Oakland, CA 94609
(510) 547-6633

Poetry, fiction, sociology, politics,
economy, education, book reviews.

A journal of black studies and re-
search, addressing such issues
as black culture, black politics,
black education, economics,
Southern Africa, etc. . . . A
journal on the cutting edge of
contemporary black thought.
Jesse Jackson, Jayne Cortez,
Johnnotta B. Cole, Gwendolyn
Brooks, Haki R. Madhubuti,
P.P. Sarduy
Unsolicited Manuscripts Received/

Published per Year:
100–150/8–10.
Payment: subscription plus 10
copies.
Reporting Time: 2 months.
Copyright held by Black World
Foundation.
1969; 4/yr; 10,000
$30/ind, $50/inst; $6/ea;
20%–40%
64 pp; 7 x 10
$1,000/page; $600/½ page; query
ISSN: 0006-4246
L-S Dist., DeBoer

BLACK WARRIOR REVIEW

Mark S. Drew
P.O. Box 2936
Tuscaloosa, AL 35486-2936
(205) 348-4518
Poetry, fiction, essays, reviews,
translations, interviews.
The **BLACK WARRIOR RE-
VIEW** publishes the best of
contemporary writing by the
best of contemporary writers.
Andre Dubus, Michael S. Harper,
John Ashbery, Jorie Graham,
Jane Miller, David Wojahn.
Unsolicited Manuscripts Received/
Published per Year: 20,000/100.
Reading Period: year–round.
Payment: $5–10/page.
Reporting Time: 1–3 months.
Copyright held by magazine; re-
verts to author upon publication.

1974; 2/yr; 1,800
$11/yr ind, $17/yr inst; $6/ea
180 pp; 6 x 9
Ad Rates: $150/page (5 x 8);
$85/½ page (5 x 3½)
ISSN: 0193-6301

THE BLOOMSBURY REVIEW

Tom Auer, Publisher;
Marilyn Auer, Assoc. Publisher
1028 Bannock St.
Denver, CO 80204
(303) 892-0620;
Fax (303) 892-5620
Reviews, graphics/artwork, poetry,
interviews, photographs, essays.
THE BLOOMSBURY REVIEW
is a "Book Magazine" that in-
cludes reviews, interviews, es-
says, poetry, profiles, and pre-
views of new titles, with an
emphasis on new titles from
small, medium-sized, and uni-
versity presses.
Harlan Ellison, Gregory Mc-
Namee, John Nichols, Linda
Hogan, Peter Wild.
Unsolicited Manuscripts Received/
Published per Year: 1,000/100.
Reading Period: year–round.
Payment: $15/review; $10/poetry;
$20/interviews.
Reporting Time: 4–6 weeks.
Copyright reverts to author.
1980; 6/yr; 50,000

$16/yr; $3/ea; 40%; less discount through distributors.

32 pp; 11¼ x 16

Ad Rates: $3,150/page (9⅞ x 15¼); $1,680/½ page (9⅞ x 7½); $890/¼ page (4⅞ x 7½ or 2⁵⁄₁₆ x 15¼ or 9⅞ x 3⅝)

ISSN: 0276-1564

BLUE UNICORN

Ruth G. Iodice, Harold Witt, Daniel J. Langton, Editors; Robert L. Bradley, Art Editor; Fred Ostrander, Contest Chairperson

22 Avon Rd.

Kensington, CA 94707

(510) 526-8439

Poetry, translation, artwork.

We are looking for excellence of the individual poetic voice, whether that voice comes through in form or free verse, rhyme or not. We want originality of image, thought and music, poems which are memorable and communicative. We publish both well-known poets and unknowns who deserve to be known better.

John Ciardi, Charles Edward Eaton, Emilie Glen, Diana O'Hehir, William Stafford.

Unsolicited Manuscripts Received/ Published per Year: 35,000/100.

Payment: in copies.

Reporting Time: 3–4 months.

Copyright held by magazine; re-

verts to author upon publication.

1977; 3/yr; 500

$14/yr, $18/yr foreign; $5/ea

56 pp; 5½ x 8½

ISSN: 0197-7016

BLUELINE

Anthony Tyler

English Dept.

SUNY

Potsdam, NY 13676

Poetry, fiction, essays, reviews, graphics/artwork, oral history, journals.

BLUELINE is dedicated to prose and poetry about the Adirondacks and other regions similar in geography and spirit. We are interested in historic and contemporary writing, from new and established writers, that interprets the region as well as describes it.

Eric Ormsby, Robert Morgan, Annie David, Joan Conner.

Unsolicited Manuscripts Received/ Published per Year: 130/31. Previously unpublished mss. need SASE for response.

Reading Period: Sept.–Nov.

Payment: in copies.

Reporting Time: 2–10 weeks.

Copyright held by magazine; reverts to author upon publication.

1993; 300

$6/yr; $6/ea; $4

100 pp; 6 x 9
ISSN: 0198-9901

BOGG

John Elsberg, George Cairncross
422 North Cleveland
Arlington, VA 22201

Poetry, prose poems, criticism, essays, reviews, interviews, graphics/artwork.

Editing is a subjective affair, and we print what takes our fancy. **BOGG** is an Anglo-American literary journal, with contributions from the U.S., Canada, England, Australia/New Zealand and India.

Ann Menebroker, Ron Androla, Harold Witt, Robert Peters, John Millett, Tina Fulker, Richard Peabody, Jon Silkin, Laurel Speer, Charles Plymell, A.D. Winans, Charles Bukowski.

Unsolicited Manuscripts Received/ Published per Year: 10,000 poems/100-150 US poems; 3-6 prose pieces; 2-3 interviews; 3-6 essays.

Payment: in copies.
Reporting Time: immediately.
Copyright held by author.
1968; 2–3/yr; 800
$12/3 issues; $4.50/ea;
   $3.50/sample; 40%
64 pp; 6 x 9
ISSN: 0882-648X

BOHEMIAN CHRONICLE

Emily W. Skinner, Ellen M. Williams
P.O. Box 387
Largo, Fl 34649-0387

Fiction, nonfiction, essays, poetry, humor.

An international newsletter/magazine promoting sensitivity in the arts, **BOHEMIAN CHRONICLE'S** primary focus is to extend an arm to communities worldwide whose voices have been quelled.

Reading Period: Dec.–Sept.
Payment: $5.00 per article; $5.00 per art used.
Reporting Time: 2 months.
Copyright: each issue is copyrighted as a whole (magazine buys first rights; SASE for guidelines.)
1991; 12/yr; 500+
$12/U.S. ea; $15/outside U.S. ea; $1/ea
12 pp; 8½ x 5½
Noncommercial. We depend on subscriptions and the sale of sample issues for our revenues.

BOMB MAGAZINE

Betsy Sussler
594 Broadway
Suite 1002A
New York, NY 10012
(212) 431-3943

Interviews, poetry, fiction, photographs, art.

BOMB MAGAZINE is a spokespiece for new art, fiction, theater and film in New York. Named after Wyndham Lewis's "Blast," it promotes and encourages intergenerational, interdisciplinary and intercultural dialogue.

Thulani Davis, Jessica Hagedorn, Gary Indiana, Roland Legiareli-Laura, Patrick McGrath, Caryl Phillips, Lynne Tillman.

Unsolicited Manuscripts Received/ Published per Year: 2,000/4.

Payment: $100.

Copyright reverts to author.

1981; 4/yr; 8,500

$18/yr; $4/ea; 40%

100 pp; 10 x 14½

Ad Rates: available on request

BOOKENDS

Chet Hagan

P. O. Box 227

Warnersville, PA 19565

(610) 678-6480

Book Review Editor:

Harry L. Eshleman

323 S. Whiteoak St.

Kutztown, PA 19530

(610) 683-5508

Library news (locally & statewide); book reviews aimed at the local market—Reading & Berks County.

Published six times a year, **BOOKENDS** is totally financed by the Friends of the Reading-Berks (PA) Public Libraries. All writing is volunteered.

John Updike, James L. Holton, Christopher Hinz, Lloyd Arthur Eshbach, Chet Hagan.

Payment: none; all volunteer contributions.

Copyright: authors, if they wish, copyright own material. the magazine is not copyright per se.

1981; 6/yr; 2,000

16+ pp; 8½ x 11

ISSN: 0893-6471.

THE BOOKPRESS

Ben Goodman

DeWitt Building

215 N. Cayuga St.

Ithaca, NY 14850

(607) 277-2254

Fax (607) 275-9221

Articles, interviews, reviews, fiction, poetry, art, photographs.

THE BOOKPRESS is a monthly cultural newspaper dedicated to promoting the discussion and exchange of ideas and opinions concerning the literary and visual arts.

Ann Druyan, Gunilla Feigenbaum,

Michael Serino, Mark Schechner, Paul West.
Unsolicited Manuscripts Received/ Published per Year: 20/3. Reading Period: Aug.–May.
Payment: varies.
Reporting Time: 1 month.
Copyright: Bookpress, Inc.
1991; 8/yr; 15,000
$10/yr
20 pp; 11 x 17
Ad Rates: $720/full page (11 x 17), $600/¾ pg, $440/½ pg, $330/⅜ pg, $240/¼pg, $180/³⁄₁₆ pg, $130/⅛pg, $70/¹⁄₁₆ pg.

BORDERLANDS: Texas Poetry Review

Editors rotate from among our permanent board members
P. O. Box 49818
Austin, TX 78765
(512) 444-7320
Original poetry, short reviews, essays on contemporary poetry.
BORDERLANDS publishes outward—looking, accessible poems on society, environment, history, other cultures, landscape, or spiritual life; and essays setting contemporary poetry in some large context, often social or political.
Stephen Dobyns, Ted Kooser, David Romtvedt, Elizabeth Socolow, Naomi Nye, William

Stafford, Laurel Speer, Walt McDonald, Patianne Rogers.
Unsolicited Manuscripts Received/ Published per Year: 2,000/200.
Payment: 1 copy.
Reporting Time: 3–4 months.
Copyright: 1st North American Rights only.
1992; 2/yr; 500
14/yr ind, $16/yr inst; $8.50/ea; 50%
100 pp; 5½ x 8½
Ad Rates: no ads at present; may trade ads later with other literary journals.
ISSN: 1065-0342
Fine Print, Ebsco

BOSTON LITERARY REVIEW (BLUR)

Gloria Mindock
Box 357
W. Somerville, MA 02144
(617) 625-6087
Poetry, short fiction (under 3,000 words).
We seek work that pushes form or content, and that has a unique, even idiosyncratic voice. 5–10 poems are welcome, as we prefer to publish several poems by each author.
Eric Pankey, David Ray, Stuart Freibert, Richard Kostelanetz.
Unsolicited Manuscripts Received/ Published per Year: 2,500/35.

Payment: 2 copies.
Reporting Time: 2–4 weeks.
Copyright reverts to author upon
  publication.
1984; 2/yr; 500
$9/yr; $5/ea
24 pp; 5½ x 13

40–48 pp; 11⅜ x 14½
Ad Rates: $800/page (10 x 14);
  $550/½ page (10 x 6¾);
  $250/¼ page (4¾ x 6¾)
ISSN: 0734-2306
Interstate, Ingram, Total

BOSTON REVIEW

Josh Cohen, Editor
33 Harrison Ave.
Boston, MA 02111
(617) 350-5353

THE BOSTON REVIEW is an
  award-winning national magazine with the distinctive voice
  of Boston—unconventional coverage of politics, culture, and all
  the arts. Meet the next generation of gifted young writers
  alongside established authors
  saying what's really on their
  minds. People like Ralph Nader,
  Henry Louis Gates, Jr., Sharon
  Olds, Sven Birkerts, bell hooks,
  Michael Dorris, Robert Pinsky.
Unsolicited Manuscripts Received/
  Published per Year: 1,000/40.
Payment: $40–$250/depending on
  length and author.
Copyright held by Boston Critic,
  Inc.; reverts to author upon publication.
1975; 6/yr; 20,000
$15/yr ind, $18/yr inst

BOTTOMFISH

Robert Scott
DeAnza College
21250 Stevens Creek Blvd.
Cupertino, CA 95014
(408) 864-8538 or 864-8547

Poetry, fiction.

BOTTOMFISH accepts lyric poems and short fiction of 5,000
  words or less. We publish some
  experimental fiction. We are
  interested only in carefully
  crafted work.
Naomi Clark, Janice Dabney, William Dickey, Edward Klein-
  schmidt, Martin Nakell.
Unsolicited Manuscripts Received/
  Published per Year: 500-
  1,000/30 poems, 6 stories.
Reading Period: year–round.
We read all year but yearly deadline is February 1; we go to
  press middle of March.
Payment: in copies.
Copyright held by magazine; reverts to author upon publication.
1975; 1/yr; 500
$4/ea; 40%

70–80 pp; 17.5 x 21 cm.
No ads

BOULEVARD

Richard Burgin, Editor
P. O. Box 30386
Philadelphia, PA 19103
(215) 568-7062

Poetry, fiction, criticism, essays,
translations, interviews, photos,
graphics.

BOULEVARD publishes excep-
tional fiction and poetry and
essays by impressive new talent
as well as established literary
voices. The editors believe a
critical dimension is essential to
an outstanding literary publication; thus, each issue publishes
essays on literature and the
other arts. **BOULEVARD** believes in the school of talent.

John Ashbery, John Barth, Joyce
Carol Oates, Alice Adams, John
Updike.

Unsolicited Manuscripts Received/
Published per Year: 6,000+/75.

Reading Period: Oct.–May.

Payment: $25–250+/poetry;
$50–250+/fiction & other prose.

Copyright held by Opojaz Inc. for
First North American Serial
Rights; reverts to author upon
publication.

1986; 3/yr; 3,000

$12/yr ind, $20/2yrs, $25/3 yrs;
$7/yr inst; $6/ea. 40%
200+ pp
Ad Rates: $150/pg, $100/½ pg
ISSN: 0885-9337
DeBoer, Ingram, Ubiquity

BOUNDARY 2

William V. Spanos
SUNY/Binghamton
Binghamton, NY 13901
(607) 798-2743

Poetry, fiction, criticism, essays,
plays, translation, interviews,
photographs, graphics/artwork.

BOUNDARY 2 publishes poetry,
fiction and literary criticism that
try to break out of the impasse
that traditional, including modernist, literature and literary
criticism have become stalled
in. We are especially interested
in providing a forum for experi-
ments in open forms that ultimately interrogate the literary
tradition and the dominant culture this tradition supports.

Armand Schwerner, Jerome Rothenberg, John Taggart, Charles
Bernstein and the
l=a=n=g=u=a=g=e poets.

Payment: none.
Reporting Time: 4–6 months.
1972; 3/yr; 1,000
$15/yr ind, $13/yr students; $25/yr
inst; $8/ea; 40%

300 pp; 9 x 5¾

Ad Rates: $100/page; $50/½ page; $25/¼ page

THE BRIDGE: a journal of fiction & poetry.

Jack Zucker; Helen Zucker, Fiction Editor; Mitzi Alvin, Poetry Editor; Marion Meilgaard, Associate Fiction Editor; Lorene Erickson, Managing Editor.

14050 Vernon St.

Oak Park, MI 48237

(313) 547-6823

Fiction, poetry, reviews (1–2).

Eclectic collection of 48% fiction, 48% poetry, 4% reviews, etc. Our writers run from national to new. We devote about 10% of each issue to Michigan writers.

Grace Bauer, X. J. Kennedy, Ruth Whitman, Daniel Hughes, Barbara Greenberg.

Unsolicited Manuscripts Received/ Published per Year: 1,000+/80.

Reading Period: year–round.

Payment: none.

Reporting Time: 3–4 months.

Copyright: first rights only.

1990; 2/yr; 700

$10/yr; $5/ea; $15/2yr; 40%

192 pp; 5½ x 8

Ad Rates: $45/page

ISSN: 1052-1569

BRIEF

Jim Hydock

P.O. Box 33

Canyon, CA 94516

(415) 376-5509

Poetry, fiction, post-modern fiction/poetry.

Subscription only. Sold in select bookstores.

Larry Eigner, Fielding Dawson, August Kleinzahler, Anselm Hollo, Martha King.

Payment: none.

Reporting Time: 2–4 weeks.

Copyright held by magazine; reverts to author upon publication.

1988; 3/yr; 250

$10/yr ind, $12/yr inst; $2.50/ea; 40%

25 pp; 5½ x 8½

No ads

THE BROOKLYN REVIEW

2308 Boylan Hall, Brooklyn College

Brooklyn, NY 11210

(718) 951-5195

Short fiction, poetry.

An annual magazine featuring established writers, while also publishing dynamic emerging voices in both fiction and poetry.

Allen Ginsberg, John Ashbery, Amy Gerstler.

Unsolicited Manuscripts Received/

Published per Year: about 5%.
Reading Period: Sept.–Nov. 15.
Payment: 2 copies.
Reporting Time: 6–10 weeks.
1974; 1/yr; 500
$5/ea
120 pp; digest-sized
No ads.

BRÚJULA/COMPASS

Isaac Goldemberg
Latin American Writers Institute
Hostos Community College
500 Grand Concourse,
Bronx, NY 10451
(718) 518-4195
Devoted to Latino Literature in the
U.S. Bilingual (Spanish & English). Publishes fiction, poetry,
reviews, personal essays, literary criticism, interviews & information on grants, calls for
manuscripts, residencies, other
magazines, opportunities for
publication, literary contests for
Latino writers.
Julia Alvarez, Luis Rafael
Sánchez, Iván Silén, Ilán Sta-
vans, Magali Alabau, Julio Or-
tega, Judith Ortiz Coffer.
Unsolicited Manuscripts Received/
Published per Year: 300/120.
Reading Period: year–round.
Payment: in-kind.
1987; 4/yr; 5,000
$20/yr; $4/ea

32 to 40 pp; tabloid
Ad Rates: $400/page; $250/½
page; $150/¼ page; $100/⅛
page; $75/¹⁄₁₆ page

BRUSSELS SPROUT

Francine Porad
P.O. Box 1551
Mercer Island, WA 98040
(206) 232-3239
Haiku Poetry, senryu, renku,
tanka, book reviews dealing
with haiku, graphics/artwork.
A journal of contemporary English
language haiku and art, with
international contributors and
subscribers. Seeking haiku and
senryu in a variety of styles and
forms, from one to four lines;
tanka, five lines. Subject matter
is open. BRUSSELS SPROUT
looks for haiku that capture
"the haiku moment" in a fresh
way.
H. F. Noyes, Marlene Mountain,
George Swede, Paul O. Williams, Elizabeth St. Jacques,
Yvonne Hardenbrock.
Unsolicited Manuscripts Received/
Published per Year: 6,000/600.
Reading Period: year–round.
Payment: none, 3–$10 editor's
awards.
Reporting Time: 3 weeks.
Copyright reverts to author upon
publication.

1980; 3/yr; 300
$16/yr domestic/Canada, $21 elsewhere; $5.50/ea, $7/ea elsewhere.
48 pp; 8½ x 5½
ISSN: 0897-7356

BUTTON
Sally Cragin
Box 876
Lunenburg, MA 01462
Poetry, fiction, sheet music, recipes, interviews, celebrity facts.
New England's tiniest quarterly of real poetry, convincing fiction and gracious living, with a readership aged 9 to 93 spanning the continent.

David Barber, William Corbett, Gary Leib, Romayne Dawnay, Birdsongs of the Mesozoic.
Unsolicited Manuscripts Received/Published per Year: 150/10–15.
Reading Period: year–round.
Payment: none, 2 one-year subscriptions; everlasting gratitude.
Reporting Time: 6–8 weeks.
Copyright reverts to author after publication.
1993; 4/yr; 800
$5/$10/yr (deluxe subscription includes objet d'art), $1.00/ea; 40%.
27 pp; 4 x 5
Thimble

C

CAFE MAGAZINE

c/o City Books
1111 East Carson St.
Pittsburgh, PA 15203
attn: Frank Carroll

CAFE SOLO

Glenna Luschei
Box 2814
Atascadero, CA 93422
(805) 243-1058

Poetry, criticism, essays, reviews,
translation, photographs,
graphics/artwork and letters to
the editor.

We seek excellence and the avant-
garde: Subconscious navigation
in strange waters and Columbus
sighting land. We print new
writers next to known ones. We
emphasize poetry, but encourage
imaginative essays and new literary art forms.

Robert Bly, Denise Levertov, Ai,
Gene Frumkin, Gary Snyder,
Lawrence Ferlinghetti, Thomas
McGrath, Brenda Hillman,
David Oliveria, and Ioanna
Carlson.

Unsolicited Manuscripts Received/
Published per year: 3000/50.

Reading Period: Oct.–Feb.

Payment: in copies.

Reporting Time: 8 weeks.

Please do not submit until you
have ordered a sample copy.

Copyright held by Solo Press.

1969; 3/yr; 500

$20/yr; $5/ea; 40%

44 pp; 8½ x 11

ISSN: 0773-1796

CALIBAN

Lawrence R. Smith
P. O. Box 561
Laguna Beach, CA 92652

(714) 497-7437

Poetry, fiction, translation, interviews, graphics/artwork.

CALIBAN has redefined the literary and artistic avant-garde by cutting across partisan lines, making different writers and artists in serious pursuit of the new aware of each other. CALIBAN also insists that the avant-garde is not the exclusive domain of white, middle-class males, bohemian or otherwise.

Berssenbrugge, Vizenor, Komunyakaa, Kingston, Wakoski.

Unsolicited Manuscripts Received/Published per Year: 2,000/20.

Payment: $15–$20, plus 2 copies.

Reporting Time: 1–2 months.

Copyright held by magazine; reverts to author upon publication.

1986; 2/yr; 1,700

$14/yr; $26/2 yr ind; $24/yr inst; $8/ea; 40%, 25% textbook orders

192 pp; 6 x 9

Ad Rates: $100/page (5 x 8)

ISSN: 0890-7269

DeBoer, BookPeople, SPD

CALLALOO

Charles H. Rowell
Department of English
Wilson Hall
University of Virginia
Charlottesville, VA 22903

(804) 924-6616

Poetry, fiction, criticism, essays, reviews, plays, translation, photographs, graphics/artwork.

CALLALOO is a quarterly journal which features the arts and literature of Africans, and Africans in the Diaspora, (the United States, the Caribbean, Latin America, Europe, Canada, and Southeast Asia & Australia). CALLALOO now also features a special section, "Cultural Criticism," which presents challenging essays by critics and theorists on all topics and areas of cultural interest.

Rita Dove, John Edgar Wideman, Maryse Condé, Judith Ortiz Cofer, Derek Walcott, K. Anthony Appiah, Caryl Phillips, Audre Lorde, Yusef Komunyakaa. Recent issues focused on Haitian arts and literature, Puerto-Rican women writers, Post Colonial discourse, and native American writers, Guyanese-British writer Wilson Harris, and the playwright George C. Wolfe.

Payment: (When grants are available from NEA.)

Copyright registered under Callaloo by Johns Hopkins University Press; transferable to author; previous copyrights with notification.

1976; 4/yr; 1400

$27/yr, $54/yr inst; $8.50/ea ind, Foreign subs. add $7 + 7% GST Canada; +$7 Mexico; $17 all other countries.

256 pp; 7 x 10

Ad Rates: $225/page (5½ x 8); $155/½ page (5½ x 4); cover 3/$250

ISSN: 0161-2496

CALLIOPE

Martha Christina

Creative Writing Program

Roger Williams University

Bristol, RI 02809

(401) 254-3217

Poetry, fiction.

Interested in both established and emerging writers, but need not have published elsewhere. Prefer concrete to abstract images, work that appeals to the emotions through the senses.

Thomas Lux, Mark Doty, Mark Cox, Lynne deCourcy, Tim Seibles, Allison Joseph.

Unsolicited Manuscripts Received/ Published per Year: about 2,000/about 50.

Reading Period: Aug. 15–Oct. 15; Jan. 15–Mar. 15.

Payment: 2 copies and subscription.

Copyright held by magazine; reverts to author upon publication.

1977; 2/yr; 450

$5/yr; $3/ea; 40%

5½ x 8½

CALYX: A Journal of Art and Literature by Women

Margarita Donnelly, Bev McFarland, Micki Reaman, Co-Managing Editors; & collective members

P.O. Box B

Corvallis, OR 97339

(503) 753-9384; Fax (503) 753-0515

Poetry, fiction, essays, translations, reviews, photographs, visual art, interviews.

Considered one of the finest literary magazines in the U.S., CA-LYX publishes work by women and presents a wide spectrum of women's experience. CALYX is committed to publishing work by women of color, working class women, lesbians, politically active women, and older women. Recipient of the 1993 & 1994 American Literary Magazines Awards. Recipient of the 1994 OSU Friends of the Library inaugural Achievement Award, & the U of O Oregon Women of Achievement Award.

Haunani-Kay Trask, Kathleen Crown, Jana Harris, Mallikā Seugputa, Shauna Singh Baldwin, & Sarah Sarai.

Unsolicited Manuscripts Received/
Published per Year:
3,500–8,000/75–100.
Reading Period: Oct. 1–Nov. 15;
Mar. 1–Apr. 15.
Payment: in copies & subscription
& small cash payments.
Reporting Time: 3–6 months.
Copyright reverts to authors at
publication.
1976; 3/volume (2/yr); 5,000
$18/yr ind, $22.50/yr inst, $30/yr
Canadian, $36/yr foreign; $8/ea
+ postage; 30%–40%
128+pp.
Ad Rates: $550/page (5¾ x 7);
$285/½ page (5¾ x 3⅜)
ISSN: 0147-1627
Small Changes, Inland, Book-
People, Fine Print, Ingram,
SPD, Airlift, Armadillo

ture a single photographer each
issue.
Laurel Speer, Laurie Taylor, Martin Robbins, Charles A. Wauga-
man.
Unsolicited Manuscripts Received/
Published per Year: 2,500/100.
Reading Period: Aug.–Apr.
Payment: each issue we award
$200 for the best poem and
$100 for the photography. All
contributors are paid in copies.
Reporting Time: 1–4 months.
Copyright held by magazine; reprint rights granted upon request
provided reprint credit is given
to the magazine.
1964; 2/yr; 700
$7/yr; $5/ea; 40%
64 pp; 5½ x 8½
ISSN: 0146-2199

THE CAPE ROCK

Harvey Hecht
English Department
Southeast Missouri State University
Cape Girardeau, MO 63701
(314) 651-2636
Poetry, photographs.
We have no restrictions on subjects or forms. Our criterion for
selection is the quality of the
work rather than the bibliography of the authors. We prefer
poems under 70 lines. We fea-

CAPRICE

James Mechem, Lynne Savitt
229 N. Fountain St.
Wichita, KS 67208-3833
(316) 683-8728
Fiction, poetry, movie reviews
Non-academic women writers,
mostly.
Ai, Sibyl James, Marge Piercy,
Ursule Molinaro, Toi Derricotte,
Lola Haskins, Alma Luz Villan-
ueva, Alicia Ostriker, Kelly
Cherry, Nikki Giovanni, Jodi
Braxton.

Unsolicited Manuscripts Received/
Published per Year: 30/8.
Reporting Time: 3 months.
1987; 12/yr
$50/yr; $5/ea
60 pp; 7 x 8 ½

THE CARIBBEAN WRITER

Erika J. Waters
University of the Virgin Islands
RR 02, Box 10,000 Kingshill
St. Croix, VI 00850
(809) 692-4152
Fax (809) 692-4152

Poetry, fiction, reviews, graphics/
artwork.

THE CARIBBEAN WRITER is
an international magazine with a
Caribbean focus. The Caribbean
should be central to the work,
or the work should reflect a
Caribbean heritage, experience,
or perspective.

Opal Palmer Adisa, Julia Alvarez,
Kamau Brathwaite, Olive Senior, Derek Walcott.

Unsolicited Manuscripts Received/
Published per Year: 600/50.

Annual deadline: Sept. 30.

Payment: 2 copies.

Copyright held by Research Publications Center; reverts to author
upon publication.

1987; 1/yr; 1,500
$9/ea; 30%
150–200 pp; 6 x 9

Ad Rates: $250/page (6 x 9);
$150/½ page; $100/¼ page
ISSN: 0893-1550

THE CAROLINA QUAR-TERLY

Amber Vogel
Greenlaw Hall CB #3520
University of North Carolina at
Chapel Hill
Chapel Hill, NC 27599-3520
(919) 962-0244

Poetry, fiction, reviews, nonfiction.

A literary journal published three
times yearly.

Barry Hannah, Denise Levertov,
Mark Doty, Stephen Dunn.

Unsolicited Manuscripts Received/
Published per Year: 4,000/60-
80.

Reading Period: year–round.

Reporting Time: 2–4 months.

First-publication rights (held by
magazine).

1948; 3/yr; 1,500
$10/yr ind, $12/yr inst; $5/ea
80 pp; 6 x 9
Ad Rates: $80/page; $60/½ page;
$40/¼ page
ISSN: 0008-6797

CARTA ABIERTA

Juan Rodriguez
Center for Mexican American
Studies

Texas Lutheran College
Seguin, TX 78155
(512) 372-6059
News/notices about the Chicano
    literary world.
An irregular, off-beat, progressive
    and at times incisive newsletter
    (rag) that keeps an eye on the
    Chicano literary world.
1975; irreg; 1,000
$20/yr; $3/ea
12 pp; 8 ½ x 11
ISSN: 0198-1021

CAT'S EAR

Jim Roland, Founding Editor;
    Scott Ludtke, Assoc. Editor;
    Jack Holcomb, Asst. Editor
Galliard Group Publishers
P.O. Box 946
Kirksville, MO 63501
(816) 785-4185
Poetry, fiction.
CAT'S EAR publishes poetry and
    fiction with an emphasis on the
    lyrical and metaphorical, always
    with an eye on future directions
    of the tradition.
Diane Wakoski, Charles Edward
    Eaton, Robert Peters, Laurel
    Speer, Naomi Shihab Nye.
Payment: 2 copies.
Reporting Time: 9 weeks.
Copyright held by Galliard Group
    Publishers, but reverts to author
    upon publication.

1992; 3/yr; 250
$10/ind, $12/inst; $4/ea; 40%
48 pp; 5½ x 8½
Ad Rates: $50/page (4 x 7);
    $30/½ page (4 x 3¼ or 2 x 7);
    $20/ page (4 x 1 or 1 x 7)
ISSN: 1062-6379

CATALYST MAGAZINE

Pearl Cleage
236 Forsyth St., Suite 400
Atlanta, GA 30303
(404) 730-5785
Fiction, nonfiction, poetry, criti-
    cism, essays.
Focuses primarily on Southern writ-
    ers, but welcomes all submissions
    in fiction, poetry, drama and criti-
    cism. The magazine presents
    writers in a format designed to
    stimulate discussion and encour-
    age the exchange of ideas.
Willie Woods, Zaron Burnett, Mari
    Evans.
Unsolicited Manuscripts Received/
    Published per Year: 800/500.
Payment: $20–$200.
Reporting Time: 6–8 months.
SASE for return of submissions
    and immediate acknowledge-
    ment of work received.
Copyright authors.
1986; 2/yr; 5,000
$10/2 yrs; $2.50/ea
96 pp; 7½ x 14
ISSN: 0896-7423

THE CATHARTIC

Patrick M. Ellingham
P.O. Box 1391
Fort Lauderdale, FL 33302
(305) 967-9378
Poetry, reviews, photographs, artwork.
THE CATHARTIC is devoted to the unknown poet, with the understanding that most poets are unknown in America. All types of poetry except those that are racist or sexist. Avoid poems over 50 lines or rhyme for the sake of rhyme. Experiment with language and form. Poems that deal with or come from the dark side; intense poems that use words sparingly and forget the poet; poems that jar the reader's sensibilities; darkly erotic poems; poems that show social awareness.
Joy Walsh, Harry Knickerbocker, Paul Weinman.
Unsolicited Manuscripts Received/Published per Year: 500+/50.
Payment: 1 copy.
Copyright reverts to author upon publication.
1974; 2/yr; 200
$5/yr; $3/ea
28 pp; 5½ x 8½
No ads
ISSN: 0145-8310

CEILIDH: AN INFORMAL GATHERING FOR STORY & SONG

P.O. Box 6367
San Mateo, CA 94403
(415) 378-2350 or (415) 591-9902
Fiction, poetry, plays, translation, photographs, graphics/artwork
Patrick Smith, John Moffitt, Traise Yamamoto, Richard Soos, Sarah Bliumis.
$7.50/yr; $2.50/ea; 40%

CENTRAL PARK

Stephen-Paul Martin; Richard Royal, Prose and Visuals; Eve Ensler, Poetry
P.O. Box 1446
New York, NY 10023
(212) 691-0890 or (212) 242-0302
Experimental fiction, narrative fiction, theory, graphics/artwork, poetry, photographs, translation, interviews, reviews.
CENTRAL PARK is moving in three main directions: poetry and fiction of an either experimental or aggressively political nature, essays in social or esthetic theory, and visual work that moves the eye to think about how it sees. Prospective contributors are advised to order a sample copy ($5) before submitting.

Marc Kaminsky, Rosmarie Wal-
drop, Rae Armantrout, Ron
Silliman, Jackson Mac Low.
Payment: 1 copy.
Reporting Time: 8 weeks.
Copyright held by magazine.
1981; 2/yr; 1,000
$8/yr; $5/ea; 40%
100 pp; 7½ x 10
Ad Rates: $100/page; $50/½ page;
$25/¼ page
Ubiquity, Edge

CHAMINADE LITERARY REVIEW

Loretta Petrie
Chaminade University of Honolulu
3140 Waialae Ave.
Honolulu, HI 96816-1578
(808) 735-4723

Poetry, fiction, criticism, reviews.
CHAMINADE LITERARY REVIEW intends to bring together work from both artists
and writers, talented new ones
along with those nationally or
internationally recognized. We
want writing from Hawaii side
by side with writing from the
mainland to demonstrate how
well our local writers compare.
We want a magazine at once
regional and cosmopolitan. We
hope to reflect the diversity of
Hawaii's people, their writers,
their interests.

Cathy Song, John Unterecker,
Phyllis Thompson, William
Stafford, Tony Quagliano.
Unsolicited Manuscripts Received/
Published per Year: 200/60+.
Payment: 1 year's subscription,
upon publication.
Copyright held by Chaminade
Press; reverts to author upon
publication.
1987; 2/yr; 350
$10/yr; $18/2 yrs (ind & inst);
$5/ea; 20%
175 pp; 6 x 9
Ad Rates: $50/page (4 x 7¼);
$25/½ page (4 x 3⅞)
ISSN: 0894-6396

CHANTS

Terrell Hunter
R 1 Box 1738
Dexter, ME 04930
(207) 924-3673

Poetry, translations of poetry.
CHANTS publishes the best poetry we can find, regardless of
style. We value intensity, originality, involvement—poems
that grab you hard and won't let
go.
Bill Shields, Jorie Graham, James
Laughlin, Michael Kreps,
Michael LaBruno.
Unsolicited Manuscripts Received/
Published per Year:
1,000/75–100.

Reading Period: year–round.
Payment: 2 copies
Reporting Time: 2–3 months,
sometimes longer.
Copyright reverts to poet.
1989; 2/yr; 500
$12/3 issues; $4/ea; 30–40%
64 pp; 6 x 9
Ad Rates: $25/½ page

THE CHARIOTEER

Pella Publishing Company
337 West 36th St.
New York, NY 10018-6401
(212) 279-9586
Poetry, fiction, criticism, essays,
reviews, plays, translation,
graphics/artwork.
Purpose: to bring to English-
speaking readers information
on, appreciation of, and translations from modern Greek
literature, with criticism and
reproductions of modern Greek
art and sculpture.
Unsolicited Manuscripts Received/
Published per Year: 6/none.
Payment: none.
Reporting Time: 3 months.
Copyright held by Pella Publishing
Company; reverts to author
upon request.
1960; 1/yr; 1,000
$15/yr; $28/2 yrs; $40/3 yrs
200 pp; 5½ x 8½
Ad Rates: $125/page (4⅛ x 7);

$75/½ page (4⅛ x 3½)
ISSN: 0577-5574

THE CHARITON REVIEW

Jim Barnes
Northeast Missouri State
University
Kirksville, MO 63501
(816) 785-4499
Poetry, fiction, essays, reviews,
translation.
Excellence in literature only. We
like the old; we like the new.
Jack Cady, Phyllis Barber, Barry
Targan, David Ray, Robert Can-
zoneri, Patricia Goedicke, Gordon Weaver, Steve Heller, Elizabeth Moore.
Unsolicited Manuscripts Received/
Published per Year:
6-8,000/100.
Payment: $5/page.
Reporting Time: 1 week–1
month.
Copyright held by Northeast Missouri State University; reverts to
author upon publication.
1975; 2/yr; 700
$9/yr, $15/2yr, $5/ea; $3/sample
copy
100 pp; 6 x 9
Ad Rates: $100/page (4 x 7);
$50/½ page (4 x 3½)
ISSN: 0098-9452

THE CHARLOTTE POETRY REVIEW

A.A. Jillani, Lisa Kerley

P.O. Box 36701

Charlotte, NC 28236

Poetry, book reviews, short–short fiction, poet interviews.

Regardless of percentages, **CPR** as a rule regularly publishes first-time poets alongside some of the best in the country. Freshness is the key here.

Tony Moffeit, William Walsh, Chuck Sullivan, Harry Brody.

Published per Year: 3,000/100.

Payment: none.

Reporting Time: 2–3 months.

Copyright reverts to author upon publication.

1992; 4/yr; 1,500

$18/yr; $4.50/ea

48 pp; 8½ x 11

Ad Rates: $35/business card

THE CHATTAHOOCHEE REVIEW

Lamar York

DeKalb College

2101 Womack Road

Dunwoody, GA 30338-4497

(404) 551-3166

Poetry, fiction, criticism, essays, reviews, interviews.

THE CHATTAHOOCHEE REVIEW promotes fresh writing and encourages as yet unacknowledged writers by giving them space in print next to their acclaimed peers.

Leon Rooke, Fred Chappell, George Garrett, Jim Wayne Miller, Peter Meinke.

Unsolicited Manuscripts Received/ Published per Year: 3,000/100.

Reading Period: year–round.

Payment: 2 copies of **THE CHATTAHOOCHEE REVIEW.**

Reporting Time: 2 months.

Copyright held by DeKalb College; reverts to author upon publication.

1980; quarterly; 1,250

$15/yr; $25/2 yrs; $4/ea; 30%

100 pp; 6 x 9

Ad Rates: $125/page (4½ x 7); $75/½ page (4½ x 3½)

ISSN: 0741-9155

CHELSEA

Richard Foerster, Alfredo de Palchi, Andrea Lockett, Joan Connor

Box 773

Cooper Station

New York, NY 10276-0773

Poetry, fiction, criticism, essays, translations, interviews, art.

Stress on style, variety, originality. No special biases or requirements. Flexible attitudes, eclectic material. Active interest, as

always, in crosscultural ex-
changes, in superior translations.
Leaning toward cosmopolitan
avant-garde, interdis-
ciplinary techniques, but no
strictures against traditional
modes. Annual competition
(send SASE for guidelines).
Daisy Aldan, Mei-mei Berssenbrugge, Alvin Greenberg, Ha
Jin, Laura Kasischke, LuAnn
Keener, Ann Lauterbach, Carl
Phillips, Ruth L. Schwartz, Susan Sonde, Ann Weinstone.
Unsolicited Manuscripts Received/
Published per Year: 4,000/60.
Payment: $5/page.
Reporting Time: immediately–4
months.
Copyright held by magazine; reverts to author upon publication.
1958; 2/yr; 1,300
$12/2 issues or 1 double issue;
$15/foreign; $6.50/ea
128 pp; 6 x 9
$125/page (4½ x 7½); $75/½
page (4½ x 3½); exchange ads
also available
ISSN: 0009-2185
DeBoer, Faxon, Ebsco

CHICAGO REVIEW
David Nicholls
5801 S. Kenwood
Chicago, IL 60637
(312) 702-0887

Poetry, fiction, criticism, essays,
reviews, translation, interviews,
photographs, graphics/artwork.
CHICAGO REVIEW is an international journal of writing and
cultural exchange published at
the University of Chicago.
Elizabeth Alexander, Alice Fulton,
Albert Goldbarth, Barry Han-
nah, Yusef Komunyakaa, Gary
Snyder, Gerald Vizenor.
Unsolicited Manuscripts Received/
Published per Year: 2,000/70.
Payment: copies/subscription.
Reporting Time: 2 months.
Copyright held by magazine;
transfers to author upon request.
1946; 4/yr; 2,500
$15/yr ind, $35/yr inst; $6/ea;
40%
128 pp; 6 x 9
Ad Rates: $150/page (4½ x 7½);
$75/½ page (2½ x 7½)
ISSN: 0009-3696
Armadillo, Bookpeople, Fine
Print, Ingram, Olson, Ubiquity

CHIRON REVIEW
Michael Hathaway
522 E. South Ave.
St. John, KS 67576-2212
(316) 549-3933
Poetry, fiction, nonfiction, reviews, all press news.
Presents the widest possible range
of contemporary creative writ-

ing, traditional and off-beat in an attractive, professional tabloid format, including artwork and photos of featured writers. Charles Bukowski, Robert Peters, Lyn Lifshin, Lorri Jackson, Antler, Joan Jobe Smith.
Unsolicited Manuscripts Received/ Published per Year: 1,825+/100.
Payment: copies.
Reporting Time: 2-6 weeks.
Copyright: author retains rights.
1982; 4/yr; 2,000
$10/ind; $3/ea; 40%
20-48 pp; 10 x 13
Ad Rates: send SASE
ISSN: 1046-8897

CIMARRON REVIEW

Gordon Weaver, Editor; Paul Bowers, Al Learst, Associate Editors; Thomas Reiter, Sally Shigley, Sharon Gerald, Doug Martin, Hugh Tribbey, Poetry Editors; Peter Donahue, Peter Theis, Dot Archibald, Leslie Fife, Jerry Erwin, Fiction Editors; E.P. Walkiewicz, Nonfiction Editor; Thomas E.
Kennedy, European Editor.
205 Morrill Hall
Oklahoma State University
Stillwater, OK 74078-0135
(405) 744-9476

Poetry, fiction, essays, reviews.
Seeks well-written material, which emphasizes attempts to find value and purpose in a dehumanized and dehumanizing world. Avoids "easy" answers of extremes and would not publish work which espouses any specific religious or political view or advocates simple escapism. It does not publish children's stories; but does publish stories about children aimed at adult understanding.
Unsolicited Manuscripts Received/ Published per Year: 2,275/12–16.
Payment: $50/prose; $15/poem.
Reporting Time: 8–12 weeks.
Copyright held by magazine.
1967; 4/yr; 450
$12/yr; $3/ea
112 pp; 6 x 9
ISSN: 0009-6849

CINCINNATI POETRY REVIEW

Jeffrey Hillard
Humanities Department
College of Mount St. Joseph
Cincinnati, OH 45233
(513) 244-4930

Poetry.
CINCINNATI POETRY REVIEW sets local writers in a national context. One fourth to one third of each issue is local; the rest is national. "Local"

means about 150 from the city. All types of poetry considered. Poetry contest held once per year. Alvin Greenberg, X.J. Kennedy, David Citino, Enid Shomer, Walter McDonald. Payment: none. Reporting Time: 4–6 weeks. Copyright held by magazine; reverts to author upon publication. 1985; 2/yr; 1,000 $9/yr; $2/ea (samples); 40%; 50% for direct purchase by dealers 72 pp; 5½ x 8½

barth, Pat Hutchings, Charlotte Mandel. Unsolicited Manuscripts Received/ Published per Year: 3,500/40- 50. Payment: 3 copies and a small cash award. Reporting Time: 3–4 months. Copyrighted. 1983; 2/yr; or one double issue; 1,500 $8/yr; $4/ea 80 pp; 5½ x 8½ ISSN: 0740-9311 Ingram

CLOCKWATCH REVIEW

James Plath, Editor; Robert, C. Bray, Lynn DeVore, James McGowan, Pamela Muirhead, Associate Editors
Dept. of English
Illinois Wesleyan University
Bloomington, IL 61702-2900
(309) 556-3352

Fiction, poetry, interviews, essays, photographs, graphics/artwork.
CLOCKWATCH REVIEW seeks to present quality work in a format lively enough to attract a popular as well as literary/academic audience. Special feature: an ongoing interview series with contemporary artists and musicians.
Bob Shacochis, Koko Taylor, Jamaica Kincaid, Albert Gold-

CLUES: A Journal of Detection

Pat Browne
Journals Department
Popular Press
Bowling Green State University
Bowling Green, OH 43403
(419) 372-2981

Articles, reviews.
A magazine focusing upon detective fiction.
Unsolicited Manuscripts Received/ Published per Year: 50–60/25.
Reading Period: year–round.
1982; 2/yr; 700
$12.50/yr; $7.75/ea

COFFEEHOUSE

Ray Foreman
P.O. Box 566

Eastlake, CO 80614

(303) 452-6108

Poetry, short stories, commentaries.

A high quality narrative poetry and short story magazine in a cooperative publishing venture with writers.

Unsolicited Manuscripts Received/ Published per Year: 600/100.

Reading Period: year–round.

Reporting time: one month

Copyright held by author.

1990; 4/yr; 300+

$4.00/2yrs (8 issues)

20 pp; digest 5½ x 8½

ISSN: 1061-5687

COLLAGES & BRICOLAGES

Marie-José Fortis

P.O. Box 86

Clarion, PA 16214

(814) 226-5799

Poetry, fiction, criticism, essays, reviews, plays, translation, interviews, photographs, graphics/ artwork (b & w).

COLLAGES & BRICOLAGES, which has published authors from the five continents, believes in innovative writer who has read the classics. At this point in time we would like to receive less egocentric, more politically engaged, pieces. 1995 will focus on George Sand. 1996 will probably focus on Beckett, Ionesco, and an absurdism that in our confused Fin-de-siecle, looks more and more like realism.

Marilou Awiakta, Eric Basso, Susan Onthank Mates, Greg Boyd, Jo Santiago, Maria Fernande Espinosa and many important non-mainstream authors.

Unsolicited Manuscripts Received/ Published per Year: 600/20-25.

Reading Period: Aug.–Nov.

Payment: 1 or 2 copies. Extras: ½ price.

1993; 1/yr; 800

$7.50/ea

120 pp; 11 x 18

Ad Rates: $50/page (9 x 16); $30/½ page (5 x 8); $15/¼ page (2½ x 4)

C & B does exchange ads with other lit mags.

COLORADO REVIEW

David Milofsky, Editor; Robert Olen Butler, George Cuomo, James Galvin, Jorie Graham, Joanne Greenberg, Michael Martone, Dan O'Brien, Carol Oles, Toby Olson, Robert D. Richardson, Jr., Alberto Rios, Contributing Editors.

Department of English
Colorado State University
Fort Collins, CO 80523

Fiction, poetry, essays, and reviews.

Although published in Colorado,
COLORADO REVIEW is
more than a regional literary
magazine. We seek to print the
best fiction, poetry, translations,
interviews, reviews, and articles
on contemporary literary subjects that we receive from a
contributorship that is national
and international. We continue
to be interested in Magical Re-
alist writing, but any writing
that is vital, highly imaginative
and highly realized in artistic
terms and that avoids mere
mannerism to embody important
human concerns will find support here.

Reg Saner, Patricia Goedicke, Bin
Ranke, Carole Oles, T. Alan
Broughton, Rita Ciresi, David
Huddle; interviews with Carolyn
Forche; Gwendolyn Brooks,
Gretel Ehrlich.

Unsolicited Manuscripts Received/
Published per Year:
7,000/varies.

Reading Period: Sept.–May.
Payment: when funding permits.
1977; 2/yr 1,000
$15/yr, $28/2 yr; $8/ea; 40%
112 pp; 6 x 9

Ad Rates: $100/page (7½ x 5);
$50/½ page

**COLUMBIA: A Magazine of
Poetry and Prose**
Rotating Editors
404 Dodge Hall
Columbia University
New York, NY 10027
(212) 854-4391

Poetry, fiction, essays.
Reading Period: year–round.
Payment: in copies; Editors'
awards also.
Reporting Time: 1–2 months.
Copyright reverts to author.
$18/3 issues; $13/2 issues; $7 ea
Approx. 220 pp; 5 x 8
Ad Rates: on request

CONFRONTATION
Martin Tucker
L.I.U. Dept. of English
C.W. Post
Greenvale, NY 11548
(516) 299-2391

Poetry, fiction, criticism, essays,
plays, translation, interviews.

We are eclectic in our tastes, pre-
ferring a mix of traditional and
experimental, of the known and
relatively unknown writers. We
have no prohibition except that
of poor literary quality.

Cynthia Ozick, Wilfrid Sheed,

Stephen Dixon, Joyce Carol
Oates, Thomas Fleming, Joseph
Brodsky.
Unsolicited Manuscripts Received/
Published per Year: 5,000/250.
Reading Period: Sept.–May.
Payment: $5 to $100.
Reporting Time: 6 weeks.
Copyright held by Long Island
University; reverts to author
upon publication.
1968; 2/yr; 2,000
$10/yr ind, $10/yr inst; $6/ea
160–190 pp; 5½ x 8½

Edgar Wideman.
Unsolicited Manuscripts Received/
Published per Year: 5,000+/10.
Payment: in copies, and $150.
Reporting Time: 4–6 weeks.
Copyright reverts to author upon
publication.
1981; 2/yr; 7,500
$18/yr; $32/2yr; $10/ea
320 pp; 6 x 9
Ad Rates: $350/page (4⅜ x 7½);
$250/½ page
ISSN: 0278-2324

CONJUNCTIONS

Bradford Morrow
Bard College
Annandale-on-Hudson, NY 12504
(914) 758-1539

Poetry, fiction, translation, interviews, photographs, graphics/
artwork, essays.

CONJUNCTIONS publishes for-
mally innovative writing, with
equal emphasis on fiction and
poetry; also essays on culture
and the arts, special features.
Editorial staff: Walter Abish,
John Ashbery, Mei-Mei Bers-
senbrugge, Guy Davenport,
Elizabeth Frank, Robert Kelly,
Kenneth Irby, William Gass,
Susan Howe, Ann Lauterbach,
Patrick McGrath, Nathaniel
Tarn, Quincy Troupe, John

THE CONNECTICUT POETRY REVIEW

Harley More, J. Claire White
P.O. Box 818
Stonington, CT 06378

Poetry, criticism, reviews, translations, interviews, excerpts from
verse plays.
Marge Piercy, John Updike, Margaret Randall, Allen Ginsberg,
Eugenio de Andrade.
Unsolicited Manuscripts Received/
Published per Year:
1,500/18–20.
Payment: $5/poem; $10/review;
$20/interview; $20/verse play.
Reporting Time: 3 months.
1981; 1/yr; 500
$3/ea
50 pp; 5¾ x 9¼
ISSN: 0277-7770

CONNECTICUT RIVER REVIEW

Ben Brodinsky
327 Seabury Dr.
Bloomfield, CT 06002
Poetry.
The **CRR** uses highest quality poetry, in which logic and emotion, picture and sound cohere, making for authentic music. All forms welcome, except haiku. Prefer poems of 40 lines or under; submit no more than 5 poems at a time.
Unsolicited Manuscripts Received/ Published per Year: 800–1,000/90–100.
Reading Period: year–round.
Payment: 1 copy.
Reporting Time: 2–8 weeks.
Copyright held by Connecticut Poetry Society; reverts to author upon publication.
1978; 2/yr; 400
$20/2 yr; $6/ea; 40%
40 pp; 6 x 9

CONTACT II

Maurice Kenny, J.G. Gosciak
P.O. Box 451, Bowling Green
New York, NY 10004
(212) OR4-0911
Poetry, reviews, criticism, translation, interviews, photographs, graphics/artwork.
Contemporary American poetry.
Janice Mirikitani, Charlotte de Clue, Carolyn Stoloff, Shalin Hai-Jew, Karoniaktatie.
Unsolicited Manuscripts Published per Year: 20%.
Payment: in copies; when payment is cash, $10/poem, $15/review.
Reporting Time: 6 months.
Copyright held by Contact II Publications; reverts to author upon publication with credit.
1976; 2/yr; 2,500
$10/ind, $16/inst; $7/ea; 40%; 50% prepaid on 10 or more.
92 pp; 7¾ x 10½
Ad Rates: $150/page; $80/½ page; $50/¼ page
ISSN: 0197-6796

CONTEXT SOUTH

David Breeden, Craig Taylor, Paul Hadella
Campus Box 4504
Schreiner College
2100 Memorial Blvd.
Kerrville TX 78028-5697
Poetry, fiction, criticism, graphics/ artwork.
A magazine based in the South, but not confined to it, **CONTEXT SOUTH** endeavors to be a collection by artists interested in pushing boundaries.
Wayne Dodd, Andrea Hollander Budy, Diane Glancy, William Greenway.

Unsolicited Manuscripts Received/
Published per Year: 1,000+/50.
Copyright held by author.
300
$12/yr; $5/ea; 40%
65 pp; 5½ x 8½
$100/page; $50/½ page; $25/¼
page
ISSN: 1045-2265

CORNFIELD REVIEW

Stuart Lishan, Editor; Ann Bower,
Fiction Editor; Terry Hermson,
Poetry Editor; Larry Sauselen,
Art Editor
OSU at Marion
1465 Mt. Vernon Ave
Marion, OH 43302
(614) 389-2361

Poetry, short stories, nonfiction
essays; original art (black &
white) and photography.
A "little" literary magazine show-
casing the Midwest experience
(but not limited to that topic).
Submissions should be of high
quality; fiction and nonfiction
should not exceed 3,500 words.
Unsolicited Manuscripts Received/
Published per Year: 600/20.
Reading Period: Sept.–Jan.
Payment: 2 copies.
Reporting Time: 2–4 months.
Copyright reverts to author.
1976; 1/yr; 1,500
$5/ea

64 pp
ISSN: 0363-4574

COTTONWOOD

George Wedge, Editor; Phil
Wedge, Poetry Editor; Ben Ac-
cardi, Fiction Editor
University of Kansas
Box J, 400 Kansas Union
Lawrence, KS 66045
(913) 864-3777

Poetry, fiction, reviews, interviews, photographs, graphics/
artwork.
COTTONWOOD uses fiction and
poetry with clear images and
interesting narratives and reviews of books by writers or
from publishers in our area. The
magazine welcomes submissions
from all parts of the country.
Robert Day, Rita Dove, Patricia
Traxler, Gerald Early, William
Stafford.
Unsolicited Manuscripts Received/
Published per Year: 3,000+/50.
Payment: 1 copy.
Reporting Time: 2–6 months.
Copyright held by magazine; reverts to author upon publication.
1965; 3/yr; 500
$15/yr; $6.50/ea; 30%
120 pp; 6 x 9
ISSN: 0147-149X

CPQ

John M. Brander
1200 E. Ocean Blvd., #64
Long Beach, CA 90802
(213) 495-0925
Poetry, translation,
graphics/artwork.
Poems may come from anywhere in the country. We like everything we've published in **CPQ**, some of it a lot, but from now on we would like to receive not only poems like those we've printed but also those which are unlike anything we've ever printed.
Jennifer Olds, William James Kovanda, Sylvia Rosxen, Joseph Kent, Aaron Kramer.
Unsolicited Manuscripts Received/ Published per Year: 150/30.
Payment: none.
Reporting Time: 2-3 months.
Copyright held by English Department, Chapman College, Orange, CA; reverts to author upon publication.
1972; 3 or 4/yr; 500
$5/ea; 20%
84 pp
No ads
Small Press Traffic, Midnight Special

CRAB CREEK REVIEW

Linda Clifton; Carol Orlock; Fiction
4462 Whitman Ave., N.
Seattle, WA 98103
(206) 633-1090
Poetry, fiction, translation, essays, graphics/artwork.
". . . well-crafted and perceptive works . . . technically proficient and sensitive poems . . . powerfully expressed images . . . tightly controlled narrative . . . diverse enough to appeal to a variety of literary tastes . . ." Literary Magazine Review. *Not accepting submissions until further notice.*
William Stafford, Rebecca Wells, Mary Kollar, Tim McNulty.
Unsolicited Manuscripts Received/ Published per Year: 400/0 until 1994.
Payment: 2 copies.
Reporting Time: 4–8 weeks.
Copyright held by CCR; reverts to author upon publication. Current publication: *Crab Creek Review Anniversary Anthology* paperbound.
1983; Currently available: *10th Anniversary Anthology,* $10.00
Back issues: $3.00; 40%; 50% through distributor Small Changes, 316 Terry N. P. O. Box 19046 Seattle, WA 98109 (206) 382-1980
Anthology 160pp; 5x8
$120/page (6 x 10); $65/½ page (6 x 5); $35/¼ page (6 x 2½); $20/⅛ page (3 x 2½)
ISSN: 07380-7008

CRAZYHORSE

Zabelle Stodola, Managing Editor; Judy Troy, Fiction Editor; Ralph Burns, Poetry Editor; Dennis Vanatta, Criticism Editor.

English Department
University of Arkansas at Little Rock
2801 S. University
Little Rock, AR 72204
(501) 569-3160

Poetry, fiction, criticism, reviews, interviews.

A literary magazine which publishes quality work by established and promising new writers.

Andre Dubus, Bobbie Ann Mason, Raymond Carver, Jorie Graham, John Updike.

Unsolicited Manuscripts Received/ Published per year: 20,000/60.

Reading Period: Sept.–Oct. for fiction.

Payment: 2 copies and $10/page.

Annual fiction and poetry awards: $500 each.

Reporting Time: 3 months.

Copyright reverts to author upon request.

1960; 2/yr; 1,000

$10/yr; $5/ea; 25%–40%

135 pp; 6 x 9

Ad Rates: $85/page; $50/½ page

ISSN: 0011-0841

CRAZYQUILT

Jim Kitchen
P.O. Box 632729
San Diego, CA 92163-2729
(619) 688-1023

Poetry, fiction, criticism, essays, plays, photographs, graphics/ artwork.

All kinds of poetry; short stories with good character development; nonfiction about writers; literary criticism; one-act plays and black and white photography and art work. Accept translations of poetry. Publish new writers as well as established authors.

Mimi Albert, Ruth Good, Gordon Grice, Louis J. Phillips, Victoria Golden McMains.

Unsolicited Manuscripts Received/ Published per Year: 500/70-80.

Payment: 2 copies.

Reporting Time: 10–12 weeks.

Copyright held by Crazyquilt Press; reverts to author upon publication.

1986; 4/yr; 180

$18.00/yr (ind & inst); $28.00/2 yrs; $6.00/ea; 40%

100 pp

ISSN: 0887-5308

CREAM CITY REVIEW

Mark Drechsler and Andrew Rivera, Editors-in-Chief; Brian Jung, Editor

P.O. Box 413
University of Wisconsin-
Milwaukee
Milwaukee, WI 53201
(414) 229-4708
Poetry, fiction, reviews, essays,
interviews, plays, photographs,
graphics/artwork.
The **CREAM CITY REVIEW** is
an eclectic literary magazine
affiliated with the University of
Wisconsin-Milwaukee; it strives
to publish the best of traditional
and non-traditional work by
new and established writers.
Tess Gallagher, Stuart Dybek,
Donald Hall, Cathy Song, David
Ignatow, Marge Piercy, Maxine
Kumin, Amy Clampitt, Derek
Walcott, Amiri Baraka, Mary
Oliver & William Stafford,
Lawrence Ferlinghetti.
Unsolicited Manuscripts Received/
Published per Year:
12,000/226+.
Reading Period: year–round, but
response time is longer in the
summer.
Reporting Time: 2–8 weeks.
Copyright held by the Board of
Regents of the University of
Wisconsin; reverts to author
upon publication.
1975; 2/yr; 2,000
$12/yr, $21/2yr; sample $5.00; 40%
300 pp; 5½ x 8½
Ad Rates: inquire with SASE

CREATIVE NONFICTION
Lee Gutkind
P.O. Box 81536
Pittsburgh, PA 15217
(412) 422-8404
Fax (412) 422-8405
Essays, memoirs, profiles written
in creative nonfiction genre.
First journal to focus on emerging
genre of creative
nonfiction/literary journalism.
Publishes essays, memoirs, profiles by new and established
writers. Readership spans entire
writing community.
Christopher Buckley, Adrienne
Rich, Michael Stephens, Margaret Gibson, Charles Simic.
Unsolicited Manuscripts Received/
Published per Year: 300/30.
Reading Period: year–round.
Payment: $5–$10 per published
page.
Copyright held by Creative Nonfiction Foundation.
1993; 4/yr; 2,000
$20/3 issues, $10/ea.
100 pp; 5½ x 8¼
$250/page; $175/½ page; discounts are available for cash,
extended runs.
ISSN: 1070-0714
DeBoer, Desert Moon

CREEPING BENT
Joseph P. Lucia
433 West Market St.

Bethlehem, PA 18018
(215) 866-5613
Poetry, reviews, fiction, essays, translation.

Hewing to no orthodoxies but reflecting an awareness of the broad spectrum of current writing and thought about writing, **CREEPING BENT** is an independent, eclectic, and adventurous magazine for serious (but not solemn or humorless) readers and writers of contemporary literature, with emphasis on poetry.

Brigit Kelly, Charles Edward Eaton, Turner Cassity, Robert Gibb, Donald Revell.
Unsolicited Manuscripts Received/ Published per Year: 1,500/varies, 0-100.
Payment: none.
Copyright held by publishers; reverts to author upon publication.
1984; 2/yr; 250
$6/yr ind, $7/yr inst; $3/ea. 40%
No ads
ISSN: 8756-0291

THE CRESCENT REVIEW

J. T. Holland
P. O. Box 15069
Chevy Chase, MD 20825
(202) 265-5103
Short stories.
Approximately 15 to 22 short stories are published per issue, no poems, essays, excerpts from novels, interviews.
Unsolicited Manuscripts
Published per Year: 15–22.
Payment: Two copies & discount on authors' copies.
Reporting Time: 4–8 weeks.
$14/1yr; $25/2yr; $8 + postage

CRITICAL TEXTS: A Review of Theory and Criticism

Joe Childers, Jon Anderson, Richard Moye, Martha Buskirk, James Buzard, Ina Lipkowitz, Susan Fraiman, Gary Hentzi, Eric Lott
602 Philosophy Hall
Columbia University
New York, NY 10027
(212) 854-3215

Articles, reviews, translations and interviews dealing with theory in the humanities.
We are an oppositional journal interested in printing articles and reviews on theoretical issues connected with the humanities and social sciences.
Payment: none.
Reporting Time: 2 months.
Copyright held by magazine.
1982; 3/yr; 850
$9/yr ind; $3.75/ea; $5/back issues
120 pp; 6 x 9
$185/page; $100/½ page

ISSN: 0730-2304
Ubiquity

CROSSCURRENTS

Linda Brown Michelson
2200 Glastonbury Rd.
Westlake Village, CA 91361
(818) 991-1694
Fiction, graphics.
CROSSCURRENTS features previously unpublished, literary short fiction. Select pieces are highlighted by photos and line drawings. Two special issues each year.
Alice Adams, Saul Bellow, Josephine Jacobsen, Joyce Carol Oates, John Updike.
Unsolicited Manuscripts Received/ Published per Year: 5,000/60.
Reading Period: June–Nov. 30.
Payment: varies, $35 minimum/story.
Reporting Time: 6 weeks.
Copyright reverts to author.
1980; 4/yr; 3,000
$18/yr; $6/ea; 40%
176 pp; 6 x 9
ISSN: 0739-2354
Faxon, Ebsco, Boley, L-S Distributors, Ingram

CUMBERLAND POETRY REVIEW

Editorial Board
P.O. Box 120128 Acklen Station

Nashville, TN 37212
(615) 373-8948
Poetry, criticism, interviews.
CUMBERLAND POETRY REVIEW is devoted to poetry and poetry criticism and presents poets of diverse origins to a widespread audience. We place no restrictions on form, subject, or style. Manuscripts will be selected for publication on the basis of the writer's perspicuous and compelling means of expression. We welcome translations of high quality poetry. Our aim is to support the poet's efforts to keep up the language.
Seamus Heaney, Lewis Horne, Emily Grosholz, Francis Blessington, Mairi McInnes.
Payment: in contributor's copies.
Reporting Time: 6 months.
Copyright held by Poetics, Inc.; reverts to author upon publication.
1981; 2/yr; 500
$14/yr ind; $17/yr inst; $7/ea sample back issue
100 pp; 6 x 9
Ads Rates: Only on exchange basis
ISSN: 0731-7980
Faxon, Swets, Ebsco, McGregor

CUTBANK

Editors
Dept. of English

University of Montana
Missoula, MT 59812
(406) 243-5231
Poetry, fiction, essays, reviews, interviews, photographs, graphics/artwork.
CUTBANK is a literary magazine with a national scope and a regional bias, often featuring new writers alongside more well-known names.
Rick DeMarinis, James Galvin, William Kittredge, Mark Levine, Greg Pape.
Unsolicited Manuscripts Received/Published per Year: 1,000/50.
Reading Period: August 15–March 15
Reporting Time: 8-12 weeks.
1973; 2/yr; 400
$12/yr; $6.95/ea; 40%
128 pp; 5 ½ x 8 ½
Ad Rates: $90/page; $45/half page
ISSN: 0734-9963

D

DECEMBER MAGAZINE
Curt Johnson
Box 302
Highland Park, IL 60035
(708) 940-4122
Fiction, nonfiction, poetry.
A magazine of the arts and opinion.
Unsolicited Manuscripts Received/
    Published per Year: 150/10.
Payment: 2 copies.
Reporting Time: 4-8 weeks.
1958; irreg.; 1,200
$25/4 issues; $6/ea; 20%
6 x 9
ISSN: 0070-3141

DEFINED PROVIDENCE
Gary J. Whitehead
P.O. Box 16143
Rumford, RI 02916
Poetry, reviews of poetry books,
    interviews with poets, poetics.
DEFINED PROVIDENCE is a
perfect-bound annual poetry
magazine devoted to publishing
new and unknown poets along-
side those poets considered to
be among the best in America.
Gary Soto, Sean Thomas Dough-
    erty, Robert Morgan, David
    Citino, Neal Bowers, Gillian
    Conoley, Jack Myers, Mark
    Doty.
Unsolicited Manuscripts Received/
    Published per Year: 1,500/30-
    40.
Reading Period: year-round.
Payment: copies.
Reporting Time: 2–8 weeks.
Copyright reverts to author upon
    publication.
1992; 1/yr; 300
$4/yr, $7/2yrs; $4/ea; 40%
72 pp; digest size
Ad Rates: $100/page (5 x 8);
    $50/½ page (5 x 4);
    $10/business card; exchanges
ISSN: 1066-2197

DENVER QUARTERLY

Bin Ramke
University of Denver
Denver, CO 80208
(303) 871-2892
Poetry, fiction, reviews, criticism, essays, interviews.
For almost thirty years the **DENVER QUARTERLY** has been publishing work by distinguished as well as promising new writers. The magazine generally publishes material reflecting on modern culture as it has developed over the past century. It is recognized as one of the premiere literary publications of the Rocky Mountain region.
James Tate, Carl Dennis, Charles Baxter, Jorie Graham, Rachel Hadas.
Unsolicited Manuscripts Received/ Published per Year: 3,000/35.
Payment: $5/page for fiction, essays, reviews; $5/page for poetry.
Copyright held by magazine.
1966; 4/yr; 900
$15/yr ind, $18/yr inst; $5/ea; 20%
160 pp; 6 x 9
Ad Rates: $150/page (5 x 8½); $75/½ page (5 x 4½)
ISSN: 0011-8869

DESCANT

Karen Mulhallen
P.O. Box 314
Station P. Toronto, ON M55 258
CANADA
(416) 603-0223
Short fiction, poetry, essays, plays, visual essays.
Literary magazine interested in all the arts and their interrelationship. Aims to publish works of excellence from established and emerging writers and artists. Quality bound.
Leon Rooke, Isabel Allende, Joseph Skvorecky, Michael Ondaatje, Margaret Atwood.
Unsolicited Manuscripts Received/ Published per Year: 700/10.
Reading Period: year–round.
Payment: varies.
Copyright: 1st Canadian Rights
1970; 4/yr; 1,200
$20/yr ind; & $31/yr inst.; $10–$13
130 pp; 5¾ x 8¾
$225/page 5¾ x 8¾-one issue; $400-two issues (B&W)
ISSN: 0382-909-X
Canadian Magazine Publishers Association

DIMENSION

A. Leslie Willson
P.O. Box 26673
Austin, TX 78755
(512) 345-0622
Poetry, fiction, essays, plays, translation, interviews, graphics/

artwork, German literature in the original and translation: post 1945.

DIMENSION concentrates on established and non-established writers from all German-speaking countries, with original works with translations. Few essays.
Friedrich Dürrenmatt, Wolfgang Hildersheimer, Günter Grass, Günter Kunert, Peter Weiss.
Payment: modest, copies for translators.
Reporting Time: varies.
Copyright held by magazine.
1968; 3/yr; 1,000
$20/yr ind, $24/yr inst; $10/ea; 20%
200 pp; 6 x 9

DJINNI (formerly NAHANT BAY)
Kalo Clarke, Kim Alan Pederson
29 Front St. # 2
Marblehead, MA 01945
(617) 639-1889
Essays, poetry, fiction, drawings, B&W photographs.
Literary magazine looking for unique voices and original style.
Unsolicited Manuscripts Received/ Published per Year:
350–400/50–60.
Reading Period: June–Dec.
Payment: 1 copy.
Reporting Time: 2–4 months.

Copyright: 1st North American Serieal Rights.
1990; 1/yr
60-100 pp; half sheet

DOG RIVER REVIEW
Laurence F. Hawkins
5976 Billings Road
Parkdale, OR 97041-9610
(503) 352-6494
Poetry, fiction, reviews, short plays, black and white art, essays.
Open to all poetic forms. Favorite poets/writers: Whitman, Jeffers, Thomas, Patchen, Cardenal, Bukowski, Celine, Bowles, Miller Burroughs, Whinkla.
David Chorlton, Richard Kostelanetz, Sheila Nickerson, Nathaniel Tarn.
Unsolicited Manuscripts Received/ Published per Year:
400–450/50–60.
Payment: in copies.
Reporting Time: immediately to 4 months.
Copyright reverts to author of publication.
1981; 2/yr; 300
$8.00/yr; $4.00/ea; 3/sample; 40%
56-64 pp; 5½ x 8½
ISSN: 0749-260X

THE DRAMA REVIEW
Richard Schechner
MIT Press Journals

55 Hayward St.
Cambridge, MA 02142
(617) 253-2866
Editorial office:
721 Broadway #626
New York, NY 10003
Fax (212) 995-4060

TDR is a quarterly journal of performance with a strong intercultural, intergeneric, and interdisciplinary focus. We consider everything from wrestling to ritual, from Peter Brook's Mahabharata to what is going on at "Downtown Beirut." **TDR** borrows from the fields of anthropology, performance theory, popular culture, ethology, psychology, and politics. We combine scholarship and journalism in the form of essays, interviews, letters and editorials.
Payment: $50–250.
Copyright held by MIT Press.
1955; 4/yr; 6,000
$20/yr students, $32/yr ind, $80/yr inst; $8/ea
160 pp; 7 x 10
ISSN: 1054-2043

E

EARTH'S DAUGHTERS: A Feminist Arts Periodical

Editors: Kastle Brill, Joan Ford,
Pat Colvard, Bonnie Johnson,
Joyce Kessel, Ryki Zuckerman
Box 41
Central Park Stn
Buffalo, NY 14215

Poetry, fiction, plays, photographs, graphics/artwork.

EARTH'S DAUGHTERS is a feminist literary and art periodical published in Buffalo, New York. We believe ourselves to be the oldest feminist arts periodical extant, having published our first issue in February, 1971. Our focus is the experience and creative expression of women.

Jimmie Canfield, Lyn Lifshin, Marge Piercy, Kathryn Machan Aal, Susan Fantl Spivack.

Unsolicited Manuscripts Received/
Published per Year:
1,000–1,500/200+.
Payment: 2 copies.
Reporting Time: 3 months.
Copyright held by magazine; reverts to author upon publication.
1971; 3/yr; 1,000
$14/yr ind, $22/yr inst; $5/ea;
30%
60 pp; 6 x 9
No ads
ISSN: 0163-0989
Ebsco, Faxon, Burroughs

1812

Dan Schwartz, Richard Lywch,
Joe Todaro
Box 1812
Amherst, NY 14226-7812

Fiction, poetry, art.
The war along the Niagara.
Unsolicited Manuscripts Received/
Published per Year: 400/25.

Payment: various/arranged.
Reporting Time: 2 months.
Copyright.
1995; 1/yr; 1,000+
100+ pp; 4½ x 11
Ad Rates: arranged

ELF: Eclectic Literary Forum
C. K. Erbes
P.O. Box 392
Tonawanda, NY 14150
(716) 693-7006
Poetry, short fiction, essays on
literary themes, critical reviews,
special features.
Professionally printed quarterly,
publishing well-crafted contem-
porary works in an uncluttered,
readable format; continuing Native American folklore. ". . . a
good choice for any literatures
collection,"—Library Journal.
Gwendolyn Brooks, William
Stafford, Joyce Carol Oates,
Nikki Giovanni, William Greenway, John Dickson, Daniel Berrigan, R. T. Smith, Dana Gioia.
Unsolicited Manuscripts Received/
Published per Year:
3,000+/100–125.
Reading Period: year–round.
Payment: 2 sample copies.
Reporting Time: 4–6 weeks.
Copyright: ELF Associates, Inc.
1991; 4/yr; 5,200
$16/yr; $5.50/ea

56–60 pp; 8½ x 11
Ad Rates: inquire for rate sheet.
ISSN: 1054-3376
Ingram, DeBoer

EMBERS
Katrina Van Tassel, Mark
Johnston, Charlotte Garrett
Box 404
Guilford, CT 06437
(203) 453-2328
Poetry.
A poetry journal. Editors are po-
ets, interested in poets' voices.
New writers encouraged. Sub-
mit 3–5 poems.
Yearly chapbook contest. Guide-
lines available.
Unsolicited Manuscripts Received/
Published per Year: 3,000/85.
Payment: 2 copies.
Reporting Time: Continuously.
Copyright held by poets; reverts
upon publication.
1979; 2/yr; 500
$11/yr; $6/ea; $3/sample
48 pp; 6 x 9
ISSN: 0731-0382

EMERGENCE
Michele Friske, Donna Maria
Chappell
P.O. Box 1615
Bridgeview, IL 60455
(708) 423-6681

Short fiction and poetry.

EMERGENCE is a literary journal by, for, and about women. A strong, active voice is the most important quality we seek.

Cris Burks, Sally Elizabeth Colford, Zoe Keithley, Betty Shiflett, Lynda Rutledge Stephenson.

Unsolicited Manuscripts Received/ Published per Year: 1,000/25.

Reading Period: June-August.

Payment: 2 copies.

Reporting Time: 3 months.

Copyright reverts to author.

1993; 1/yr; 1,000

$6/yr; $8/ea; 40%

136 pp; 7 x 10

Ad rates: $100/full page

ISBN: 0-9635187-1-2

Fine Print Distributors

THE EMRYS JOURNAL

Jeanine Halva-Neubauer

P.O. Box 8813

Greenville, SC 29604

(803) 294-2066

Poetry, fiction, essays.

Our journal is interested in publishing the work of new writers, especially that of women and other minorities. We are interested in maintaining a high literary standard.

Maxine Kumin, Carole Oles, Linda Paston, Amy Clampitt,

Pattiann Rogers.

Unsolicited Manuscripts Received/ Published per Year: 1,000/18.

Payment: in copies.

Reporting Time: 6 weeks.

Copyright held by The Emrys Foundation.

1984; 1/yr; 400

$10/ea; 40%

No ads

EPOCH

Michael Koch

251 Goldwin Smith Hall

Cornell University

Ithaca, NY 14853

(607) 255-3385

Poetry, fiction.

EPOCH is primarily a journal of fiction, poetry and essays. Publish work by a wide range of writers, some established, some just beginning their careers.

Harriet Doerr, Rick DeMarinis, Stuart Dybek, Thylias Moss, Lee K. Abbott, Alice Fulton.

Reading Period: Sept. 15—April 15.

Payment: $5/magazine page (prose); 50¢/line (poetry). These are minimum payments. We pay more when we have the funds.

Reporting Time: 1 month.

Copyright held by Cornell University; reverts to author upon publication.

1947; 3/yr; 1,000
$11/yr; $5/ea
128 pp; 6 x 9
Ad Rates: $180/page (5 x 8);
  $100/½ page (3 x 8)
ISSN: 0145-1391
DeBoer

EUROPE PLURILINGUE/ PLURILINGUAL EUROPE

Françoise Wuilmart, Editor-in-chief; Nadine Dormoy, Director of Publication; Albert Russo, Assistant Editor.
Nadine Dormoy
44 rue Perronet
92200 Neuilly, FRANCE
(331) 46.24.12.76

Articles, essays, interviews, poetry and short prose, pluridisci-plinary.

All material should involve any of the 12 nations of the European union, their culture and languages and must be written in any of its 10 official languages, i.e.: English, French, German, Spanish, Italian, Portuguese, Danish, Dutch, Greek, Gaelic—High specialization in every field required.

George Steiner, Umberto Eco, Hugo Claus, Jacques Darras, Renzo Titone, Jean-Pierre Faye, Eduardo Lourenco, Theodoze Zeldin,

Harald Weinzich, Hilde Domin.
Unsolicited Manuscripts Received/ Published per Year: dozens/20.
Payment: 2 copies of the issue.
Reporting Time: 2–3 months—
  send 3 IRC (international reply coupons) with mss.
Copyright is property of the re-view, but may be negociated with author.
1991; 6 as of 1994; 1,000
$30/yr; $15/ea; published twice a year. 15%; postage included, checks to be made out and sent to: Liliane Lazar, 37 Hill Lane, Roslyn Heights, NY 11517, but mss *must* be sent to Nadine Dormoy—44 rue Perronet— 92200 Neuilly, FRANCE.
150+ pp; 15cm x 20cm.
Ad Rates: upon request
ISSN: 1161-8884

THE EVERGREEN CHRONICLES

Jim Berg, Senior Editor; Susan Raffo, Managing Editor
P.O. Box 8939
Minneapolis, MN 55408
Essays, short fiction, plays, poetry, visual art.
A journal of gay and lesbian arts and cultures.
Lev Raphael, Ruthann Robson, Terri Jewell, Rane Arroyo.

Unsolicited Manuscripts Received/
Published per Year: 500/50.
Payment: $50 and copy.
Reporting Time: 3 months.
Copyright: First run rights only.
1985; 3/yr; 2,000
$15/yr; $7.95/ea
80–100 pp; 6¾ x 8¾
Ad Rates: Write for rates.
ISSN: 1043-3333
Fine Print, Inland

EXCURSUS LITERARY ARTS JOURNAL

Giancarlo Malchiodi and a revolv-
ing collective
P.O. Box 1056
Knickerbocker Station
New York, NY 10002
Poetry, fiction, creative non-
fiction.
Eclectic. Quality work in varied
styles.
First issue due Fall 1995, no con-
tributors determined yet.
Unsolicited Manuscripts Received/
Published per Year: est. 400/40.
Reading Period: Sept.–June.
Payment: in copies.
Copyright held: magazine has first
time rights, then reverts.
1995; 1/yr; 1,000–1,200
$10.00/yr; $12.00/ea
104 pp; 8½ x 11

EXHIBITION

Karen Perry, Editor
261 Madison Ave. S.
Bainbridge Island, WA 98110
(206) 842-7901
Short fiction, essays, poetry, art-
work.
Seek work which is innovative
and challenging from Pacific
Northwesterners.
Unsolicited Manuscripts Received/
Published per Year: 600/45+.
Payment: 2 copies.
2/yr; 1,000
$5/ea
35 pp; 8½ x 11
Ad Rates: available on request.

EXQUISITE CORPSE

Andrei Codrescu
P.O. Box 25051
Baton Rouge, LA 70894
Poetry, criticism, essays, reviews,
translation, photographs,
graphics/artwork, polemics, letters, reports from many countries.
A review of books and ideas. We
are a print cafe, hopeful that
vigorous dialogue on general
culture is still possible in Man-
darin US. We encourage honesty, combativeness and open-
ness. We have published wideranging polemics, as well as
essays on various matters of

literary interest. Our foreign bureaus report on goings-on in several European and Asian cities. We also publish translations, and reprint important but overlooked texts. Our contributors are both famous and unknown.

Lawrence Ferlinghetti, Hayden Carruth, Maggie Estep, James Laughlin, Laura Rosenthal.

Unsolicited Manuscripts Received/ Published per Year: 10,000/500.

Payment: some payment to contributors.

Reporting Time: 1 month.

Copyright held by authors.

1983; 6/yr; 5,500

$20/yr; $3.50/ea

28 pp; 6 x 15½

ISSN: 0740-7815

Inland

EYEBALL
Jabari Asim, Andrea M. Wren
P.O. Box 8135

St. Louis, MO 63108

(314) 947-6313

Poetry, fiction, essays, reviews, interviews, art.

EYEBALL exists to defend and extend the quest of literature to function as a unifying force in a world challenged by disorder and division.

Gwendolyn Brooks, Dennis Brutus, Paul Beatty, Kevin Powell.

Unsolicited Manuscripts Received/ Published per Year: 50-100/20+.

Payment: 2 copies.

Reporting Time: within 1 year.

Copyright reverts to author.

1992; 2/yr; 2,000

$7/yr; $3.50/ea

48 pp; 13 x 10¾

Ad Rates: negotiable

ISSN: 1063-9675

F

F MAGAZINE
John Schultz
1405 West Belle Plaine
Chicago, IL 60613
(312) 281-7642
Fiction, criticism, essays, reviews, translations, interviews.
F MAGAZINE has the contemporary purpose of being devoted to the publication of fiction that is part of a literary movement toward a synthesis of fiction techniques, emphasizing story—content, imagery, character, voice, style, a rich exploration of points of view, forms, dimensions of time, dramatic and self relationships. Award winning fiction.
Andrew Allegretti, Betty Shiflett, Beverlye Brown, Gary Johnson, Shawn Shiflett, John Schultz, Charles Johnson, Harry Mark Petrakis, Cyrus Colter, Paul Carter Harrison.
Reading Period: Sept. 1–May 15.
Payment: varies, from $5/page.
Reporting Time: 4 months.
Copyright held by magazine; reverts to author upon publication.
2/yr; 1,500
$6.95/ea; 40%
210 pp; 6 x 9
Ad Rates: Contact CLMP for information.
ISBN: 0-936959-00-2
Ingram, DeBoer

FARMER'S MARKET
Jean C. Lee, John E. Hughes.
P.O. Box 1272
Galesburg, IL 61402
Poetry, fiction, essays, translation, graphics.
A national, award-winning magazine, publishing quality literary

work reflective of Midwestern literary traditions and consciousness.

Philip Dacey, Mark Jacobs, Elizabeth Klein, John Knoepfle, Elisabeth Stevens, Elaine Fowler Palencia.

Unsolicited Manuscripts Received/ Published per Year: 2,000/40.

Payment: 2 copies and author's discount.

Reporting Time: 8–12 weeks.

Copyright held by author.

1982; 2/yr; 500

$10/yr; $6/ea; 40%

100-200 pp; 5½ x 8½

No ads

ISSN: 0748-6022

(FEED.)

P.J. Mark, Editor; Judy Rutkin, Editorial Asst; Steve Wiley, Photography Editor; Tara Eng, Art Director

P.O. Box 1567

Madison Square Station, New York, NY 10003

Poetry, fiction, artwork.

(FEED.) is an affordable paperback arts journal documenting the new movement of writing and art. (FEED.) encourages (and is partial to) those underrepresented: queer, feminist, ethnic, etc., but is open to all experience.

Dale Peck, Amudha Rajendran, Gretchen Elkins, Michael J. Mintz, Mark Jacobson.

Payment: 5 copies plus next 2 issues, discount on additional copies.

Reporting Time: prompt.

Copyright held by magazine; reverts to author.

1993; 1,000

$16/yr ind, $22/yr inst; $5/ea; 40%

varies; 6 x 9

Ad Rates: call for rates.

ISSN: 1072-5431

DeBoer, Fine Print

FELL SWOOP

X.J. Dailey

3003 Ponce De Leon St.

New Orleans, LA 70119

(504) 943-5198

Poetry, fiction, essay, drama, art, photographs.

The All Bohemian Revue, **FELL SWOOP** is a guerilla/gorilla venture exploring the edge of 'acceptability' in contemporary writing. We like a good laugh at anyone's expense, especially our own.

Richard Martin, Elizabeth Thomas, Andrei Codrescu, Ed Dorn, Clara Talley-Vincent, R. Speck.

Unsolicited Manuscripts Received/

Published per Year: 1,000/25.
Reading Period: year–round.
Payment: in copies.
Reporting Time: immediately.
Copyright reverts to author upon
publication.
1983; 3/yr; 1,000
$8/yr; $3/ea
pp varies; 8½ x 11
ISSN: 1040-5607

FICTION

Mark Mirsky, Editor; Caryn Stab-
insky, Managing Editor
c/o Dept. of English
The City College
138th & Convent Ave.
New York, NY 10031
(212) 650-6319
Prose fiction, translations.
FICTION represents no particular
school of fiction other than the
inventive and the innovative.
We publish the difficult, the
experimental, the unusual, with-
out excluding the well known.
Amdahl, Brodkey, Oates, Minot,
Macauley, Mirsky, Cherry.
Unsolicited Manuscripts Received/
Published per Year:
2,000–3,000/20–30.
Reading Period: Oct.–May.
Payment: $25 and copies.
Reporting Time: 3–6 months.
Copyright: Fiction, Inc. Reverts to
author on request.

1972; 2/yr; 3,000
$20/3 yr; $6.95/ea; 50%
200 pp; 9 x 6
Ad Rates: negotiable
ISSN: 74470 80497
Ingram, DeBoer

FICTION INTERNATIONAL

Harold Jaffe
Department of English
San Diego State University
San Diego, CA 92182
(619) 594-5443 or (619) 594-5469
Fiction, reviews, essays, visuals.
FICTION INTERNATIONAL's
twin biases are toward postmod-
ernism and progressive politics,
either integrated or apart. We
especially welcome writing from
the "Third World" (both abroad
and at home), and we favor writ-
ing that cuts through or fuses or
ignores the canonical genres.
Note: Special issues advertised in
Poets & Writers or *American
Book Review.*
Robert Coover, Claribel Alegria,
Gerald Vizenor, Michel Serres,
Marianne Hauser, Pierre Guyo-
tat, Margaret Randall, Roque
Dalton.
Unsolicited Manuscripts Received/
Published per Year: 500-700/20-
30.
Reading Period: Sept.–Dec. 15.
Payment: copies.

Reporting Time: 1–3 months.
$12/yr ind, $24/yr inst; $6/ea; 40%
McPherson, Blackwell North
American, Faxon, Baker & Taylor

Ad Rates: $100/page
ISBN: 015-0630
Canadian Magazine Publishers
Association

THE FIDDLEHEAD
Don McKay
Campus House, UNB P.O. Box
4400
Fredericton, New Brunswick,
E3B5A3
CANADA
(506) 453-3501
Short fiction, poetry, book re-
views. (Canadian books only)
Canada's oldest continuing literary
magazine, with a world-wide
circulation. Any good writing,
from any place, will be wel-
come here.
Christine Barton, Jim Meirose,
Ruth Warat.
Unsolicited Manuscripts Received/
Published per Year:
2,000/20–25. Include SASE
with International coupons or
Canadian stamps.
Payment: $10/page
Reporting Time: 4–6 months.
Copyright: First serial rights
only—copyright remains with
author.
1945; 4/yr; 800
$18/yr; $6/ea; 30%
120–128 pp; 6 x 9

FIELD
Stuart Friebert, David Young
Rice Hall
Oberlin College
Oberlin, OH 44074
(216) 775-8408
Poetry, criticism, essays, reviews,
translation.
We look for the best in contempo-
rary poetry, poetics and transla-
tions and emphasize essays by
poets themselves on the craft.
Marianne Boruch, Margaret At-
wood, W. S. Merwin, Robert
Bly, Charles Simic, James Tate,
Shirley Kaufman, Miroslav
Holub.
Unsolicited Manuscripts Received/
Published per Year: 25,000/100.
Reading Period: year–round.
Payment: $20–30/page.
Reporting Time: 2 weeks.
Copyright held by Oberlin Col-
lege; reverts to author upon
publication.
1969; 2/yr; 2,500
$12/yr, $20/2 yrs; $6/ea; 20–30%
100 pp; 5½ x 8½

FINE MADNESS

Sean Bentley, Louis Bergsagel,
Christine Deavel, John Malek,
John Marshall
P.O. Box 31138
Seattle, WA 98103-1138
Poetry, fiction.
We look for poetry that shows wit,
imagination, love of language,
technical skill and individual
style.
Pattiann Rogers, Peter Wild, Caroline Knox, Mark Svenvold, Tess
Gallagher, Albert Goldbarth.
Unsolicited Manuscripts Received/
Published per Year: 1,500/50.
Payment: copies.
Reporting Time: 3 months.
Copyright held by magazine; reverts to author upon publication.
1980 3 every 2 years; 1,000
$9/yr; $5/ea
80 pp; 5½ x 8
ISSN: 0737-4704
Small Changes, Ubiquity, Armadillo, Fine Print

FIRST INTENSITY

Lee Chapman
P.O. Box 140713
Staten Island, NY 10314-0713
Poetry, short fiction.
Robert Kelly, Diane di Prima,
Barry Gifford, Kenneth Irby,
Lucia Berlin.
Unsolicited Manuscripts Received/
Published per Year: 200/60.
Reading Period: year-round.
Payment: 2 copies.
Reporting Time: 6–8 weeks.
Copyright held by First Intensity,
reverts to authors upon publication.
1993; 2/yr; 250
$17/yr, $9/ea; 40%
130 pp; 6 x 9
Small Press Distribution

FIVE FINGERS REVIEW

John High, Aleka Chase, Thoreau
Lovell
P.O. Box 15426
San Francisco, CA 94115
Poetry, fiction, essays.
The FIVE FINGERS REVIEW
seeks to publish fresh, innovative writing and artwork that is
not necessarily defined by the
currently "correct" aesthetic or
ideology. FIVE FINGERS REVIEW welcomes work that
crosses or falls between genres.
In addition to new fiction and
poetry, FIVE FINGERS REVIEW presents essays, interviews, and translations. Each
issue explores a theme; recent
issues have focused on spirituality and the avant–garde, the
new lyric and shifting narrative,
and new writing from Moscow
to San Francisco.

Francisco Alarcon, C. D. Wright, Norman Fischer, Mikhail Epshtein, Leslie Scalapino, Lyn Hejinian, David Levi–Strauss, Thaisa Frank, Keith Waldrop, Rosmarie Waldrop, Peter Gizzi, Aleksei Parschikov.
Unsolicited Manuscripts Received/ Published per Year: 1,000/75.
Payment: in copies.
Reporting Time: 3 months.
Copyright held by magazine; reverts to author upon publication.
1984; 2/yr; 1,000–1,500
$15/yr, $28/2yr, $12 inst; $9/ea; 40%
150–250 pp; 6 x 9
Ad Rates: $150/page (4½ x 7½); $100/½ page (4½ x 3½ or 2 x 7½); $75/¼ page (2 x 3½)
BookPeople, Inland, SPD, L-S
· Distributors, Spectacular Diseases (UK)

and experimental prose. Volumes I-IV, First Series is now complete.
Diane di Prima, Gary Snyder, Michael McClure, Robert Bly, Christina Zawadiwsky, Frank Stewart, Lawrence Ferlinghetti, Joanne Kyger, Sam Hamill, Cole Swensen, Arthur Sze.
Unsolicited Manuscripts Received/ Published per Year: 100/0.
Payment: in copies.
Reporting Time: 4 weeks.
Copyright held by publisher; reverts to author upon publication.
1976; irreg.; 2,000
All issues $15/ea; 40% 5 or more copies, 20% 1–4 copies
160 pp; 8½ x 11
ISSN: 0147-1686
SPD, BookPeople

FLOATING ISLAND

Michael Sykes
P.O. Box 341
Cedarville, CA 96104
(916) 279-2290

Poetry fiction, photography in folio format, graphics/artwork.
Expansive, eclectic, very wideranging with center on West coast of North America—special interest in photography and graphic arts, lyric poetry

THE FLORIDA REVIEW

Russell Kesler
English Department
University of Central Florida
Orlando, FL 32816
(407) 823-2038

Poetry, fiction, essays, reviews.
We publish stories with heart that aren't afraid to take risks. Experimental fiction is welcome, so long as it doesn't make us feel stupid. We look for clear, strong poems filled with real things, real people, real emo-

tions, poems that might conceivably advance our knowledge of the human heart.

Stephen Dixon, Jane Ruiter, Liz Rosenberg, Karen Fish, Michael Martone.

Unsolicited Manuscripts Received/ Published per Year: 2,500/40.

Reading Period: year–round.

Payment: small honoraria are awarded when possible.

Reporting Time: 2–3 months.

Copyright held by University of Central Florida; reverts to author upon publication.

1972; 2/yr; 1,000

$7/yr ind, $11/2 yrs ind, $9/yr inst, $13/2 yrs inst; $4.50/ea; 40%

128 pp; 5½ x 8½

Ad Rates: exchange ads only

ISSN: 0742-2466

Fine Print

FLYWAY (formerly POET AND CRITIC)

Stephen Pett
203 Ross Hall
Iowa State University
Ames, IA 50011
(515) 294-2180

Poetry, fiction, literary nonfiction, reviews.

FLYWAY publishes poems, stories, excerpts from novels, personal essays, reviews (3,000 words or less), and photographs. All creative work will be accompanied by brief commentary from its author. Commentary will be requested of those whose work is accepted.

We try to be receptive to all work, asking only that it have ambition and display a sense of craft.

Michael Martone, Jane Smiley, Neal Bowers, Mary Swander, Ray Young Bear, Fern Kupfer, and Joe Geha.

Reading Period: Sept.–May.

Payment: 1 copy.

Reporting Time: 3 days–2 months.

Copyright held by Iowa State University; reverts to author upon publication.

1995–96; 3/yr; 1,000

$18/yr ind, $18/yr inst; $8/ea; 40%

96 pp; 6 x 9

Ad Rates: upon request; exchanges with other magazines

ISSN: 0032-1958

FOLIO

Department of Literature
American University
Washington, DC 20016
(202) 885-2973

Poetry, fiction, reviews, translations, black & white art & photography.

FOLIO prints quality fiction and poetry by established writers as well as those just starting out. We like to comment on submissions when time permits. Prose limit: 4,500 words. SASE required.

Henry Taylor, Linda Pastan, William Stafford, Jean Valentine, Simon Perchik, Kermit Moyer, Myra Sklarew.

Unsolicited Manuscripts Received/ Published per Year: 1,300/6 stories/prose; 30 poems.

Reading Period: Aug.–April.

Payment: prizes of up to $75 awarded for best fiction and poem.

Copyright reverts to author upon publication.

1984; 2/yr; 400

$10/yr; $5/ea; 30%

70 pp; 6 x 9

DeBoer

FOOTWORK: The Paterson Literary Review (PLR)

Maria Mazziotti Gillan

Cultural Affairs Department

Passaic County Community College

1 College Boulevard

Paterson, NJ 07505-1179

(201) 684-6555

Poetry, fiction, review, graphics/ artwork.

PLR is a high quality literary quarterly.

Laura Boss, William Stafford, Marge Piercy, David Ray.

Unsolicited Manuscripts Received/ Published per Year: 10,000/200.

Payment: in copies.

Reading Period: Jan.–Mar.

Reporting Time: 6 months.

Copyright held by Passaic County College; reverts to author upon publication.

1979; 1/yr; 1,000

$10/yr ind, $12/yr inst; $10/ea; 40%

290 pp; 8½ x 11, perfect-bound

Ad Rates: $300/page (8½ x 11); $150/½ page (8½ x 5); $100/¼ page (4 x 2½)

FORKROADS: A Journal of Ethnic American Writing

David Kherdian

Box 159

Spencertown, NY 12165

Poems, stories, plays, profiles, studies, memoirs by and reviews of ethnic American writers.

The first multi-ethnic magazine to publish all American writers whose work is informed—at least in part—by another culture.

Luis J. Rodriguez, Michael Lally, Lawson Fusao Inada, Piri Thomas, Norbert Krapf.

Payment: $50.00 poems & reviews: $200.00 stories, interviews.
Reporting Time: 6 weeks generally.
Copyright held by Forkroads Publishing Company.
1995; 4/yr; 5,000
$20/yr ind, $6/ea; 55%
96–122 pp; 7⅝ x 9¼
Ad Rates: send for prospectus

THE FORMALIST

William Baer
320 Hunter Drive
Evansville, IN 47711

Contemporary metrical poetry and translations.
Devoted entirely to formal, metrical verse and publishing contemporary poetry and translations that participate in the great tradition of metrical poetry from Chaucer to Wilbur.
Howard Nemerov, Richard Wilbur, Mona Van Duyn, Derek Walcott, Maxine Kumin, John Updike.
Unsolicited Manuscripts Received/ Published per Year: 5,000+/160+.
Reading Period: year–round.
Payment: 2 copies.
Reporting Time: within 2 months.
Copyright: yes.
1990; 2/yr; growing
$12/yr, $22/2 yr; $6.50/ea; contact publisher

128pp; 6 x 9
No advertising
ISSN: 1046-7874

THE FOUR DIRECTIONS

Joanna and William Meyer
P.O. Box 729
Tellico Plains, TN 37385
(615) 524-8612

American Indian authors, poets and writers.
To provide a forum for American Indian writers; to provide a positive publishing experience; to assist in development of Indian writers and develop a market and readership for Native American Writers.
Raven Hail, E. James Hillsburg, Whitefeather.
Unsolicited Manuscripts Received/ Published per Year: Numerous/100+.
Payment: 2 cents/word for stories and articles; $10/full page poem; $5/half page poem.
Reporting Time: 4–6 weeks.
Copyright: first serial rights.
1992; 4/yr
$21/yr; $6/ea; 40%
64 pp; 8 ½ x 11
Ad Rates: $145/page; $100/½ page; $70/¼ page; inside covers: $170 back, $195 front

FOUR QUARTERS

John J. Keenan, Editor; John P.
Rossi, Associate Editor
La Salle Univ.
1900 W. Olney Avenue
Philadelphia, PA 19141
(215) 951-1610
Poetry, fiction, essays, vignettes,
book reviews.
A magazine of contemporary cul-
ture aimed at college-educated
readers. Publishes nonspecial-
ized articles, essays, fiction, and
poetry.
Seamus Heaney, Joyce Carol
Oates, James Merrill, John
Lukacs, John Hollander, J.D.
McClatchy.
Unsolicited Manuscripts Received/
Published per Year: 500/35+.
Reading Period: Jan.–June 30.
Payment: on acceptance.
Reporting Time: 6 weeks.
Copyright held by La Salle Univ.;
assignable to author.
1951; 2/yr
$8/yr; $4/ea; 40%
64 pp; 7 x 10
Ad Rates: $100/page
ISSN: 0015-9107

FRANK: An International Jour-
nal of Contemporary Writing
and Art

David Applefield, Editor/Publisher
104 rue Edouard Vaillant
93100 Montreuil
FRANCE
(331) 48.59.66.58; Fax (331)
48.59.66.68
Poetry, fiction, translations, interviews, graphics/artwork, essays,
photographs.
FRANK is a highly eclectic journal open to both established and
emerging talent which emphasizes internationalism. The journal encourages both literary and
visual work that takes risks but
does not ignore the value of
intellectual traditions. Contemporary Chinese, Congolese,
Turkish, Nordic, Philippino,
Belgian and Pakistani writing.
Vaclav Havel, Samuel Beckett,
Italo Calvino, James Tate, Allen
Ginsberg, Paul Bowles, Robert
Coover, Raymond Carver, Rita
Dove, Stephen Dixon, Sony
Labou Tansi, Frederick Bar-
thelme, Phillip Glass.
Unsolicited Manuscripts Received/
Published per Year: 1,000/30.
Payment: $5/page plus two copies.
Copyright held by author.
1983; 2/yr; 4,000
$30/4 issues ind, $60/4 issues inst;
$9.95/ea; 33%–40%
224 pp; 5½ x 8½
Ad Rates: $1,000/page (5 x 8);
$500/½ page (4½ x 3½);
$300/¼ page (2½ x 3½)

ISSN: 0738-9299; ISBN:
2-908171-09-0

FREE FOCUS

Patricia D. Coscia

JAF Station

Box 7415

New York, NY 10116-4630

Women's poetry.

FREE FOCUS is a small-press
magazine which focuses on the
educated women of today and
needs stories and poems. The
poems can be as long as 2
pages or as short as 3 lines. No
X-rated material. Poems should
be single-spaced on individual
sheets.

Patricia D. Coscia, Ed Janz.

Unsolicited Manuscripts Received/
Published per Year: 500/200.

Payment: 1 copy.

Reporting Time: 6 months.

Copyright held by editor.

1985; 2/yr; 500

$4/yr; $2/ea

20 pp; 8 x 14

Ad Rates: $1/column; $3/page

ISSN: 0447-5667

FREE LUNCH

Ron Offen

P.O. Box 7647

Laguna Niguel, CA 92607-7647

Poetry.

Unsolicited Manuscripts Received/
Published per Year: 2,500/75.

Reading Period: Sept. 2–May 31.

Copyright held by Free Lunch
Arts Alliance.

1989; irregular; 1,200

Magazine is free to all serious
U.S. Poets living in the U.S.
send SASE for details. Will not
consider more than 3 poems per
submission.

Others: $12/yr; $5 ea

32 pp; 5½ x 8½

Ad Rates: $100/page (4 x 8);
$60/½ page (4 x 4); $35/¼
page (2 x 2)

FUEL MAGAZINE

Ms. Andy Lowry

P.O. Box 146640

Chicago, IL 60614

(312) 235-5096

Fiction, art & poetry.

FUEL is an eclectic home for risk
takers and truth seekers. Aca-
demics beware—we want to be
a zine not a literary journal.

Nicole Panter, Bill Shields, Denise
Dee, Larry Oberc, Dan Nielson.

Unsolicited Manuscripts Re
ceived/Published per Year:
1,500/150–200.

Payment: 1 copy.

Reading Period: year round, varies as each issue fills.
Reporting Time: 2–4 weeks.
Copyright held by author.
1992; 4/yr; 3000
$10/4 copies; $3/ea
40 pp; 8½ x 5½
Ad Rates: vary, generally trade w/other publications.
Fine Print, Sugar Distribution

FURIOUS FICTIONS

Joseph Lerner
P.O. Box 423665
San Francisco, CA 94102
(415) 431-0461
"Flash" or short-short fiction.

FURIOUS FICTIONS is the leading literary journal devoted to showcasing the best new short-short or "flash" fiction in the U.S. today.
Molly Giles, Diane Glancy, Tom Whaler, Jacques Servin.
Unsolicited Manuscripts Received/ Published per Year: 6,000/60.
Reading Period: year–round.
Payment: 1 year subscription.
Reporting Time: 2 weeks–2 months.
Copyright: First serial rights.
1992; 3/yr; 1,500
$12/yr; $3.95/ea
36 pp; 8½ x 11
ISSN: 1065-7983
Ubiquity, Desert Moon, Fine Print

G

GAIA: A JOURNAL OF LITERARY & ENVIRONMENTAL ARTS

Robert S. King, Editor-in-Chief
P.O. Box 709
Winterville, GA 30683
(706) 542-0811
Poetry, fiction, essays,
graphics/artwork.
GAIA is a quarterly with emphasis on environmental themes.
E.G. Burrows, Stuart Friebert,
Paul Grant, Ann Struthers, Martha M. Vertreace.
Payment: 1 year sub.
Reporting Time: 2 months.
Copyright held by Whistle Press,
Inc.
1993; 4/yr; 450
$9/yr (ind & inst); $4/ea; 40%
44 pp

THE GALLEY SAIL REVIEW

Stanley McNail
1630 University Ave., #42
Berkeley, CA 94703
(415) 486-0187
Poetry, reviews.
GSR seeks excellence in contemporary poetry, without regard for schools, cliques, or "movements." It values sincerity and honors craftsmanship. It tries to encourage poetry that speaks to the human condition in this modern world, and to develop a wider appreciation of poetry as an essential art in society.
Martin Robbins, Michael Culross,
Laurel Ann Bogen, Harold Witt,
Carol Hamilton.
Payment: in copies.
Copyright held by magazine; reverts to author upon publication.
1958; 3/yr; 400

$8/yr ind, $15/2 yr ind, $15/2 yr
  inst; $3/ea; 40%
40 pp; 8½ x 5½
ISSN: 0016-4100

GAS: HIGH OCTANE
POETRY

Kevin Opstedal & Tom Clark
3164 Emerson
Palo Alto, CA 94306
(415) 493-5903
Poetry.
GAS prints only premium high-
  octane poetry guaranteed to rid
  you of those psychic knocks &
  pings. Free cranial liposuction
  with fill-up.
Ed Sanders, Alice Notley,
  Bukowski, Dorn, Eileen Myles.
Payment: copies.
Reporting Time: 1–2 weeks.
Copyright reverts to individual
  authors upon publication.
1990; irregular; 100
$30/sub; $10/ea; 40%
130 pp; 9 x 7½
Ad Rates: $100/page; $50/½ page;
  $25/¼ page
ISSN: 1058-532X
BookPeople, Last Gasp

A GATHERING OF THE
TRIBES

Steve Cannon, Jenny Seymore,
  Christian Haye, Melanie Best

P.O. Box 20693
Tompkins Square
New York, NY 10009
Poetry, fiction, essays, reviews,
  interviews, graphics/artwork,
  photographs.
TRIBES is a multicultural, maga-
  zine of writing on the arts
  which reflects the richness and
  diversity of America's cultural
  heritage.
Jessica Hagedorn, Ishmael Reed,
  Hernandez Cruz, Jayne Cortez,
  Al Young.
Payment: none.
Copyright held by authors.
1991; 2/yr; 1,500
$15/yr ind, $20/yr inst; $4.50/ea;
  40%
80 pp; 8½ x 11
Ad Rates: $275/page (6¼ x 8½);
  $150/½ page (6¼ x 4¼)
ISSN: 1058-9112

GEORGETOWN REVIEW

Steven Carter
400 E. College St.
Box 227
Georgetown, KY 40324
(502) 863-7567
Fiction and Poetry.
A literary review looking to publish honest, quality fiction and
  poetry.

Unsolicited Manuscripts Received/
Published per Year:
1,000–1,500/60–80.
Reading Period: Sept. 1–May 1.
Payment: 2 copies.
Reporting Time: 2–4 months.
Copyright reverts to author upon
publication.
1993; 2/yr; 1,200
$10/yr; $5/ea; 55%
112 pp; 5¼ x 8¼
Ad Rates: $75/page; $32.50/½
page.
Fine Print, DeBoer

THE GEORGIA REVIEW

Stanley W. Lindberg
University of Georgia
Athens, GA 30602-9009
(706) 542-3481

Poetry, fiction, essays, reviews,
graphics/artwork.

An international journal of arts
and letters with a special interest in current American literary
writing; seeking interdisciplinary thesis-oriented essays—not
scholarly articles—and engaging
book reviews, plus the best in
contemporary poetry and fiction; authors range from Nobel
laureates and Pulitzer Prize winners to the as-yet unknown and
previously unpublished.

Rita Dove, Stephen Dunn, Eudora
Welty, Fred Chappell, Seamus
Heaney, Mary Hood, Louise
Erdrich, Wayne Dodd, Emily
Hiestand.

Unsolicited Manuscripts Received/
Published per Year: 17,000/100

Payment; $3/line for poetry;
$35/printed page for prose.

Reporting Time: 8–12 weeks.

Reading Period: year-round, but
no submissions accepted during
June, July, or August.

Compilation copyright entered by
the University of Georgia,
which has purchased first serial
rights; all other rights are retained by individual authors.

1947; 4/yr; 7,000
$18/yr; $7/ea
208 pp; 6¾ x 10
Ad Rates: $350/page (4¾ x 7½);
$225/½ page (4¾ x 3⅝)
ISSN: 0016-8386
DeBoer, Ubiquity, Fine Print,
Anderson News

THE GETTYSBURG
REVIEW

Peter Stitt
Gettysburg College
Gettysburg, PA 17325-1491
(717) 337-6770

Poetry, fiction, essays, graphics/
artwork.

THE GETTYSBURG REVIEW

is an interdisciplinary magazine of arts and ideas, which features the highest quality poetry, fiction, essays, essay-reviews, and graphics by both beginning and established writers and artists. Two special interests are the publication of serial fiction and the inclusion of a full-color graphics section in each issue. Essays are in a variety of disciplines, with a wide range of subject matter.

E.L. Doctorow, Charles Simic, Philip Levine, Alison Baker, Hayden Carruth, Linda Pastan, Rita Dove, Charles Wright, Marilyn Nelson Waniek, Richard Wilbur, Joyce Carol Oates.

Unsolicited Manuscripts Received/ Published per Year: 4,000/85.

Reading Period: Sept.–June.

Payment: $25/page prose; $2/line poetry; upon publication.

Copyright held by Gettysburg College; reverts to author upon publication.

1988; 4/yr; 4,200

$18/yr ind, $18/yr inst; $32/2 yr; $45/3 yr; $7/ea; 40%

170 pp; 6¾ x 10

Ad Rates: $225/page (5 x 7½)

ISSN: 0898-4557

Eastern News

GIORNO POETRY SYSTEMS

John Giorno
222 Bowery
New York, NY 10012
(212) 925-6372

Poetry.

Magazine in three formats: LP record, Compact Disc, and Cassette. Video Pak series is a magazine in video format.

Laurie Anderson, William Burroughs, Patti Smith, Diamanda Galas, Nick Cave.

Payment: $500 royalty advance, and 12% of the retail price of each record sold.

1972; 4/yr; 10,000

$8.98/single album; $12.98/double album; $8.98/cassette; $13.98/ compact disc; $39.95/video cassette; 40%—55%

GLIMMER TRAIN STORIES

Linda Davies, Susan Burmeister-Brown
812 SW Washington St. #1205
Portland, OR 97205
(503) 221-0836

Quarterly short story magazine printed on acid-free, recycled stock. Each story is illustrated.

Many unknowns as well as Charles Baxter, Ellen Gilchrist, Mary McGarry Morris, Richard Bausch, Ann Beattie.

Unsolicited Manuscripts Received/
Published per Year: 12,000/32.
Payment: $550 upon acceptance.
Reporting Time: 3 months.
Copyright reverts to author upon
publication.
1991; 4/yr; 19,500
$29/yr; $9/ea; 40%
168 pp; 5¾ x 9¼
No advertising
Ingram, IPD, Pacific Pipeline, De-
Boer, Ubiquity, BookPeople,
ANCO, Fine Print

GRAB-A-NICKEL
Barbara Smith
Alderson-Broaddus College
Philippi, WV 26416
(304) 457-1700

Poetry, fiction, reviews, photographs, graphics/artwork.

GRAB-A-NICKEL is a tabloid
journal of poems, fiction, book
reviews, photographs and drawings. Open submissions; priority
given to Appalachian writers
and subject matter. There is en-
couragement of new writers of
any age or background. It is a
product of a college community's writers' workshop.
Barbara Smith, John McKernan,
Eddy Pendaris, Mark Rowh, T.
Kilgore Splake, Llewellyn
McKernan, Jim Wayne Miller.

Unsolicited Manuscripts Received/
Published per Year:
450–500/200.
Payment: in copies.
Copyright held by author.
1977; 2–3/yr; 1,000
25¢/ea
16–20 pp; 11½ x 14

GRADIVA
Luigi Fontanella
P.O. Box 831
Stony Brook, NY 11790
(516) 632-7448 or (516) 632-7440

Poetry, essays, reviews, translation, interviews.

GRADIVA is an international
journal of modern Italian literature that focuses on literary
criticism and theory. All contributions are published in English
or Italian. Creative works written in other languages are published with translation.
Umberto Eco, Edoardo Sanguineti,
Mario Luzi, Alfredo Giuliani,
Andrea Zanzotto.
Unsolicited Manuscripts Received/
Published per year: 50+/4.
Payment: in copies, subscription.
Copyright held by magazine; reverts to author upon publication.
1986; 2/yr; 3,000
$25/yr
100 pp; 5½ x 8½

Ad Rates: $100/page (5½ x 8½); $60/½ page (5½ x 4¼); $35/¼ page (2¾ x 4¼)

GRAHAM HOUSE REVIEW

Peter Balakian, Bruce Smith
Box 5000
Colgate University
Hamilton, NY 13346
(315) 824-1000, ext. 262
Poetry, essays, translations, interviews.
We publish the best poetry and poetry in translation we can get. We have just begun an interview series and will publish essays in the future. We pay scrupulous attention to production, and have an international interest in selecting material.
Seamus Heaney, Derek Walcott, Madeline De Frees, David Wagoner, Maxine Kumin, Carolyn Forché.
Unsolicited Manuscripts Received per Year: 10,000.
Payment: in copies.
Reporting Time: 1–2 months.
Copyright held by magazine; reverts to author upon publication.
1976; 1/yr; 1,750
$7.50/yr ind, $7.50/inst; $7.50/ea; 20%
125 pp; 8½ x 5½

GRAIN

Geoffrey Ursell, Elizabeth Philips, Edna Alford, Judith Krause, Catherine Macaulay
Box 1154
Regina, Saskatchewan, S4P3B4
CANADA
(306) 757-6310; Fax (306) 565-8554
Literary and visual art.
GRAIN publishes the best new previously unpublished fiction, poetry, and other genres from across Canada and around the world.
Unsolicited Manuscripts Received/ Published per Year: Hundreds/80.
Reading Period: year–round.
Payment: $30—$100 (Canadian).
Reporting Time: 2–4 months.
Copyright remains with author.
1973; 4/yr; 1,525
$19.95/yr; $6.95/ea; 40%
144 pp; 6 x 9
Ad Rates: $250/page; $150/½ page; $100/¼ page
ISSN: 0315-7423
Canadian Magazine Publishers Association

GRAND STREET

Jean Stein
131 Varick St., Room 906
New York, NY 10013
(212) 807-6548

Poetry, fiction, essays, interviews, art.

Andrei Bitov, Henry Green, Toni Morrison, William T. Vollmann, Paul Auster, John Ashbery, Nina Berberova.

Unsolicited Manuscripts Received/ Published per Year: 3,500/10.

Reading Period: year–round.

Payment: inquire.

Reporting Time: 6–8 weeks.

Copyright: one-time first-serial rights only; author retains copyright.

1981; 4/yr; 6,000

$40/yr ind, $55/yr foreign; $12.95/ea

270 pp; 7 x 9

Ad Rates: $450/page

ISSN: 0734-5496

D.A.P./Distributed Art Publishers

GRASSLANDS REVIEW

Laura B. Kennelly

NT Box 13706

Denton, TX 76203

(817) 565-2126/ or 565-2127

Poetry and fiction.

Publishes poetry and fiction from known and unknown authors chosen by students in adult learners' creative writing group. Send manuscripts only in October or March.

Jendi Reiter, James Hoggard, Robert Weaver.

Unsolicited Manuscripts Received/ Published per Year: 300/64.

Reading Period: Oct. & Mar. (postmarks only).

Payment: in copies.

Reporting Time: 3–4 months.

Copyright reverts to author.

1988; 2/yr; 300

$8/yr ind, $15/yr inst; $2.50/ea

90 pp; 5 x 9

Ad Rates: $20/½ page, plus subscription

GREAT RIVER REVIEW

Orval Lund

211 West Seventh St.

Winona, MN 55987

(507) 454-6564

Poetry, fiction, criticism, reviews, graphics.

Dedicated to publishing the best in fiction, creative prose, and poetry, and to showcasing the work of new, emerging and established writers. Specially interested in Midwestern writers. **GREAT RIVER REVIEW** is accepting no unsolicited manuscripts until further notice.

Unsolicited Manuscripts Received/ Published per Year: 1,200/50.

Reading Period: year–round.

Payment: in copies.

Reporting Time: 1–3 months.

Copyright reverts to author.
1977; 2/yr; 1,200
$10/yr; $6/ea
280 pp; 6 x 8
Ebsco, Faxon, Aquinas

GREEN FUSE POETRY

Brian Boldt
3365 Holland Dr.
Santa Rosa, CA 95404
(707) 544-8303

Contemporary free verse.
We focus on environmental themes and issues of war and peace in a 64-page, digest size format; perfect-bound.
Antler, John Brandi, David Chorlton, Dorianne Laux, Denise Levertov, Laurel Speer.
Unsolicited Manuscripts Received/ Published per Year: 4,000/100.
Payment: 1 copy, more to featured poets.
Reporting Time: Within 12 weeks.
Copyright reverts to author upon publication.
1984; 2/yr; 600
3 issues for $14; $4.50
64 pp; digest; perfect-bound

GREEN MOUNTAINS REVIEW

Neil Shepard, Poetry Editor and General Editor; Tony Whedon, Fiction Editor

Johnson State College
Johnson, VT 05656
(802) 635-2356

Poetry, fiction, essays, reviews, interviews, translations, photographs.
GMR publishes work by promising newcomers and well-known writers from across the country.
Galway Kinnell, Denise Levertov, Larry Levis, David St. John, Ellen Lesser, David Wojahn.
Unsolicited Manuscripts Received/ Published per Year: 2,000/60.
Reading Period: Sept.–May.
Payment: in copies.
Reporting Time: 1–3 months.
Copyright held by magazine; reverts to author upon publication.
1987; 2/yr; 1,300
$12/yr; $6/ea; 40%
144–172 pp; 6 x 9
$150/page; $75/½ page
ISSN: 0895-9307
Ubiquity, Fine Print, Armadillo

THE GREENSBORO REVIEW

Jim Clark
Department of English
Univ. North Carolina-Greensboro
Greensboro, NC 27412
(910) 334-5459; Fax (910) 334-3281
Poetry, fiction.
Contemporary and experimental.

We want to see the best being written regardless of theme, subject or style.

Ellen Herman, Peter Taylor, Greg Johnson, Peter Meinke, Lane von Herzen, Jere Hoar, Molly Giles, Robert Morgan, Greg Kuzma, Thomas Lux.

Unsolicited Manuscripts Received/ Published per Year: 1,000–1,200 fictions/12–20.

Payment: in copies.

Reporting Time: 2–4 months.

Copyright held by magazine; reverts to author.

1966; 2/yr; 5–600

$8/yr, $16/2 yrs, $20/3 yrs; $4/ea

120–180 pp; 6 x 9

ISSN: 0017-4084

Adam Zagajewski, Ann Beattie, Barry Hannah, Lydia Davis, Michael S. Harper, Gail Wronsky, X. J. Kennedy, Stephen Dixon, Caila Rossi, Richard Howard; interviews with Czeslaw Milosz, Walter Hopps, Amy Hempl, and others.

Unsolicited Manuscripts Received/ Published per Year: 780/60

Payment: copies.

Copyright held by magazine; reverts to author upon publication.

1987; 2/yr; 1,000

$12/yr subscription, $7/ea; $5/back issue; $12/Barthelme Memorial

140 pp; 9 x 6

No ads

ISSN: 0896-2251

GULF COAST

Polly Koch, Eric Williamson
Department of English
University of Houston
Houston, TX 77204-3012

Poetry, fiction, essays, interviews, art criticism, articles.

GULF COAST encourages submission of high-quality, wellcrafted work that takes risks, whether formally inventive or intensifying a form's inherent strengths, with an acute awareness of its own language—all styles & subjects.

GULF STREAM MAGAZINE

Lynne Barrett, Editor; Associate Editors: Christopher Gleason, Blythe Nobleman.
FIU, North Miami Campus
North Miami, FL 33181
(305) 940-5599

Poetry, fiction, essays.

GSM publishes high quality fiction, poetry and essays. We are open to experimental and mainstream work. No more than 5 poems. Limit prose to 25 pages.

Gerald Costanzo, Ann Hood, Stuart Dybek, Dara Wier.

Unsolicited Manuscripts Received/
Published per Year: 1,000/50.
Reading Period: Sept.–April.
Payment: in copies.
Reporting Time: 1–3 months.
Copyright held by magazine; First
North American serial rights.
1989; 2/yr; 350
$7.50/yr; $4/ea; 40%
96 pp; 8½ x 5½

GYPSY

Belinda Subraman, S. Ramnath
10708 Gay Brewer Drive
El Paso, TX 79935
(915) 592-3701

Fiction, reviews, graphics/artwork,
essays, poetry.
We are an international family of
independent literary and visual
artists. We seek to enlarge our
family and support. Please write
for current themes and guidelines. In general, we are interested in writing of lasting value,
usually dealing with human
rights and experience. Currently
doing double issue book edi-
tions. Inquire before submitting.
Prices vary.
Peter Wild, Laurel Speer, James
Purdy, Albert Huffstickler, Gerald Locklin.
Unsolicited Manuscripts Received/
Published per Year: 5,000±/180±.
Reporting Time: 6–12 weeks.
Copyright: Vergin' Press.
1984; 2/yr; 1,000
Ad Rates: $100/page; $55/½ page;
$30/¼ page
ISSN: 0176-3148

H

ISSN: 1060-0469

HABERSHAM REVIEW

David L. Greene, Lisa Hodgens
Lumpkin, co-editors
Piedmont College
P.O. Box 10
Demorest, GA 30535
(706) 778-3000
Fiction, Poetry

HABERSHAM REVIEW is a
general literary journal with a
regional focus (Southeastern
U.S.) Each issue features an
unpublished work by and an
interview with a prominent
Southern writer.
D.C. Berry, Judith Cofer, Rose-
mary Daniell, Mary Hood, Terry
Kay, Frank Gannon
Unsolicited Manuscripts Received/
Published per Year: 900/40.
Payment: copies.
Reporting Time: 4 months ±.
Copyright held by Piedmont Col-
lege; reverts to author upon
publication.
1991; 2/yr; 500
$12/yr; $6/ea; 40%
96 pp; 6 x 9
Ad Rates: $500/page (5 x 8+);
$250/½ page (2½ x 4±)
ISSN: 1060-0469

**HAIGHT ASHBURY
LITERARY JOURNAL**

Joanne Hotchkiss, Alice Rogoff,
Will Walker
558 Joost Avenue
San Francisco, CA 94127
(415) 584-8264

The magazine began with six editors of extremely diverse socio-
economic and ethnic back-
grounds. The magazine
encompasses diversity of view-
point, racial, sexual as well as
style, tending to confront the

difficult and painful of human experiences as well as the higher reaches of emotional experiences. The Journal publishes both local writers and other interested writers.

Eugene Ruggles, Mona Lisa Saloy, Peter Plate, Jack Hirschman, Laura del Feugo, Leslie Simon, Edgar Silex.

Unsolicited Manuscripts Received/ Published per Year: 800/100.

Reading Period: Oct.–Dec., Mar.–June

Payment: in copies.

Reporting Time: 2–4 months.

Copyright held by author.

1980; 1½/yr; 2-3,000

$35/lifetime subs; $3/ea by mail; $6/2 issues; $12/4 issues

16 pp; 11 x 17¼

Ad Rates: $150/page (10 x 17); $75/½ page (7½ x 9); $50/¼ page (9 x 5); $40, $30, $20 for smaller ads

HAMBONE

Nathaniel Mackey
134 Hunolt Street
Santa Cruz, CA 95060
(408) 426-3072

Poetry, fiction, criticism, reviews, plays, translation, interviews, photographs, graphics/artwork.

Cross-cultural work emphasizing the centrifugal.

Edward Kamau Brathwaite, Susan Howe, Geoffrey O'Brien, Gustaf Sobin, Jay Wright.

Payment: copies.

Reporting Time: 1–4 months.

Copyright held by magazine: reverts to author upon publication.

1974; 1/yr; 600

$14/2 issues ind; $18/2 issues inst; $8/ea; 40%

200 pp; 5½ x 8½

ISSN: 0733-6616

Small Press Distribution

HAMMERS

Nat David
1718 Sherman #203
Evanston, IL 60201
(708) 328-7555

Poetry.

An end of the millennium irregular poetry magazine.

Beatriz Badikian, John Dickson, Michael Warr, Luis Rodriquez, Albert Huffstickler.

Unsolicited Manuscripts Received/ Published per Year: 1,000/100.

Payment: 1 free copy.

Reporting Time: 1–2 months.

1990; 2/yr; 500

$5/ea; 40%

7 x 8½

THE HAMPDEN-SYDNEY POETRY REVIEW

Tom O'Grady
P.O. Box 126

Hampden-Sydney, VA 23943
(804) 223-8209

Poetry.

A small, carefully-printed correspondence among poets which attempts to print the unknown with the known.

David Ignatow, Robert Pack, Patricia Goedicke, David Huddle, Lewis Turco.

Payment: in copies.

Copyright held by Tom O'Grady; reverts to author upon publication.

1975; 2/yr; 500

$5/yr ind; $5/yr, $12/3-yr inst; $5/ea; 1990 Anthology 328 pp. $12.95; 40%

60 pp; 5 x 9

No ads

HANGING LOOSE

Robert Hershon, Dick Lourie, Mark Pawlak, Ron Schreiber

231 Wyckoff Street
Brooklyn, NY 11217
(212) 206-8465

Poetry, fiction, translation, graphics/artwork.

Our interests continue to center on finding new writers and then staying with them, often to the point of book publication. (Book mss and artwork by invitation only.)

Paul Violi, Kimiko Hahn, Steven Schrader, Donna Brook, Gary Lenhart.

Payment: some payment to contributors.

Reporting Time: 2–3 months.

Copyright held by magazine; reverts to author upon publication.

1966; 3/yr; 1,500

$12.50/yr ind, $15/yr inst; $5/ea + $1.50 postage; 20%–40%

96 pp; 7 x 8½

ISSN: 0440-2316

Ubiquity, SPD, Fine Print, Book-People

HANSON'S SYMPOSIUM: Of Literary & Social Interest

Eric Hanson

113 Merryman Court
Annapolis, MD 21401
(410) 626-0744

Poetry, fiction, essays, humor, interviews, dialogues, and various features.

A magazine of general interest, we are striving to combine the traditionally separate aspects of literary and social journals into one magazine.

Unsolicited Manuscripts Received/ Published per Year: 2,000/50.

Payment: $30–$100, plus 1 copy.

Reporting Time: 2 weeks.

Copyright held by Hanson Publishing, reverts to author.

1988; 2/yr; 1,500

$5/ea; 40%
80 pp; 8½ x 11
No ads

HAPPINESS HOLDING TANK

Albert Drake
9727 S.E. Reedway
Portland, OR 97266
(503) 771-6779

Poetry, very short fiction, essays, reviews, interviews, etc. . . .
HHT is an eclectic magazine, and publishes a wide variety of poetry—free verse, forms, narrative, lyric, found poetry, visual poetry, etc. . . . Emphasis is on the well-made poem that expresses a sense of humanity.

Earle Birney, Vern Rutsala, William Stafford, William Matthews, Judith Goren, Lee Upton.
Unsolicited Manuscripts Received/ Published per Year: 1,000+/100.
Payment: in copies.
Reporting Time: 2 weeks–2 months.
Copyright held by author.
1970; 1/yr; 300
$2/ea
pp and size varies
Have never had paid ads.

HAWAII REVIEW

Michelle Viray
UH Mānoa
Department of English
1733 Donaghho Rd.
Honolulu, HI 96822
(808) 956-8548

Poetry, fiction, criticism, essays, reviews, plays, translations, interviews, photographs, graphics/artwork.
Ursule Molinaro, Ian MacMillan, Nell Altizer, John Unterecker, Michael McPherson, William Pitt Root, Frank Stewart.
Unsolicited Manuscripts Received/ Published per Year: 1,000/100.
Payment: $10–75, plus 2 copies; more for cover art.
Reporting Time: 30–120 days.
Copyright held by magazine; reverts to author upon publication.
1973; 3/yr; 2,000
$15/yr; $5/ea
100–180 pp; 5½ x 9
Ad Rates: $100/page
ISSN: 0093-9625

HAYDEN'S FERRY REVIEW

Salima Keegan
ASU Matthews Center
Tempe, AZ 85287-1502
(602) 965-1243

Poetry, fiction, nonfiction.
Nationally distributed magazine publishing quality literary art.
HFR promotes work of emerging and established writers of

fiction, poetry, and creative
nonfiction.
David St. John, Ken Kesey, Maura
Stanton, Raymond Carver, Nor-
man Dubie, Rita Dove, Charles
Wright, Jean Valentine, Naomi
Shihab Nye, John Ashbery.
Unsolicited Manuscripts Received/
Published per Year: 6,000/60.
Reading Period: year–round.
Payment: copies.
Reporting Time: 3–5 months.
Copyright reverts to author.
1986; 2/yr; 1,000
$10/yr; $6/ea
128; 6 x 9
ISSN 0887-5170

THE HEARTLANDS TODAY
The Firelands Writing Center
Nancy Dunham & Larry Smith,
 Managing Editors
Firelands College,
Huron, Ohio 44839
(419) 433-5560

Photography, personal essays, fiction (4,000 wds), poems.
We feature a theme from the contemporary Midwest—The Heartlands Today—for each volume
(annual). The writing must be
set in the Midwest, though it
need not treat the Midwest. We
look for writing of character
and place. Theme for 1994;

community and what it means
in the Midwest.
Gary Snyder, Scott R. Sanders,
Carolyn Banks, Antler.
Unsolicited Manuscripts Received/
Published per Year: 400/40.
Reading Period: Jan.–June.
Payment: $10 and 2 copies.
Reporting Time: 2 months.
Copyright: we buy first rights (in
some cases second), return
rights to author.
1991; 1/yr; 850
$8.50/yr; $8.50/ea
160; 6 x 9
ISSN: 1066-6176

**HELLAS, A Journal of Poetry
& the Humanities**
Gerald Harnett
304 South Tyson Avenue
Glenside, PA 19038
(215) 884-1086

Poetry, classics, Renaissance &
modern literary studies.
We provide a unique forum for the
poetry, theory and criticism of
poets working in meter–"The
new formalism," or, as our advertising describes that movement, "The New Classicism."
Timothy Steele, Richard Moore,
Joseph Malone, Frederick
Turner, Dana Gioia.
Unsolicited Manuscripts Received/
Published per Year: 5,000 po-

ems, 100 articles/60-70 poems, 20-25 articles.

Copyright: First North American serial rights only.

1990; 2/yr; 700

$14/yr, $24/2 yrs; $8.75/sample (p.p.) 40%

176 pp; 6 x 9

$175/page (4 x 7); $100/½ page (4 x 3½)

ISSN: 1044-5331

HERESIES: A Feminist Publication on Art and Politics

Heresies Collective, Inc.

P.O. Box 1306

Canal Street Station

New York, NY 10013

(212) 227-2108

Essays, experimental writing, short fiction, interviews, poetry; page art, photography, graphic art, all visual arts.

HERESIES is the longest-lived feminist art journal still publishing. Thematic, political focus. "We believe that what is commonly called art can have a political impact and that in the making of art and all cultural artifacts our identities as women play a distinct role . . . A place where diversity can be articulated."

Unsolicited Manuscripts Received/ Published per Year: 3,000/25–35.

Reading Period: year–round.

Payment: nominal.

Reporting Time: 8–12 months.

Copyright reverts to author upon publication.

1977; 1–2/yr; 6,000

Four issues - $27/ind, $38/inst; $8/ea; 40%

112 pp; 8½ x 11

Ad Rates: $400/page

ISSN: 0146-3411

BookPeople, Inland, Ingram, Small Changes, Fine Print, Desert Moon, Marginal Distribution

HIGH PLAINS LITERARY REVIEW

Robert O. Greer, Jr.

180 Adams St., Suite 250

Denver, CO 80206

(303) 320-6828

Fiction, essays, poetry, reviews, criticism, interviews.

Designed to bridge the gap between commercial magazines and an outstanding array of academic quarterlies. A handsomely produced literary magazine that is intended to be more broadly based than academia without being commercially "targeted." A journal designed to display the absolute best of craft. O. Henry award winning fiction appeared as early as Vol. 1, No. 1.

Richard Currey, Nancy Lord, Marilyn Krysl, Darrell Spencer, Tony Ardizzone, Julia Alvarez, Rita Dove.

Unsolicited Manuscripts Received/ Published per Year: 4,000/85.

Payment: $5/page prose; $10/page poetry.

Reporting Time: 8 weeks.

Copyright held by magazine; reverts to author upon publicaton.

1986; 3/yr; 1,100

$20/yr; $7/ea; 40%

140 pp; 6 x 9

Ad Rates: $100/page; $50/½ page

ISSN: 0888-4153

DeBoer, Ubiquity, Fine Print

HIRAM POETRY REVIEW

Hale Chatfield and Carol Donley

Box 162

Hiram, OH 44234

(216) 569-5330

Poetry, criticism, essays, reviews, interviews. Photographs, graphics, and artwork by invitation only.

Unsolicited Manuscripts Received/ Published per Year: 6,000/50.

Reporting Time: 8–16 weeks.

Copyright reverts to author upon publication.

1967; 2/yr; 500

$4/ea; 40%–60%

40 pp; 6 x 9

ISSN: 0018-2036

HOB-NOB

Mildred K. Henderson

994 Nissley Rd.

Lancaster, PA 17601

(717) 898-7807

Short fiction, nonfiction, poetry, reviews, letters, cartoons.

HOB-NOB is a small literary publication of 52+ pages with material from contributors from around the world, of all ages and levels. Includes separate "Family Section" for (and by, when available) children. New contributors may submit during January & February only. Please send SASE for guidelines before submitting.

Fulbright scholar Sanford Pinsker, other college professors.

Payment: free copy on first appearance (at least). Small payment for cartoons & certain artwork.

Reporting Time: A few weeks, especially for rejections—maybe longer for acceptances (or return of material not sent during reading period). Waiting time until publication for new contributors: more than 2 years.

Copyright: Yes—first rights only—all rights revert to author

or poet after that.
1969: 4/yr; 300+
$8/yr; $2.50/ea
52–56 pp; 8½ x 11
Ads are free to subscribers, ex-
changers, or purchasers of issue

THE HOLLINS CRITIC

John Rees Moore
P.O. Box 9538
Hollins College, VA 24020
(703) 362-6317 or 362-8268

Poetry, critical essays, reviews,
graphics/artwork.

A non-specialist periodical concen-
trating on the work of a single
contemporary poet, fiction
writer or dramatist in each issue. Cover picture, essay of
about 5,000 words, brief ac-
count of author, check-list of
publications, several poems and
a section of brief book reviews.
Peggy H. Lewis, Tom Hansen,
Susan Rea, John Quinn.
Payment: $200/essay (by permis-
sion of editor only); $25/poems.
Copyright held by magazine.
1964; 5/yr; 650
$6/yr; $2/ea—US
20 pp; 7 x 10
ISSN: 0018-3644

Stuyvesant Station
New York, NY 10009
(718) 769-2854

Poetry, fiction, criticism, reviews,
translation, interviews, photographs, news.

We publish poetry, reviews of
books, art exhibits, theater,
news of the literary and small
press scene, interviews and fiction. Occasional pull-out section
of single poet's work.

Cornelius Eady, Norman Rosten,
Will Inman, William Packard,
Antler, Lyn Lifshin, Paul
Genega, Richard Kostelanetz.
Unsolicited Manuscripts Received/
Published per Year: 320
(poetry)/60
Payment: in copies and subscrip-
tion.
Reporting Time: 2–4 months.
Copyright held by magazine; re-
verts to author upon publication.
1979; 3–4/yr; 1,000
$8/yr ind, $8/yr inst, $15/2 yrs;
$2/ea; 40%
24 pp; 10 x 15
Ad Rates: $150/page (10 x 15);
$75/½ page (10 x 7½);
$37.50/¼ page (5 x 7½)
DeBoer, Fine Print

HOME PLANET NEWS

Donald Lev and Enid Dame
P.O. Box 415

HOPEWELL REVIEW

c/o Arts Indiana, Inc.
47 S. Pennsylvania, Suite 701

Indianapolis, IN 46204

(317) 632-7894

Poetry, short fiction, personal essay.

HOPEWELL REVIEW is an annual collection of poetry, short fiction and personal essays by Indiana writers.

Alice Friman, Susan Neville, Scott Russell Sanders, Mari Adams, Yusef Komunyakaa.

Unsolicited Manuscripts Received/ Published per Year: 1,500/40.

Payment: $35/poem; $150/short fiction, personal essay. 3 $500 awards of excellence.

Copyright held by Arts Indiana, Inc., reverts to author upon publications.

1989; 1/yr; 8,000

$6.95/ea

128 pp

ISSN:1069-6636

HOWLING DOG

M. P. Donovan

2913 Woodcock Ct.

Rochester, MI 48306

(810) 752-8511

Poetry, fiction, graphics/artwork.

Our purpose is to have an effect similar to the howl of a dog with its foot caught in a fence. We desire something that may not be pleasant or permanent, but will still be heard by every-

one in the neighborhood.

John Sinclair, M. L. Liebler, Hank Malone, Larry Goodell.

Unsolicited Manuscripts Received/ Published per Year: 5,000/100.

Payment: in copies.

Reporting Time: 6 months or more.

Copyright held by authors.

1985; 2/yr; 500

$10/yr; $5/ea; 40%

64 pp; 6 x 9

Ad Rates: $80/page (4 x 8); $40/½ page (4 x 4); $20/¼ page (2 x 4)

ISSN: 0888-3521

THE HUDSON REVIEW

Paula Deitz, Frederick Morgan

684 Park Ave.

New York, NY 10021

(212) 650-0020

Poetry, fiction, criticism, essays, reviews.

We publish both new and established writers. We have no university affiliation, and we are not committed to any narrow academic aim or to any particular political perspective. We focus on the area where literature and poetry bear on the intellectual life of the time.

Reading Period: nonfiction Oct. 1–Mar. 31; fiction June 1–Nov. 30; poetry April 1–Sept. 30.

Payment: 2½¢/word for prose;
50¢/line for poetry.
Reporting Time: 1–3 months.
Copyright held only on assigned
reviews.
1948; 4/yr; 4,500
$24/yr; $7/ea
160 pp; 6 x 9¼
Ad Rates: $300/page (4½ x 7½);
$200/½ page (4½ x 3⅝);
$150/¼ page (2⅛ x 3⅝)
ISSN: 0018-702X
Eastern News

HUNGRY MIND REVIEW

Bart Schneider
1648 Grand Ave.
St. Paul, MN 55105
(612) 699-2610
Essays, reviews, interviews, and
photographs.
HUNGRY MIND REVIEW pub-
lishes book reviews, essays, and
forums on particular focuses.
HUNGRY MIND REVIEW
reviews large, small, and uni-
versity presses, focusing on
mid- and backlist titles.
Robert Bly, Lewis Hyde, Herbert
Kohl, Phillip Lopate, William
Stafford, Bill McKibben, Gerald
Early, Maxine Hong Kingston,
Michael Dorris, Quentin Crisp, E.
Annie Proulx.
Unsolicited Manuscripts Received/
Published per Year: 600/0.

Payment: varies.
Copyright held by David Un-
owsky, dba **HMR**.
1986; 4/yr; 30,000
$13.00/yr ind; $15/yr Canada and
inst; free/ea
56 pp; 9¾ x 15
Ad Rates: $1,625/page; $900/½
page; $475/¼ page; $295/⅛
page; $175/¹⁄₁₆ page
ISSN: 0887-5499
We distribute free of charge to
over 600 independent bookstores across the U.S. and
Canada.

HURRICANE ALICE: A Feminist Quarterly

Pat Cumbie, Carolyn Law
Lind Hall
207 Church Street, SE
Minneapolis, MN 55455
(612) 625-1834
Reviews, essays, criticism, fiction,
poetry, graphics/artwork.
HURRICANE ALICE provides a
feminist review of culture. It
prints reviews of books by and
about women, critical essays
having a feminist
perspective—especially essays
on literature, film, dance, and
the visual arts—fiction, some
poetry and graphics.
Alice Walker, Toni McNaron, Peter Erickson, Meridel Le Sueur,

Susan Griffin, Pearl Cleage,
Beth Brant.
Unsolicited Manuscripts Received/
Published per Year: 750/60.
Reading Period: year–round.
Payment: in copies.
Reporting Time: 1–3 months.
Copyright reverts to author upon
publication.
1983; 4/yr; 700
$12/yr; $10/yr students/seniors;
$20/yr libraries; $2.50/ea
12–16 pp; 11 x 17
Ad Rates: $75/⅙ page; $45 (3 x
4); $20 (3 x 2)
Ubiquity, L-S Distributor, Olson,
Fine Print

HYPHEN

John Boyer, Publisher; Mark Inge-
bretsen, Editor
c/o John Boyer
348 S. Ahrens
Lombard, IL 60148

(312) 465-5985
Fax (312) 465-5985
Fiction, nonfiction, poetry, art-
work, photography
Art and literature that won't bore
you senseless.
Dwight Okita, Cin Salach, Rosa-
lind Cummings, Margriet Smul-
ders, Michael McNeilly
Unsolicited Manuscripts Received/
Published per Year: 1200/48.
Reading Period: year–round
Payment: 2 copies.
Reporting Time: 2–6 months
Copyright held by: currently
changing ownership
1992; 4/yr; 1,200
$14/yr; $4/ea; 50%
Ad Rates: $250/page, $200 2x,
$150 3x; $200/½ page, $150
2x, $100 3x; $150/¼ page,
$100 2x, $75 3x
ISSN: 1058-3297
Fine Print, Speed Impek, Desert
Moon.

I

IKON

Susan Sherman
P.O. Box 1355
Stuyvesant Station
New York, NY 10009

Poetry, fiction, essays, translation, interviews, photographs, graphics/artwork.

IKON is a cultural, political, feminist magazine, showing the experiences of third world, lesbian, Jewish and working women, all women in the diversity of our experience. **IKON** is about making connections through the words and images of women themselves in their essays, articles, paintings, photographs, fiction, art, songs and poems.

Audre Lourde, Kimiko Hahn, Beth Brant, Grace Paley, Adrienne Rich.

Payment: subscription and 2 copies.

Reporting Time: 90 days.

Copyright held by magazine; reverts to author upon publication.

1982; 2/yr; 1,750

$10/yr ind, $15/yr inst; $6/ea; 40%

140 pp; 7 x 9

THE ILLINOIS REVIEW (Formerly Illinois Writers Review)

Jim Elledge
4240/Department of English
Illinois State University
Normal, IL 61790-4240
(309) 438-7705

Creative writing of all genres, as well as essays and reviews.

The **ILLINOIS REVIEW** seeks poems, prose poems, short-short stories, stories, novel excerpts, one act plays, translations, essays, and book reviews. Open to mainstream and alternative, to established and unknown, and to marginalized writers. Our only bias is excellence.

Reading Period: Aug. 1–May 31.

Payment: two copies and year's subscription.

Reporting Time: 1–2 months, SASE required.

Copyright reverts to author upon publication.

1993; 2/yr; 500

Individuals and Institutions may subscribe to the journal in one of two ways: as a member of Illinois Writers, Inc.: $15/yr ind, $20/yr inst; or to the journal itself: $10/yr ind, $15/yr inst; 40%

Ad Rates: $100/page (4½ x 7); $50/½ page (4½ x 4)

ISSN: 0733-9526

Illinois Literary Publishers' Association

IMAGE: A Journal of the Arts and Religion

Publisher and Editor Gregory Wolfe

3100 McCormick Ave.

Wichita, KS 67213

(316) 942-4291 ext. 325

(316) 942-9658 (Fax)

Short stories, novel excerpts, poetry, memoirs, essays, interviews.

IMAGE is the only national journal dedicated to exploring and illustrating the relationship between faith and art through world-class fiction, visual art, poetry, essays, music, and other arts.

Larry Wolwode, Ron Hansen, Denise Levertov, Doris Betts, Robert Bly.

Unsolicited Manuscripts Received/ Published per Year: 400/25.

Reading Period: year-round.

Payment: usually 5 copies of the journal, occasionally a fee.

Reporting Time: 3 weeks.

Copyright held by Hillsdale Review, Inc.

1989; 4/yr; 700

$30/yr, $10/ea; 30%

136 pp; 7 x 10

Ad Rates: $500/page; $300/½ page; $700/inside back cover. Discounts for multiple placements.

DeBoer, Ubiquity, Bookpeople

IMAGINE: INTERNATIONAL CHICANO POETRY JOURNAL

Tino Villanueva

89 Massachusetts Ave., Suite 270

Boston MA 02115

(617) 267-2592

Poetry, mostly; limited number of

articles/interviews; book reviews & book notices.

Poetry in any language provided the original language text is accompanied by a English or Spanish translation. Any mode, no restrictions on form, subject or style.

Jimmy Santiago Baca, García Márquez, Gary Soto, Isabel Allende, Bernice Zamora, Frida Kahlo, Rudolfo Anaya, Luis Valdez, Luis Jiménez.

Payment: small fee plus two author's copies.

Reporting Time: 4–6 months.

Copyright reverts to authors, artist, or photographer upon publication.

1984; 2/yr; 1,000

$8/yr ind, $14/2 yr ind, $12/yr inst, $18/2 yr inst; $4.50/ea; newstand price; back issues vary count; 35%

75–99 pp; 6 x 9

ISSN: 0747-489X

SPD

IN THE COMPANY OF POETS

Jacalyn Robinson

P.O. Box 10786

Oakland, CA 94610

(510) 568-2531

Poetry, short stories, essays, visual art.

E. Donald Two-Rivers, Selma Glasser, Patrick Fitch.

Unsolicited Manuscripts Received/ Published per Year: Approx. 350/120.

Payment: 3 copies.

Reporting Time: 3-6 months.

Copyright: US & Int'l.

1991; 6/yr; 20,000

$16/yr

approx. 62 pp; 8 x 10

ISSN: 1055-0038

INDIANA REVIEW

Gretchen Knapp, Cara Diaconoff, Shirley Stephenson

316 North Jordan Ave.

Indiana University

Bloomington, IN 47405

(812) 855-3439

Fiction, poetry, essays, book reviews, occasional drama, interviews.

We have no prejudices of style or content, but will publish only those poems and short stories which demonstrate: 1) keen sense of craft; 2) insight into the human condition. Writers should send their best work only. We prefer stories of rich texture to those that depend on a gimmick.

Dean Young, Philip Levine, Kathy Acker, Pamela Painter, George Saunders, Martin Espada, Amy Gerstler, Ursula K. LeGuin, Maureen Seaton.

Unsolicited Manuscripts Received

per Year: 5,000 (poetry and prose).

Payment: $5 per page.

Reporting Time: 2 weeks–4 months.

Copyright held by magazine; reverts to author upon publication.

1976; 2/yr; 2,000

$12/yr ind, $15/yr inst; $7/ea

200 pp; 6 x 9

Ad Rates: $150/page (6 x 9); $85/½ page (6 x 4½)

ISSN: 0738-386X

Ingram, DeBoer

INTERIM

A. Wilber Stevens, Editor; John Heath–Stubbs, English Editor; George Bruce, Scottish Editor; Associate Editors: James Hazen, Joe McCullough

Department of English

University of Nevada

Las Vegas, NV 89154

Poetry, fiction.

INTERIM prints the best poetry and short fiction we can find, plus occasional reviews. It is the revival, under its original editor, of the magazine published and edited in Seattle in 1944–55.

William Stafford, John Heath-Stubbs, X.J. Kennedy, Stephen Stepanchev, Gladys Swan.

Unsolicited Manuscripts Received/

Published per Year: 3,000-3,400/60.

Reading Period: year–round.

Payment: contributor's copies plus a two-year subscription.

Copyright held by magazine; reverts to author upon publication.

1944; 2/yr; 750

$16/3 yrs; $8/yr; $14/yr inst; $5/ea; 40%

48–64 pp; 9 x 6

ISSN: 0888-2452

INTERNATIONAL POETRY REVIEW

Mark Smith-Soto

Dept. of Romance Lang.

UNC-Greensboro

Greensboro, NC 27412

Unpublished translation with contemporary original language poem. Contemporary English language poetry with international or cross cultural theme preferred, graphics.

Coleman Barks, Charles Edward Eaton, William Stafford, Pureza Canelo, Ana Istarú, Clara Janés.

Unsolicited Manuscripts Received/ Published per Year: 1,200/100.

Payment: in copies.

1975; 2/yr; 400

ind.: 2 yrs $18; 3 yrs $25; libraries: 2 yrs $27; 3 yrs $40; $5/ea; 20%

100 pp; 5½ x 8½

Ad Rates: $50/page; $25/½ page

INTERNATIONAL QUARTERLY

Van Brock, Editor-in-Chief; Catherine Reid, Fiction; Kim Garcia, Poetry; Holly Iglesias, Nonfiction

P.O. Box 10521

Tallahassee, FL 32302-0521

(904) 224-5078

(904) 224-5127 (Fax)

Fiction, nonfiction, poetry, art.

IQ is a multicultural journal of contemporary work from around the world, in English and translation.

Carmen Naranjo, Guillermo Nuñez, Adonis, Dennis Brutus, Bei Dao.

Unsolicited Manuscripts Received/ Published per Year: 800/160.

Reading Period: year-round.

Payment: in copies.

Reporting Time: 6–8 weeks.

Copyright: First North American Serial rights then reverts to author.

4/yr; 3,000

$22/yr; $38/2 yrs; $6/ea

180–200 pp; 7½ x 10

Full Page 4x=$515/each ad. Half page 4x=$295/each ad. Quarter page 4x=$160/each ad.

ISSN: 1060-6084

INVISIBLE CITY

John McBride, Paul Vangelisti

P.O. Box 2853

San Francisco, CA 94126

(415) 527-1018

Poetry, criticism, translation, graphics/artwork, visual poetry.

A book series, formerly tabloid, of poetry, translation, visuals and statements published whenever enough good material is available: focusing on current U.S. writing, some concrete poetry and Italian writing—focused on "the internal tension of language."

Adriano Spatola, Giulia Niccolai, Ernst Meister, John Thomas, Stanislaw Baranczak, Antonio Porta, Emilio Villa; and now DAYBOOK by Robert Crosson, with DIVISION appended, remarks, criticism & such.

Unsolicited Manuscripts Received/ Published per Year: 365/?.

Reading Period: year-round.

Payment: copies and then some.

Reporting Time: 2 months.

Copyright reverts to author upon publication.

1971; 1–2/yr; 1,000

$10/yr ind, $15/yr inst

80+ pp; 5 x 9

ISSN: 0034-2009

THE IOWA REVIEW

David Hamilton
308 EPB
University of Iowa
Iowa City, IA 52242
(319) 335-0462
Poetry, fiction, criticism, essays, reviews, interviews.
We look for new as well as established writers and are usually pleased, on the whole, with what we are able to publish.
Unsolicited Manuscripts Received/ Published per Year: 8,000/100.
Reading Period: Sept.–Apr.
Payment: $1/line for poetry; $10/page for prose.
Reporting Time: 2–3 months.
Copyright held by the University of Iowa; reverts to author upon publication.
1970; 3/yr; 1,500
$18/yr ind, $20/yr inst; $6.95/ea; 30%
200 pp; 6 x 9
Ad Rates: $150/page (5½ x 8½)
ISSN: 0021-065X
Ingram

IOWA WOMAN

Marianne Abel, Editor; Sandra Adelmund, Poetry Editor
P.O. Box 680
Iowa City, IA 52244
(319) 987-2879
Fiction, essays, reviews, interviews, poetry, news briefs, features, ads, memoirs, graphics/artwork.
Rooted in the Midwest, **IOWA WOMAN** publishes award-winning women writers everywhere. National readership.
Send SASE for annual writing contest guidelines.
Judy Ruiz, Enid Shomer, Ingrid Hill, Alice Friman, Natalie Kusz.
Unsolicited Manuscripts Received/ Published per Year: 4,000+/80+.
Payment: $5/page, copies, ad discounts.
Reporting Time: 3 months.
Copyright held by magazine; reverts to author upon publication.
1980; 4/yr; 2,500
$18/yr, $24/yr Canada & Pan America; $30/yr other; $6/ea; 30%
48 pp; 8⅛ x 10⅞
ISSN: 0271-8227

irresistible impulse

Camille Blanchette
711 Belmont Pl. E., #201
Seattle, WA 98102-4451
Fiction, poetry, essays, humor, interviews, line art
Literary and art magazine. Focus: sharing human experiences, increasing communication and community, providing informa-

tion about progressive issues, and entertaining. Multicultural, anti-discriminatory.

Unsolicited Manuscripts Received/ Published per Year: 150/15

Reading Period: year–round.

Payment: copies.

Reporting Time: 2–3 weeks.

Copyright reverts to author/artist.

1982; 2/yr; 150

$8/yr; $4/ea; 40%

60 pp; 7 x 8½

Small Changes

THE ITHACA WOMEN'S ANTHOLOGY

Editorial Board; Rotating board of editors.

P.O. Box 582

Ithaca, NY 14851

Poetry, fiction, translation, photographs, graphics/artwork, criticism.

THE ITHACA WOMEN'S ANTHOLOGY was originally established as an annual collection of creative work, by, for and about women. The types of work we publish include essays, interviews, criticism, journal entries, fiction, and poetry as well as graphics of all kinds. Our commitment is to provide a medium for women to creatively express their concerns, to coin varied and new voices, while emphasizing the highest in artistic quality.

Unsolicited Manuscripts Received/ Published per Year: 200/30+.

From Ithaca and the New York State region.

Payment: copies.

Copyright held by magazine; reverts to author upon publication.

1976; 1/yr; 400

$6/ea; 40%

J

JACARANDA REVIEW

Katerine Swiggart
Department of English
2225 Rolfe Hall
University of California
Los Angeles, CA 90024
(213) 825-4173

Poetry, fiction, essays, reviews
 translation, interviews.

We try to publish the best fiction,
 poetry, and essays we can find.
 A potential contributor should
 read an issue or two to see what
 we mean by that. We feature in
 each issue an interview with a
 major writer and, usually, a
 supplement featuring work of
 special interest to us.

Jorge Luis Borges, Carolyn
 Forché, Allan Gurganus, Zbig-
 niew Herbert, Billy Collins,
 Graig Raines.

Unsolicited Manuscripts Received/
Published per Year:
 hundreds/1%.
Payment: three copies.
Copyright held by University of
 California; reverts to author
 upon publication.
1985; 2/yr; 1,000
$10/yr ind, $14/yr inst; $6/ea;
 40%
120 pp; 5½ x 8
Ad Rates: $75/page (5½ x 8);
 $50/½ page (5½ x 4); $25/¼
 page (2¾ x 4)

JAMES WHITE REVIEW

P. Willkie, C. Mayhood
P.O. Box 3356
Butler Quarter Station
Minneapolis, MN 55403
(612) 339-8317

Poetry, fiction, criticism, reviews,
 memoirs, photographs,
 graphics/artwork.

We are a gay men's literary quarterly.

David Feinberg, Essex Hemphill, Lev Raphael, Assotto Saint, Stan Leventhal.

Unsolicited Manuscripts Received/ Published per Year: 1,000/100.

Reading Period: after deadlines: Feb 1, May 1, Aug 1, Nov 1

Payment: $50/story, $10/poem.

Reporting Time: 6–8 weeks.

Copyright held by magazine; reverts to author upon publication.

1983; 4/yr; 4,500

$12/yr ind, $12/yr inst; $3/ea; 40%

20 pp; 11 x 15

Ad Rates: $400/page; $200/½ page; $120/¼ page

JEOPARDY MAGAZINE

Richard Law, Editor; Joanna Nesbit, Managing Editor; Sean Anderson, Kris Huss, Fiction Editors; Derek Martin, Non-Fiction Editor; Ken Efta, Ethan Yarbrough, Poetry Editors

132 College Hall

Western Washington University

Bellingham, WA 98225

(206) 650-3118

Nonfiction, fiction, poetry, art, photography.

Annie Dillard, Barry Lopez, Richard Hugo.

Unsolicited Manuscripts Received/

Published per Year: 1,000-1,500/100.

Payment: Two copies.

Reporting Time: 1–4 months.

Copyright reverts to author.

1963; 1/yr; 2,000

$4.75/ea

120-200 pp; book–sized

JORDAN CREEK ANTHOLOGY

Jo Van Arkel

900 N. Benton

Springfield, MO 65802

(417) 865-8731

Fiction, poetry, interviews.

We publish short stories and poetry which are literary, contemporary, experimental, humorous, or regional, with an emphasis on the Midwest to the South. No genre or formula.

John Mort, Paul Ramsey, Debra Thornton, Wilma Yeo.

Unsolicited Manuscripts Received/ Published per Year: 300/15–20.

Reading Period: Sept.–May.

Payment: copies.

Reporting Time: 6 weeks.

Copyright: first time rights.

1987; 1/yr; 500

$12/3 yr; $4/ea; $2/resale

80 pp

THE JOURNAL

Kathy Fagan, Poetry Editor; Michelle Herman, Fiction Editor

164 West 17th Ave.
Department of English
The Ohio State University
Columbus, OH 43210
(614) 292-4076
Poetry, fiction, reviews.
THE JOURNAL attempts to provide an outlet for good writing by Ohio writers and writers from around the country. We seek out good work and attempt to attract the best new writers. The editorial staff works to publish and distribute poetry, fiction, nonfiction, and reviews, the sole criterion for which is excellence.
Maurya Simon, J. R. Hummer, Jonathan Holden, Eric Pankey, and Linda Bierds.
Reporting Time: 4–6 weeks.
Copyright held by Ohio State University.
1972; 2/yr; 1,100
$8/yr; $4.50/ea; 40%
80-100 pp; 6 x 9
ISSN: 1045-084X

Randolph, NJ 07869-2086
(201) 328-5471
Poetry by New Jersey poets, essays, occasional quotations.
A magazine dedicated to the best poetry written by poets who live in New Jersey or who have lived or worked here at some time.
Kenneth Burke, Grace Cavalieri, Lesley Choyce, Alfred Starr Hamilton, Michael Weaver, Cat Doty, Joe Weil.
Unsolicited Manuscripts Received/Published per Year: 800-1,000/75-100.
Payment: 2 copies/published poem.
Reporting Time: 6 months.
Copyright: County College of Morris.
1976; 2/yr; 700
$7/yr; $4/ea; 25%
48-64 pp; 5½ x 8½
ISSN: 0363-4205
DeBoer

JOURNAL OF NEW JERSEY POETS
Sander Zulauf, Editor; North Peterson, Sara Pfaffenroth, Associate Editors; Wendy Jones, Charles Luce, Art Editors.
214 Center Grove Rd.
County College of Morris

JUST A MOMENT
Gertrude S. Eiler
P.O. Box 40
Jamesville, NY 13078
(315) 423-9268
Short stories, poetry.
Established to be a vehicle for writers of talent and ability

whether previously published or not.

Edwidge Danticat (1st book due out April, 1994), L. E. McCullough, Bradley White, Ann T. Beacham, Edith C. Johnson.

Unsolicited Manuscripts Received/Published per Year: 500/Approx. 56

Payment: Choice of free subscription or 4 free copies of issue in which published + 20% discount on more copies of issue in which published.

Reporting Time: 1–3 months.

Copyright: One time copyright. Rights revert to author.

1990; 4/yr; 500

$18/yr; $5/ea; 40%

73–94 pp; 8½ x 5½

K

**KALEIDOSCOPE: International
Magazine of Literature, Fine
Arts, and Disability**

Darshan C. Perusek, Ph.D., Editor-
in-Chief; Gail Willmott, Senior
Editor
United Disability Services
326 Locust Street
Akron, OH 44302
(216) 762-9755

Poetry, photographs, graphics/
artwork, fiction, essays, reviews.
KALEIDOSCOPE Magazine has
a creative focus that examines
the experience of disability
through diverse forms of literature and the fine arts. Works
should not use stereotyping,
patronizing, or offending language about disability.
Diana Hume George, Andre Dubus, Tony Ardizzone, Sandra
Lindow, Sheryl L. Nelms, and
Harriet Doerr.

Unsolicited Manuscripts Received/
Published per Year: 500/30.
Payment: $25–$100 fiction, up to
$25 for body of poetry.
Reporting Time: Acknowledged
within 2 weeks; up to 1 month
of deadline for rejection or acceptance.
Copyright held by Kaleidoscope;
reverts to author upon publication.
1979; 2/yr; 1,500
$9/yr, $17/2 yrs ind; $14/yr, $22/2
yrs inst; $5.00/ea; $4/sample
copy (prepaid); 20%–50%
64 pp; 8½ x 11
ISSN: 0748-8742
Ubiquity, Fine Print

**KALLIOPE: A Journal of Wom-
en's Art**

Mary Sue Koeppel
Florida Community College

3939 Roosevelt Boulevard
Jacksonville, FL 32205
(904) 381-3511
Poetry, fiction, essays, reviews,
interviews (3 annually), photographs, graphics/artwork.
The purpose of **KALLIOPE** is to
offer support and encourage-
ment to women in the arts. We
are open to experimental forms
of short fiction, poetry, prose
and art as well as traditional
formats. Editors like to see
work that challenges the reader
and addresses the complex relationships women have with each
other, men, children and society.
Marge Piercy, Elisavietta Ritchie,
Edith Perlman, Enid Shomer,
Colette Inez, Louise Fishman,
Colette, Tess Gallagher.
Unsolicited Manuscripts Received/
Published per Year: 1,000/100.
Reading Period: Sept.–June.
Payment: 3 copies or 1 yr subscription to writers and artists.
Reporting Time: 2–3 months.
Copyright held by magazine; re-
verts to author upon request.
1978; 3/yr; 1,250
$12.50/yr ind, $21/yr inst; $7/ea
last issues; $4/ea early issues;
40%
80 pp; 7¼ x 8½
No ads
ISSN: 0735-7885
Ingram

KANSAS QUARTERLY
Ben Nyberg, John Rees, G. W.
Clift
Kansas State University
Manhattan, KS 66506-0703
(913) 532-6716
Poetry, fiction, criticism, transla-
tion, interviews, photographs,
graphics/artwork.
A cultural arts and literary maga-
zine emphasizing but not re-
stricted to the culture, history,
art and writing of Mid-America
but with international interests.
David Kirby, John Bovey, Stephen
Dixon, Jonathan Holden, Peter
LaSalle, Susan Fromberg
Schaeffer, Jerry Bumpus, Lex
Williford, Annabel Thomas.
Unsolicited Manuscripts Received/
Published per year: 5,000/180.
Reading Period: year–round.
Payment: 2 copies and two series
of annual awards.
Reporting Time: 2–6 months.
Copyright held by magazine; re-
verts to author upon request.
1968; 4/yr; 1,500
$20/yr; $6/ea; 10%–40%
152+ pp; 6 x 9
Ad Rates: $100/page (4½ x 7½);
$60/½ page (4½ x 3¾); $35/¼
page (2¼ x 3¾)
ISSN: 0022-8745

KARAMU

Peggy L. Brayfield

Department of English

Eastern Illinois University

Charleston, IL 61920

(217) 581-5614

Poetry, short fiction, creative non-fiction prose, black and white graphics.

Quality writing for a literate audience who enjoy fiction, poetry, and other creative pieces.

John Dickson, Sheila Golburgh Johnson, Richard Willett, Zan Bockes, John Thompson.

Unsolicited Manuscripts Received/ Published per Year: Approx. 150 stories, 1,400 poems/approx. 6-7 stories, 30-35 poems.

Payment: 1 copy of issue containing work, extras at reduced price.

Reporting Time: 2-3 months, longer if work is under serious consideration.

Copyright: First serial rights.

1966; 1/yr; 400

$7.50/yr; $4/sample copy, $5/2 sample copies

128 pp; 5 x 8

Ad Rates: inquire

ISSN: 0022-8990

THE KENYON REVIEW

David H. Lynn, Editor; Cy Wainscott, Managing Editor

Kenyon College

Gambier, OH 43022

(614) 427-3339

Poetry, fiction, essays, reviews, interviews, plays, translations, memoirs.

THE KENYON REVIEW seeks excellent writing more than any particular kind or style. We seek to present a balanced diversity of perspective/orientation. We invite offers to review books and proposals for interviews. First publication rights required. No multiple submissions read. We discourage submissions from writers who have not read a recent issue.

Hayden Carruth, Toi Derricote, Kate Braverman, Adrienne Rich, Herbert Blau, Rafael Campo, Ursula K. LeGuin.

Unsolicited Manuscripts Received/ Published per Year: 5,000/60.

Reading Period: Sept.–Mar.

Payment: $10/page, prose; $15/page, poetry; $10 (translator) $5 (author)/page, translations.

Reporting Time: 3 months.

Copyright reverts to author.

1939; 3/yr; 5,000

$22/yr ind, $30/yr inst; $8/ea

185 pp; 7 x 10

Ad Rates: $285/page (4⅜ x 8); $175/½ page (4⅜ x 3⅞); exchanges considered

ISSN: 0163-075X

Inland, Ingram, Fine Print, De-
Boer, Ubiquity

KINESIS

Leif Peterson
P.O. Box 4007
Whitefish, MT 59937
(406) 844-3047
Fiction, poetry, essays, reviews.
A monthly journal of fiction, po-
etry, essays, and reviews.
Luci Shaw, John Leax, Rick
Newby, Lowell Jaeger.
Unsolicited Manuscripts Received/
Published per Year: 1,600/100.
Reading Period: Jan.–Dec.
Payment: 5 copies and 1 year sub-
scription
Reporting Time: 6 weeks.
Copyright held by author.
1992; 12/yr; 5,000
$20/yr, $3/ea; 33%
48 pp; 8½ x 11
Ad Rates: $350/page (7¼ x 9);
$200/½ page; $120/¼ page (3½
x 4½); $60/⅛ page (3½ x 2¼)
ISSN: 1056-781X
Tower Magazines, Ubiquity

KIOSK

Mary Obropta, Editor-in-Chief;
Robert Rebein, Fiction Editor;
A. M. Allcott, Poetry Editor
English Department
302 Clements Hall

SUNY at Buffalo
Buffalo, NY 14226
(716) 636-2575
Poetry, fiction, experimental prose.
KIOSK welcomes submissions of
creative prose and poetry. We
are interested in originality and
craftsmanship. We subscribe to
no orthodoxy; quality is our top
concern.
Recent issues have included Carol
Berge, Charles Bernstein, Raymond Federman. Especially interested in new writers.
Unsolicited Manuscripts Received/
Published per Year: 800/25-35.
Reading Period: Sept.–Apr.
Payment: 2 copies.
Author retains all rights.
1986; 1-2/yr; 500
Guidelines with #10 SASE;
sample issue with large SASE
and 6 1st class stamps, if available.
130 pp; 5½ x 8½
No ads

KUMQUAT MERINGUE

Christian Nelson
P.O. Box 5144
Rockford, IL 61125
(815) 968-0713
Poetry and very short prose.
Dedicated to the memory of Rich-
ard Brautigan.
Gina Bergamino, Antler, Lynne

Douglass, Ianthe Brautigan.
Unsolicited Manuscripts Received/
Published per Year:
Thousands/130-180.
Payment: copies.

Reporting Time: 6 to 8 weeks.
1991; 3/yr; 500
$4/ea
32-40 pp; digest

L

LACTUCA

Michael Selender
159 Jewett Avenue
Jersey City, NJ 07304-2003
(201) 451-5411

Poetry, fiction, black and white art.

Our bias is toward work with a strong sense of place or experience. Writing with an honest emotional depth and writing that is dark or disturbing are preferred over safer material. Work with a quiet dignity is also desired. Subject matter is wide open and work can be rural or urban in character. We don't like poems that use the poem, the word, or the page as images or writing about being a poet/writer (though work about dead poets/writers is o.k.).

Sherman Alexie, Charles Bukowski, Joe Cardillo, Adrian C. Louis, Sheryl Nelms.

Unsolicited Manuscripts Received/Published per Year: 2,000+/120.

Reading Period: year-round, but Nov.–Feb. is best. We will not be accepting new material until late 1995 or early 1996.

Payment: in copies.

Copyright held by magazine; reverts to author upon publication.

1986; 1–3/yr; 750

$10/3 issues; $17/6 issues; $4/ea; 40% bookstores, 55% distributors

72 pp; 7 x 8½

No ads

LANGUAGE BRIDGES QUARTERLY

Eva Ziem
P.O. Box 850792
Richardson, TX 75085
(214) 530-2363

Poetry, fiction, criticism, essays, reviews, plays, translations, photographs, artwork.

LBQ is the only fully bilingual Polish-English literary magazine in the USA. All texts are printed in Polish with English translation or vice-versa. **LBQ** creates, by presenting American writers as well, a bridge between Polish and American writers, as well as readers for cross cultural dialogue.

Prof. Danuta Mostwin, Prof. Lisowski, Prof. Ewa Thompson, Valeriu Butulescu.

Unsolicited Manuscripts Received/ Published per Year: 50/25.

Reporting Time: 2-3 weeks.

Copyright held by magazine.

1988; 4/yr; 250

$20/yr ind; $6/ea

24 pp; 8 x 11 ½

Ad Rates: $100/page; $50/½ page; $25/¼ page

ISSN: 1053-9913

LATIN AMERICAN LITER-ARY REVIEW

Yvette E. Miller

121 Edgewood Ave., 1st Flr.

Pittsburgh, PA 15218

(412) 371-9023; Fax (412) 371-9025

Criticism, essays, interviews, reviews. We now publish articles in Spanish and Portugese in addition to English.

The Journal in English devoted to the literatures of Latin America.

Payment: varies.

Reporting Time: 3 months.

Copyright held by magazine.

1972; 2/yr + special double issue; 1,200

$22/yr ind, $38/yr inst; $30/yr ind. foreign; $40/yr inst. foreign; $16/ea, back issues; 10%

150 pp; 250 pp special issue; 6 x 9

Ad Rates: $215/page (4½ x 7½); $140/½ page (4½ x 3¾); $95/¼ page (4½ x 2¼)

ISSN: 0047-4134

Ebsco, Faxon, Turner

THE LAUREL REVIEW

William Trowbridge, David Slater, Beth Richards

GreenTower Press

Department of English

Northwest Missouri State University

Maryville, MO 64468

(816) 562-1265

Poetry, fiction, creative non-fiction.

THE LAUREL REVIEW is national in scope and prints the best work received, regardless of style or author's reputation. Stephen Dunn, Sydney Lea,

Katherine Soniat, Carol Bly, Albert Goldbarth.
Unsolicited Manuscripts Received/ Published per Year: 4,000/70.
Reading Period: Sept.–May.
Payment: 2 copies and subscription.
Reporting Time: 1 week–4 months.
Copyright held by GreenTower Press; reverts to author upon request.
1960; 2/yr; 900
$8/yr, $14/2 yrs; $5/ea; 40%
124 pp; 6 x 9
Ad Rates: $80/page (6 x 9); $40/½ page (6 x 4½); exchange also
ISSN: 0023-9003

THE LEDGE POETRY & FICTION MAGAZINE

Timothy Monaghan
64-65 Cooper Ave.
Glendale, NY 11385-6150
Poetry, fiction and photography.
THE LEDGE seeks superior poetry, fiction and photographs. No biases. Work that shows craft and heart stands best shot here. THE LEDGE also sponsors an Annual Poetry Chapbook Contest and Annual Poetry and Fiction Contests. Send SASE for details.
Terri Brown-Davidson, Philip

Miller, Stephanie Dickinson, Sean Thomas Dougherty and Tony Gloeggler.
Unsolicited Manuscripts Received/ Published per Year: 1,500/50.
Reading Period: year–round.
Payment: 1 copy.
Reporting Time: 6 weeks; longer if under serious consideration.
Copyright reverts to author.
1988; 2/yr; 1,150
$9/yr, $15/2 yr; 20%
128 pp; 5 ½ x 8 ½
ISSN: 1046-2724
DeBoer

LIGHT QUARTERLY

Box 7500
Chicago, IL 60680
Light verse (metrical and non-metrical) satire, humor, cartoons and line drawings.
LIGHT QUARTERLY is the only publication in the United States devoted exclusively to light verse and satire.
John Updike, Donald Hall, X. J. Kennedy, William Matthews, Gavin Ewart, William Stafford, W. D. Snodgrass.
Unsolicited Manuscripts Received/ Published per Year: 1,000/2,500.
Payment: 2 copies of issue they appear in; 1 copy for foreign contributors.
Reporting Time: 1–3 months.

1992; 4/yr; 1,200
$16/yr; $6/ea; $4/back issue
32 pp; 8½ x 11
Write for ad rates.
ISSN: 1064-8186
Ubiquity

LILLIPUT REVIEW

Don Wentworth
207 S. Millvale Ave., #3
Pittsburgh, PA 15224
Poetry
Short poems, ten lines or less.
David Chorlton, Vogn, Steven Do-
ering, Sheila E. Murphy.
Unsolicited Manuscripts Received/
Published per Year: 1,100/5% of
all received
Reading Period: year–round.
Payment: 2 copies of issue in
which work appears.
Reporting Time: 4–8 weeks.
Copyright: Magazine uses first
rights, reverting back to author
upon publication.
1989; 12/yr; 200-250
$5/6; $1 ea. or SASE; 50%
16 pp; 4½ x 3⅝ or 3½ x 4¼

LIPS

Laura Boss
P.O. Box 1345
Montclair, NJ 07042
(201) 662-1303
Poetry.

LIPS publishes the best contem-
porary poetry submitted. No
biases.
Michael Benedikt, Gregory Corso,
Maria Gillan, Allen Ginsberg,
Robert Phillips, Marge Piercy,
Ishmael Reed.
Payment: in copies.
Reporting Time: 1 month.
Copyright held by magazine; reverts
to author upon publication.
1981; 2/yr; 1,000
$10/yr ind, $13/yr inst; $5/ea;
40%
88 pp; 5½ x 8½
ISSN: 0278-0933
Anton Mikofsky

LITERAL LATTÉ

Jenine Gordon, Jeff Bockman
61 East 8th Street
Suite 240
New York, NY 10003
(212) 260-5532
Short stories, poems, personal es-
says and art.
The highest quality prose, poetry
and art distributed FREE in cof-
feehouses and bookstores in
New York City (and by sub-
scription elsewhere).
Michael Brodsky, Stephen Dixon,
Carole Maso, Carol Muske,
John Updike.
Unsolicited Manuscripts Received/
Published per Year: 4,500/90.

Reading Period: year-round.
Payment: $25–$250.
Reporting Time: 2 months.
Copyright reverts to author upon publication.
1994; 6/yr; 12,000
$25/yr, $5/ea
28 pp; 11 x 17

THE LITERARY CENTER QUARTERLY

Ken Smith, Scott Davidson, Neile Graham, Jim Gurley
P.O. Box 85116
Seattle, WA 98145
(206) 547-2503
Reviews, essays, poetry, interviews.
We are a small quarterly hoping to offer a voice for North West writers of all genres.
John Marshall, K. C. Brown, Joseph H. Hudson.
Copyright reverts to authors.
4/yr; 2,000
$15/yr
16–32 pp; 8½ x 11
Write for ad rates and sizes

LITERARY MAGAZINE REVIEW

G. W. Clift, J. E. Roper
Department of English
Kansas State University
Manhattan, KS 66506
(913) 532-6716
Reviews and essays concerning literary magazines.
LITERARY MAGAZINE REVIEW is devoted almost exclusively to objective reviews of the specific contents of issues of magazines which publish at least some short fiction or poetry.
David Kirby, Ben Nyberg, Ben Reynolds.
Unsolicited Manuscripts Received/Published per year: 10/0.
Reading Period: year–round.
Payment: copies.
Reporting Time: queries only, please.
Copyright reverts to author upon publication.
1982; 4/yr; 600+
$12.50/yr; $4/ea; 40%
60 pp; 8½ x 5½
No ads
ISSN: 0732-6637

THE LITERARY REVIEW

Walter Cummins, Editor-in-Chief; Martin Green, Harry Keyishian, William Zander, Editors; Jill Menkes Kushner, Managing Editor
Fairleigh Dickinson University
285 Madison Avenue
Madison, NJ 07940
(201) 593-8564

Poetry, fiction, criticism, essays, reviews, translation, interviews, graphics/artwork.

New writing in English and translation. We're looking for a unique blend of craft and insight.

Susan Moon, Tom Hansen, Jane Bradley, T. Alan Broughton.

Unsolicited Manuscripts Received/ Published per Year: 3,500/200.

Reading Period: year–round.

Payment: 2 copies.

Reporting Time: 8–12 weeks.

Copyright held by Fairleigh Dickinson University; reverts to author upon publication.

1957; 4/yr; 2,000

$18/yr; $5/ea; 40%

128 pp; 6 x 9

Exchange ads

ISSN: 0024-4589

an additional slant toward African American lyrical and musical contribution.

Quincy Troupe, E. B. Rodmund, Henry Miller.

Unsolicited Manuscripts Received/ Published per year: 50/3.

Payment: varies.

Reporting Time: 12 weeks before publication.

Copyright reverts to author.

1988; 2/yr; 6,500–25,000

Literati $10/ea; Blues Annual $5/ea; 40%

112 pp; Blues Annual, 8½ x 11; Literati, 6½ x 9½

Ad Rates: please call.

ISBN: (Blues Annual) 0-944802-05-3

ISSN: (Literati) 1054-9404

Ingram

LITERATI INTERNATIONALE
Original Chicago Blues Annual

L. McGraw Beauchamp, A. C. McGraw-Beauchamp
1133 N. Damen Ave.
Chicago, IL 60622
(312) 862-1313

LITERATI is multi-arts/cultural, featuring: fine art, reproductions, photos, poems and essays. The original Chicago Blues Annual is the same as above with

LONG NEWS: In the Short Century

Barbara Henning, Art Editor; Miranda Maher, Contributing Editors: Don David, Lewis Warsh, Paul Buck, Chris Tysh, Michael Pelias, Tyrone Williams
P.O. Box 150-455
Brooklyn, NY 11215

Writing, art, poetry, experimental prose.

LONG NEWS: in the Short Century aims to publish experimental work that challenges the basic tenets of realism and expressionism.

Nicole Brossard, Fanny Howe, Sadiq Muhammad, Lorenzo Thomas.

Unsolicited Manuscripts Received/ Published per year: 100/2.

Reporting Time: 60 days.

Copyright reverts to author after publication.

1991; 1/yr; 1,000

$12/2 issues, $22/4 issues; $6/ea; 40%

185 pp; 5 x 8½

CPAD: 74470-80899

DeBoer, SPD, Fine Print, Spectacular Diseases, (UK)

LONG POND REVIEW

Russell Steinke, William O'Brien, Anthony Di Franco

Suffolk Community College

533 College Rd.

Selden, NY 11784

(516) 451-4153

Poetry, fiction, essays, reviews, interviews, photographs, graphics/artwork.

LONG POND REVIEW publishes the finest work submitted by established, emergent, and beginning writers. **LPR** has been recognized as an outstanding small press in **The Pushcart Prize II** (1977–78), **IV** (1979–80), **V** (1980–81), **VI**

(1981–82), **VII** (1982–83), and **IX** (1984–85).

Fred Chappell, David Citino, Colette Inez, Linda Pastan, Jim Barnes, William Stafford, Michael Blumenthal.

Payment: 1 contributor's copy.

Reporting Time: 2–6 months.

Copyright held by author.

1975; 1/yr; 500

$3/ea ind, $5/ea inst

72–88 pp; 6 x 9

Ad Rates: $75/page; $40/½ page

LONG SHOT

Nancy Mercado, Danny Shot

P.O. Box 6238

Hoboken, NJ 07030

Poetry, fiction, photographs, graphics/artwork.

"Writing From The Real World."

Allen Ginsberg, Amiri Baraka, Gregory Corso, June Jordan, Tom Waits, Miguel Algarin.

Unsolicited Manuscripts Received/ Published per Year: 3,000/20.

Payment: in copies.

Reporting Time: 12 weeks.

Copyright held by magazine; reverts to author upon publication.

1982; 2/yr; 2,000

$20/2 yrs; $6/ea; 40%

192 pp; 5½ x 8½

Ad Rates: $150/page (5 x 8½); $90/½ page (5 x 4¼)

ISSN: 0895-9773

DeBoer, Ubiquity, Fine Print,
I.P.D., Desert Moon, Inland

THE LONG STORY

R. Peter Burnham
18 Eaton St.
Lawrence, MA 01843
(508) 686-7638
Fiction.

We are interested strictly in long
stories (8,000–20,000 words, or
roughly 20–50 pages)—bias is
left wing and concern for human struggle for dignity etc.,
but quality is the main criterion.
Unsolicited Manuscripts Received/
Published per Year: 400/6-7.
Reading Period: year–round.
Payment: 2 copies.
Reporting Time: 2 weeks–2
months.
Copyright held by magazine; reverts to author upon publication.
1983; 1/yr; 900
$5/yr; $5/ea; 40%
160–200 pp; 5½ x 8½
ISSN: 0741-4242
Ingram

LOOK QUICK

Joel Scherzer, Robbie Rubinstein
P.O. Box 222
Pubelo, CO 81002
Poetry, fiction, reviews, photo-
graphs.

Emphasis is on free verse, blues
lyrics and brief vignettes. We
have also published material
relating to the Beats. Not reading unsolicited manuscripts.
Payment: in copies.
Copyright held by Quick Books;
reverts to author upon publication.
1975; irreg; 200
$3/ea
24–32 pp; 5½ x 8½

LOONFEATHER: A Magazine of Poetry, Short Prose & Graphics

Betty Rossi, Marsh Muirhead,
Elmo Heggie
P.O. Box 1212
Bemidji, MN 56601
(218) 751-4869
Poetry, Fiction, Graphics.

LOONFEATHER is primarily but
not exclusively a regional literary magazine publishing the
works of both emerging and
established writers. Our purpose
is to promote good writing and
encourage emerging artists by
publishing their work; sponsor-
ing readings, workshops, and
exhibits; and supporting fellow
artists/writers/organizations. Our
regional focus is northern Minnesota, Minnesota, and the surrounding states and Canada.

Edith Rylander, Robert Bly, Connie Sanderson, Philip Dacey, Joyce Penchansky, Thom Ward.
Unsolicited Manuscripts Received/ Published per Year: 200/65.
Reporting Time: Within four months following deadline for submissions.
Copyright held by magazine, reverts to author upon publication.
1979; 2/yr; 200–250
$7.50/yr; $4/ea; 40%
48 pp; 6 x 9
Ad Rates: $360/page; $180/½ page; $45/¼ page
ISSN: 0734-0699

LOST AND FOUND TIMES
John M. Bennett
137 Leland Ave.
Columbus, OH 43214
(614) 846-4126

Avant-garde, experimental, visual, language, collaborative, and other beyond the pale literature. Also graphics.
More poetry than prose. Any language; emphasizing English and Spanish.
Susan Smith Nash, Al Ackerman, N. Vassilakis, S. Murphy, Jake Berry.
Unsolicited Manuscripts Received/ Published per Year: many/few
Payment: 1 copy.
Reporting Time: immediate.

Copyright retained by authors and artists.
1975; 2/yr; 350
$20/5; $5/ea; 40%
Approx. 56 pp; 8½ x 5½
Small Press Traffic, Printed Matter

LOUISIANA LITERATURE: Literature/Humanities Review
David Hanson, Editor; William Parrill, Norman German, Associate Editors
SLU 792
Southeastern Louisiana University
Hammond, LA 70402
(504) 549-5022

Poetry, fiction, reviews of Louisiana-related books, articles on LA writing and culture.
We are interested in publishing essays and photo articles on Louisiana writing, history or art, but nothing full of jargon. Creative work we will take from anywhere on any topic.
Lewis P. Simpson, Diane Wakoski, Shirley Ann Grau, Kelly Cherry, Louis Gallo.
Unsolicited Manuscripts Received/ Published per Year: 1,500/40.
Reading Period: Sept.–May.
Payment: in copies.
Reporting Time: 1 month.
Copyright held by author.
1984; 2/yr; 650
$10/yr; $5/ea; 40%

100 pp; 6½ x 9½
Query for ad rates
ISSN: 0890-0477

LUZ EN ARTE Y LITERATURA

Veronica Miranda
P.O. Box 571062
Tarzana, CA 91357-1062
(818) 907-1454

Poetry, short stories, translations, art, etc.

LUZ is an international bilingual (Spanish/English) magazine featured mainly creative writing but also articles and interviews of writers and artists.

Carlota Caulfield, Ester de Izaguirre, Luis Benítez, Juana Rosa Pita, Enrique Jaramillo Levi.

Unsolicited Manuscripts Received/ Published per Year: 100/20
Payment: 1 copy.
Reporting Time: 3 weeks–1 months.
Copyright reverts to authors after publication.
1992; 2/yr; 500
$25/yr; $14/ea; 50%
100 pp; 8½ x 5½
Ad Rates: $400/page; $200/½ page; $100/¼ page
ISSN: 1067-0084

LYNX

Jane Reichhold, Editor
P.O. Box 1250
Gualala, CA 95445
(707) 882-2226; Fax: (707) 884-1235

Renga, tanka, criticism, essays, reviews, translation, interviews, black and white graphics, features.

LYNX is for linking poets and is the only magazine dedicated to renga and tanka. Renga (linked verse) was an outgrowth of tanka, the oldest poetry form still active in Japan, and has now invaded and captured North America.

Marlene Mountain, Hiroaki Sato, Anne McKay, Lorraine Ellis Harr, David Rice.

Unsolicited Manuscripts Received/ Published per Year: 400/120
Reporting Time: 1 week.
Copyright reverts to contributors.
1987; 3/yr; 300
$15/yr
80 pp; 4¼ x 11
ISSN: 1049-4502

LYRA

Lourdes Gil, Iraida Iturralde
P.O. Box 3188
Guttenberg, NJ 07093
(201) 861-1941 or (201) 869-2558

Poetry, fiction, criticism, interviews, essays, photographs, graphics/artwork.

We publish in English, French,

Spanish, Italian, as we are committed to raising the level of communication among contemporary writers and artists in North America and other parts of the world.
Mario Benedetti, Elizabeth Macklin, Virgilio Piñera, Alan West, Tom Whalen.
Payment: in copies.
Copyright held by magazine; reverts to author upon publication.
1987; 4/yr; 700
$15/yr ind, $18/yr inst; $4/ea; 40%
32 pp; 8½ x 11
Ad Rates: $200/page; $125/½ page; $70/¼ page. Also, on exchange.
ISSN: 0897-6716
Faxon, Slusa, Giralt

THE LYRIC
Leslie Mellichamp
307 Dunton Drive SW
Blacksburg, VA 24060
(703) 552-3475
Poetry.
We use rhymed verse in traditional forms, for the most part, about 36 lines max. We print only poetry, no opinions, no reviews. Our themes are varied, ranging from religious ectasy to humor to raw grief, but we feel no compulsion to shock, embitter, or confound our readers.
John Robert Quinn, Barbara Loots, R.L. Cook, R.H. Morrison, Neill Megaw, Paul Ramsey, Alfred Dorn, Rhina P. Espaillat.
Unsolicited Manuscripts Received/Published per Year: 2,500/200.
$800 in prizes annually.
$10/yr; $3/ea

M

THE MACGUFFIN

Arthur J. Lindenberg
Schoolcraft College
18600 Haggerty Road
Livonia, MI 48152-2696
(313) 462-4400 ext 5292 or 5327
Poetry, fiction, essays, photo-
    graphs, graphics/artwork.
We publish poetry, fiction, and
    essays of the highest quality.
    We have no biases with regard
    to style, but we are committed
    to seeking excellence. Prose
    submissions should be less than
    4,000 words.
Joe Schall, Tom Sheehan, Wendy
    Bishop, Jim Daniels, Carol
    Morris.
Unsolicited Manuscripts Received/
    Published per Year: 1,200/80.
Reading Period: Aug.–May.
Payment: 2 copies.
Reporting Time: 12 weeks.
Copyright held by Schoolcraft
College; reverts to author upon
    publication.
1984; 3/yr; 600
$12/yr ind, $10/yr inst; $4.50/ea;
    40%
144 pp; 5½ x 8½
No ads

MAGAZINE OF SPECULA-
TIVE POETRY

Mark Rich and Roger Dutcher
P.O. Box 564
Beloit, WI 53512
Poetry, reviews, and commentary
    on poetry.
Speculative poetry is the equiva-
    lent to speculative fiction, that
    confluence of post-modernism
    and science fiction in the sixties
    and seventies of the US and
    UK.
Brian Aldiss, David Memmott,

Jane Yolen, Steve Rasnic Tem, Robert Frazier.
Unsolicited Manuscripts Received/ Published per Year: 300-400/10.
Payment: 3¢/word; min. $3.00/poem.
Reporting Time: 1–8 weeks.
Copyright: First North American Serial Rights purchased, all rights revert to author.
1984; irregular; 200
$11/yr; $3.50/ea
22 pp; 5½ x 8½
ISBN: 8755-8785

MAGIC REALISM

C. Darren Butler
PYX Press
Box 620
Orem, UT 84059-0620
Magic realism, exaggerated realism, glib fantasy.
We accept a wide range of material related to mythopoeic literature including magic realism, exaggerated realism, literary fantasy, genre/dark fantasy, and glib fantasy of the sort found in folktales, fables and myths.
Unsolicited Manuscripts Published per Year: 60.
Reading Period: year-round.
Payment: $2 per magazine page plus copy.
Reporting Time: 3–6 months.
Copyright: held by contributers

1990; 2/yr; 700
$14.95/3 issues; $5.95/ea
80 pp
ISSN: 1061-2386

THE MALAHAT REVIEW

Derk Wynand, Editor, Marlene Cookshaw, Associate Editor
Box 1700
University of Victoria
Victoria, British Columbia, CANADA V8W2Y2
(604) 721-8524
Fiction, poetry.
A "generalist" literary magazine, open to new and celebrated writers. Meticulously edited, eclectic and elegant.
Tim Findley, Michael Ondaatje, Diane Williams.
Unsolicited Manuscripts Received/ Published per Year: 1,200/60.
Payment: $25 per magazine page.
Reporting Time: 3 months.
Copyright reverts to author; we buy first rights in English.
1967; 4/yr; 2,000
$20/yr (US); $7/ea (US)
132 pp; 6 x 9
ISSN: 0025-1216
Director

MANHATTAN POETRY REVIEW

Elaine Reiman-Fenton, Editor
FDR Box 8207

New York, NY 10150
(212) 355-6634
Poetry.

MANHATTAN POETRY REVIEW is dedicated to a celebration of excellence in contemporary American poetry, welcomes unsolicited manuscripts, and presents a balance of new and established poets in each issue. It was founded as a community of poets and readers to demonstrate the diversity of fine poetry in America today.
Unsolicited Manuscripts Received/ Published per Year: 1,200/50.
Reading Period: Sept.–Nov., Jan.–July.
Payment: none.
Reporting Time: 12–16 weeks.
Copyright reverts to author.
1992; $7.50 per issue, no subscriptions (foreign = U.S. $12.50)
52–60 pp; 5½ x 8½
ISSN: 885-9205

THE MANHATTAN REVIEW
Philip Fried
440 Riverside Dr., #45
New York, NY 10027
(212) 932-1854
Poetry, interviews, photographs, reviews.
We try to include American and foreign writers, and we focus on foreign writers with something

to offer the current American scene. We like to think of poetry as a powerful discipline engaged with many other fields. Peter Redgrove, Edmond Jabès, Christopher Bursk, A.R. Ammons, Stanislaw Baranczak, Bei Dao, Duoduo, Adam Zagajewski.
Unsolicited Manuscripts Received/ Published per Year: 400/1-4.
Payment: none.
Reporting Time: 8–10 weeks.
Copyright held by Philip Fried.
1980; 1/yr; 500
$10/ind. per volume (two issues); $14/inst. (2 issues)
64 pp
ISSN: 0275-6889

MANNA
Roger A. Ball, Brad Cutler, Rebecca Bradley
2966 West Westcove Dr.
West Valley City, UT 84119-5940
Short poetry with concise imagery.
Poetry magazine for beginning and intermediate poets publishing shorter poetry with clean imagery, strong content and quality writing. Accepts some rhyme, prefers free verse.
Patricia Higginbotham, Lyn Lifshin, Michael Estabrook, Albert Huffstickler.
Unsolicited Manuscripts Received/

Published per Year: 500+/200+.
Reading Period: year–round.
Reporting Time: under 3 weeks.
Copyright: Magazine copyrighted, first time rights only, reverts to author after publication.
1978; 2/yr; 200
$6/yr; $3.50/ea
35-40 pp; half legal
ISSN: 0886-5957

MĀNOA: A Pacific Journal of International Writing

Frank Stewart
English Department
University of Hawaii
Honolulu, HI 96822
(808) 956-3070 or 956-7808

Fiction, poetry, essays, reviews, interviews, translations, art, natural history essays.

US fiction and poetry, not limited to Pacific writers or themes; also features original translations of recent work from Pacific Rim nations.

W. S. Merwin, Kim Chiha, Ann Beattie, Tim O'Brien, Joyce Carol Oates, Barry Lopez, Alberto Ríos, Naomi Shihab Nye, Norman Dubie.

Unsolicited Manuscripts Received/ Published per Year: 2,800/80.

Payment: copies, plus up to $25 per page prose; more for poetry, reviews.

Reporting Time: 6–8 weeks.
Copyright reverts to author on publication.
1989; 2/yr; 2,150
$18/yr ind, $22/yr inst; 50%
240+ pp; 7 x 10
Ad Rates: $150/page; $95/½ page
ISSN: 1045-7909

THE MASSACHUSETTS REVIEW

Mary Heath, Paul Jenkins, Jules Chametzky
Memorial Hall
University of Massachusetts
Amherst, MA 01003
(413) 545-2689

Poetry, fiction, criticism, translation, interviews, photographs, graphics/artwork.

A quarterly of literature, the arts and current affairs; special art sections and special issues devoted to Feminism, Black literature, Ethnicity, Latin America, contemporary Ireland, etc. ocasionally featured. S.A.S.E. with all mss & inquiries.

Ariel Dorfman, Marilyn Hacker, Seamus Heaney, Joyce Carol Oates, Octavio Paz.

Unsolicited Manuscripts Received/ Published per Year: 3,500–4,000/80–100.

Payment: $50 prose, 35¢/line poetry ($10 min.).

Reporting Time: 3 months.
Copyright held by magazine; reverts to author upon publication when requested.
1959; 4/yr; 1,700
$15/ind, $20/inst; $5/ea + 75¢ postage; 40%
172 pp; 6 x 9
Ad Rates: $125/page (4⅛ x 7); $75/½ page (4⅛ x 3½)
Special university press rate: $100/2 full pages
ISSN: 0025-4878
DeBoer, Ubiquity, Fine Print

M/E/A/N/I/N/G
Susan Bee and Mira Schor
60 Lispenard St.
New York, NY 10013
(212) 431-3697
Art criticism and theory, artist statements, art book reviews.
A journal of contemporary art issues and theory; we publish writings by visual artists, art historians, and art critics.
Robert C. Morgan, Johanna Drucker, Charles Bernstein, Richard Tuttle, Nancy Spero, Daryl Chin, Emma Amos, Whitney Chadwick.
Unsolicited Manuscripts Received/ Published per year: 20/1 or 2.
Payment: small fee and issues for authors.

Copyright held by magazine.
1986; 2/yr; 1,000
$12/yr; $6/ea
56 pp; 8 ½ x 11
ISSN: 1040-8576
Ubiquity, SPD, DeBoer

MEN AS WE ARE
Jonathan Running Wind
P.O. Box 150615
Brooklyn, NY 11215-0615
(718) 499-2829
Fiction, poetry, essays, feature stories.
Deeply honest, vulnerable illumination of the masculine experience. A celebration and a lament of who we are today. Compassionate portrayals of our negative characteristics; models of how we can be at our highest.
James Oshinsky, Paul Milenski, David Thorn.
Unsolicited Manuscripts Received/ Published per Year: 1,000/30–50.
Payment: yes.
Reporting Time: 3–6 months.
Copyright held 90 days, then reverts to author; non-exclusive anthology rights.
1994; 1/yr; 1,200
$12/4 issues; $3/ea
48 pp; 8 ¼ x 10⅞
Ad Rates: $350/page; ¾, ½, ¼, ⅛, 1/12 page also available.

ISSN: 1067-9707
Bookpeople, Fine Print

METAMORFOSIS
Erasmo Gamboa, Lauro Flores
Chicano Studies Program
American Ethnic Studies Dept.
B523 Padleford Hall, GN-80
University of Washington
Seattle, WA 98195
(206) 543-5401
Poetry, fiction, criticism, essays,
reviews, translation, interviews,
photographs, graphics/artwork.
METAMORFOSIS welcomes
submissions of poetry, drama,
critical articles, book reviews,
and artwork (black and white 8
x 10 photographs) with SASE.
Shifra Goldman, Pedro Rodriguez,
Alfredo Arreguin, Margaret
Randall, Bobby Paramo.
Payment: none.
Copyright held by the Center; re-
verts to author upon publication.
1977; 2/yr; 500
$10/yr ind, $15/yr inst; $5/ea
50 pp; 8 ½ x 10
ISSN: 0273-1606

METAXY
Bob Lobis, Publisher; Janet Shep-
herd, M.D., Editor; Kelly Baily,
Art Director

1630 30th Street, #278
Boulder, CO 80301
(303) 666-5773
(303) 665-7252 (Fax)
Poetry, fiction, essays, reviews,
photographs.
METAXY publishes poetry and
fiction illuminated in a graphi-
cally dynamic format through
generous use of illustrations.
METAXY also publishes psy-
chologically informed essays
that explore the "Poetic Basis of
Mind." It is our hope to create
new audiences for poetry and
literary fiction by presenting
them in a visually stimulating
environment.
John Brown, Luellen Fletcher,
Marilyn Krysl, Dan Noel, Randall Schroth.
Payment: none.
Reporting Time: 8–12 weeks.
Copyright held by Metaxy, Inc.,
then reverts to author upon publication.
1993; 4/yr; 1,500
$20.00/yr ind; $20.00/yr instit.,
$6.00/ea, 40%
60 pp; 8 ½ x 11

METROPOLITAN
J. L. Bergsohn
6307 N. 31st St.
Arlington, VA 22207
Poetry and fiction.

We showcase the talents of Washington-area writers. Hilary Tham, M. A. Schaffner, Elisavietta Ritchie. Unsolicited Manuscripts Received/ Published per Year: 700/230–50. Payment: contributor's copy. Reporting Time: 2–4 weeks. Copyright reverts to author upon publication. 1991; 4/yr; 250 $8/yr; $2/ea 50 pp; 8 ½ x 5½

MICHIGAN QUARTERLY REVIEW

Laurence Goldstein
3032 Rackham Building
University of Michigan
Ann Arbor, MI 48109
(313) 764-9265

Interdisciplinary essays, fiction, poetry.
A general interest academic journal publishing essays and reviews in all areas, as well as fiction and poetry.
Donald Hall, Margaret Atwood, E.L. Doctorow.
Unsolicited Manuscripts Received/ Published per Year: 3,000/40.
Payment: $8-$10/printed page.
Reporting Time: 4-6 weeks.
Copyright reverts to author after first publication.
1962; 4/yr; 1,800

$18/yr; $5/ea; 40%
160 pp; 6 x 9
Ad Rates: $100/page
ISSN: 0026-2420
DeBoer, Fine Print, Ubiquity

MID-AMERICAN REVIEW

George Looney, Wayne Barham, Robert Early
English Department
Bowling Green State University
Bowling Green, OH 43403
(419) 372-2725

Poetry, fiction, translations, essays, book reviews, interviews.
MAR publishes poetry using strong, evocative images and fresh language; fiction which is both character and language-oriented; translations of contemporary writers; essays and book reviews on contemporary authors.
Jack Driscoll, Stephen Dunn, Philip Graham, Susan Neville, Frankie Paino, Greg Pape, Alberto Ríos.
Unsolicited Manuscripts Received/ Published per Year: 3,500+/90.
Reading Period: Sept.–May
Payment: copies and $10/page, up to $50.
Reporting Time: 1–4 months.
Copyright held by magazine; reverts to author upon publication.
1979; 2/yr; 1,000
$12/yr, $20/2 yrs; $7/ea

200 pp; 5½ x 8½
Exchange ads, 5 x 8
ISSN: 0747-8895

128 pp; 6 x 9
Ad Rates: $80/page, $50/½ page,
$50/¼ page

MID COASTER
Peter Blewett
2750 N. 45th St.
Milwaukee, WI 53210–2429
Poetry, fiction.
Unsolicited Manuscripts Received/
Published per Year: 500-
1,000/25
Payment: in copies.
Reporting Time: up to 8 weeks.
Copyright held by author.
1987; 1/yr; 800
$4.50/ea; 40%
36 pp; 8½ x 11
ISSN: 0892-970X

MIDLAND REVIEW
205 Morrill
Stillwater, OK 74078
(405) 744-9474
Poetry, fiction, photography, art-
work, essays.
Journal of contemporary literature,
literary criticism, and art.
Fritz Hamilton, Ionna-Veronica
Warwick, Mark Cox.
Unsolicited Manuscripts Received/
Published per Year: 400/50.
Payment: contributor copy.
1985; 1/yr; 200
$6/ea; $3/5 or more

MILDRED
961 Birchwood Ln.
Niskayuna, NY 12309

MINDPRINT REVIEW
Ron Pickup
P.O. Box 62
Soulsbyville, CA 95372
(209) 532-7045
Poetry, fiction, photographs, translations, graphics/artwork.
We publish quality prose, fiction,
poetry, translations, B&W photography and graphics of both
well-established and emerging
writers, artists and photographers. Our submission base is
Northern California, but our
publication reflects a national/
international cross section of
work. Each issue forms a thematic focus pertaining to humanity or philosophy, but submissions are never limited to
any subject, style or persuasion.
Quality is our criteria for acceptance.
Rosalie Moore, John Oliver Simon, Lo Fu, Agusti Bartra, Jack
Hirschman.

Payment: in copies only, upon publication.

Copyright held by magazine; reverts to author upon publication. 1983; 1/yr; 600 $7/yr ind, $7/yr inst; $6.50/ea, $7.50 by mail; 40%; consignment 128 pp; 6 x 9

Ad Rates: $240/page (4 x 7¾); $120/½ page (4½ x 4); $60/¼ page (4½ x 2½ or 2½ x 3¾)

ISSN: 1040-2233

Bookpeople

Published per Year: 1,500-2,000/50–75.

Payment: in copies.

Reporting Time: 60–90 days.

Copyright held by magazine; reverts to author upon publication. 1960; 2/yr; 1,600 $12/yr ind, $24/yr inst; $7.50/ea 200 pp; 5½ x 8 ½

Ad Rates: $100/page (5 x 7); $150/2 pages; $60/½ page (5 x 3½); $30/¼ page (2 x 3)

ISSN: 0026-5667

THE MINNESOTA REVIEW

Jeffrey Williams
the minnesota review
Dept. of English
East Carolina Univ.
Greenville, NC 27858
(919) 328-6388;
Fax (919) 328-4889

Poetry, fiction, criticism, essays, reviews, translations, interviews.

THE MINNESOTA REVIEW is a journal of committed writing. We are particularly interested in new work that is progressive in nature, with special commitment to the areas of socialist and feminist writing.

Jean Franco, Richard Ohmann, Michael Bérubé, Elizabeth Hahn, Joan Frank, Bruce Robbins.

Unsolicited Manuscripts Received/

MISSISSIPPI MUD

Joel Weinstein
1505 Drake Avenue
Austin, TX 78704
(512) 494-5459
For Fiction:
Rob Spillman
211 First Avenue
New York, NY 10003
(212) 995-5161

Poetry, fiction, photographs, graphics/artwork.

MISSISSIPPI MUD presents lucid, elegant writing and art from the *ne plus ultra* of the American scene.

Katherine Dunn, Joyce Thompson, Fred Pfeil, Todd Grimson, Christina Zawadiwsky, Tom Spanbauer.

Unsolicited Manuscripts Received/

Published per Year: 150/20.
Payment: cash, on publication,
depending on length or scale.
Reporting Time: 6–8 months.
Copyright held by magazine; reverts to author upon publication.
1973; 2–3/yr; 1,500
$19/4 issues, $6/ea
48 pp, 11 x 17

MISSISSIPPI REVIEW

Frederick Barthelme
Southern Station, Box 5144
Hattiesburg, MS 39406
(601) 266-4321

Fiction, poetry, criticism, translation, interviews.

MISSISSIPPI REVIEW is a literary magazine published by the
Center for Writers at the University of Southern Mississippi.
The editors combine solicited
and unsolicited works of well-
known and new writers in an
innovative format, producing
three numbers a year. Although
MR publishes mostly fiction
and poetry, the editors are interested in literature in translation,
interviews, and literary criticism.

Elizabeth Tallent, William Gibson,
E.M. Cioran, Amy Hempel,
Tama Janowitz.

Unsolicited Manuscripts Received/

Published per Year: 1,200/30-
40.
Reading Period: Sept.–May.
Payment: in copies.
Reporting Time: 8–12 weeks.
Copyright held by magazine; re-
verts to author upon publication.
1976; 2/yr; 2,000
$15/yr; $12/ea
120 pp; 5½ x 8½
Ad Rates: $100/page; $50/½ page;
exchange
ISSN: 0047-7559
DeBoer, Fine Print

MISSISSIPPI VALLEY REVIEW

John Mann, Tama Baldwin
Department of English
Western Illinois University
Macomb, IL 61455
(309) 298-1588

MVR publishes poetry, fiction,
and essays without regard to
any special slant of theme. Special issues (such as "the literature of witness" issue of Spring
'92) are published occasionally.
We encourage work by both new
and experienced writers.

Recent contributors include Edward Allen, R. Nikolas Macioci,
Ronald Wallace, Ralph J. Mills,
Michael Water, Ami Sands Bro-
doff, Anna Rabinowitz, and Patricia Henley.

Unsolicited Manuscripts Received/
Published per Year: 1,500/75.
Reading Period: Sept.–May.
Payment: in copies.
Reporting Time: 3 months.
Copyright held by author.
1971; 2/yr; 500
$12/yr; $6/ea
96 pp; 9 x 6
ISSN: 0270-3521

MISSOURI REVIEW

Speer Morgan, Greg Michalson
University of Missouri
1507 Hillcrest Hall
Columbia, MO 65211
(314) 882-4474

Poetry, fiction, essays, reviews,
interviews, special features of
literary interest, cartoons.
Reading Period: year–round.
Payment: $20/page; (average) up
to $500.
Reporting Time: 10–12 weeks.
Copyright held by the University
of Missouri; reverts to author
upon request.
1978; 3/yr; 6,000
$15/yr; $6/ea; 40%
224 pp; 6 x 9
Ad Rates: $250/page
ISSN: 0191-1961
ISBN: 1-879758

MOBIUS

Fred Schepartz
1149 E. Mifflin

Madison, WI 53703
(608) 255-4224
Short fiction, poetry, occasional
essays.
Fiction and poetry which uses social change as a primary or sec-
ondary theme. Doesn't have to
be overtly political as long as it
has something to say. Otherwise
anything goes.
William Steigerwaldt, Gay Davidson, R. Russell, Bonnie Brown,
Andrea Musher.
Payment: Copies.
Reporting Time: 8-10 weeks.
Copyright: Reverts to author upon
publication.
1989; 4/yr; 1,500
$12/yr ind, $3.50/ea; 40%
32pp; 8 ½ x 11
Ad Rates: $150/page (7 ½ x 10);
$80/½ page (3 x 9)

MODERN HAIKU

Robert Spiess
P.O. Box 1752
Madison, WI 53701
(608) 233-2738

Haiku, essays, reviews.
We publish only quality haiku in
which felt-depth, insight and
intuition are evident. Good university and public library subscription list includes foreign.
Paul O. Williams, Geraldine Little,
William J. Higginson, Cor van

den Heuvel, Wally Swist, Patricia Neubauer, James Kirkup.
Unsolicited Manuscripts Received/ Published per Year: 14,000/850.
Payment: $1/haiku on acceptance; $5/page for articles.
Reporting Time: 2 weeks.
Copyright held by Robert Spiess; reverts to author upon publication.
1969; 3/yr; 700
$14.85/yr; $5.25/ea
108 pp; 5½ x 8½
ISSN: 0026-7821

modern words

Garland Richard Kyle
350 Bay Street, No. 100
Box 325
San Francisco, CA 94133

Gay and lesbian poetry, fiction, and essays (plus b&w photos). A thoroughly queer international literary journal.
D. Dentinger, Robert Kaplan, Bia Lowe, Gerry Gomez Pearlberg, K.M. Soehnlein, and David Watmough.
Unsolicited Manuscripts Received/ Published per Year: 800/26.
Reading Period: year-long.
Payment: 1 free copy and $10.00 per page.
Reporting Time: prompt.
Copyright held by modern words

then reverts to author upon publication.
1994; 2/yr; 1,000
$25/3 issues; $10/ea; 40%
106–132 pp; 4½ x 7
Ad Rates: $150/page (3½ x 5½)
Small Press Distributors, Alamo Square, Fine Print

THE MONOCACY VALLEY REVIEW

William Heath, Editor
Dept. of English
Mount Saint Mary's College
Emmitsburg, MD 21727
(301) 447-6122

Fiction, poetry, photographs, graphics, artwork, criticism, interviews, essays. Our motto is: "the magazine that is always local but never provincial." We welcome singular voices and particular visions that create a real world and dramatize what matters.
Holly St. John Bergon, Roser Caminals, Mary Noel, John Grey, Roberta Bevington, Barbara Petoskey, Maxine Combs.
Reading Period: Dec.–Jan.
Payment: $10-25 for each poem, story, or artwork accepted (funds permitting).
$8/2 issues; $5/ea

MONOGRAPHIC REVIEW/ REVISTA MONOGRAFICA

Genaro J. Pérez, Janet Pérez
Box 8401
U.T. Permian Basin
Odessa, TX 79762
(915) 552-2306;
Fax (915) 552-2374
E-Mail; Perez_G @Gusher.pb.u-texas.edu

Literature and criticism of the Hispanic world.

A professional journal of criticism in the Hispanic literatures, monographic in character, devoted to areas neglected by mainstream journals. Recent topics: The Erotic, The Comics, Women Poets, Science Fiction, Detective Fiction

David W. Foster, John Dowling, Manuel Andújar, Noel Valis, Paul Ilie.

Unsolicited Manuscripts Received/ Published per Year: 50/25.
Reading Period: Aug. and Sept.
Payment: complimentary copy.
Reporting Time: 2 months.
Copyright: Perez & Perez
1985; 1/yr
$35/yr
pp varies
ISSN: 0885-7512

MOSAIC: A Journal for the Interdisciplinary Study of Literature

Dr. Evelyn J. Hinz
208 Tier Building
University of Manitoba
Winnipeg, Manitoba, R3T 2N2
CANADA
(204) 474-9763; Fax (204) 261-9086

Interdisciplinary study of literature.

MOSAIC is a scholarly journal dedicated to the "interdisciplinary study of literature"—the examination of literary works from antiquity to the present from the perspective of other disciplines.

Unsolicited Manuscripts Received/ Published per Year: 200/30–32.
Payment: none.
Reporting Time: 4 months.
Copyright held by magazine.
1967; 4/yr; 1,000
$22/yr, $38/2 yr, $53/3 yr (US/CANADA); $10/sample
138 pp; 6 x 9 ¼
Ad Rates: $150/page; $90/half page B/W
ISSN: 0027-1276
Hignell Printers (CANADA)

MOUNT OLIVE REVIEW

Pepper Worthington, Editor; Janie Jones Sower, Assistant Editor; Susan Kurjiaka, Assistant Editor; Happy Taylor, Circulation Manager

634 Henderson Street

Mount Olive, NC 28365

(919) 658-2502

Poetry, fiction, criticism, essays, reviews, plays, interviews, photographs, graphics/artwork.

The **MOUNT OLIVE REVIEW** is a cutting-edge phenomenon with an emphasis of combining academic scholarship and creative, mainstream literature. The journal is theme oriented each year and welcomes book reviews, essays, short stories, poetry, interviews, and criticism as they all relate to the stated theme.

Copyright held by Mount Olive College

1987; 1/yr; 3,500

40%

300+ pp; 7 x 10 ½

Ad Rates: $150/page (10 x 6); $75/half page (5 x 3); $35/¼ page (3 x 2)

ISSN: 0893-8288

MR. COGITO

John M. Gogol

Humanities

Pacific University

Forest Grove, OR 97116

Poetry, photographs, graphics/artwork.

Poetry in English, including translations; photographs, graphics. We like poems that surprise and move us with their language, sound and invention. **MR COGITO** specializes in publishing translations of East Central European poetry: i.e., Polish, Russian, Ukrainian Lithuanian, Latvian, Estonian, Czech, Slovak, Bulgarian, Rumainian, Greek, Serbian, Croatian, and German. Also interested in Native American poets and poems on Native American themes.

Baranczak, Herbert, Martinaitis, Cholin, Frajlich, Krynicki, Swirszczynska, Musial, Ficowski, Jastrun, Sujica, Poswiatowska, Orban, Richter, Marcenas, etc.

Unsolicited Manuscripts Published per Year: 1%.

Reading Period: year–round.

Payment: 1 copy.

Reporting Time: 1–3 months.

Copyright held by magazine; all but anthology rights revert to author upon publication.

1973; irregular; 500

$10/3 issues; $3.50/ea

24–28 pp; 4¼ x 11

ISSN: 0740-1205

Ebsco, Faxon, Dawson

N

NASSAU REVIEW

Dr. Paul A. Doyle, Managing Editor
English Dept.
Nassau Community College
State University of New York
Garden City, NY 11530
(516) 572-7792
Poetry, fiction, criticism, essays.
Unsolicited Manuscripts Received/
  Published per Year:
  600–700/30–35.
Reading Period: Sept.–Feb.
Payment: none.
Reporting Time: 5–7 months.
Copyright held by Nassau Com-
  munity College; reverts to au-
  thor upon publication.
1964; 1/yr; 1,200
Free.
92–95 pp; 6½ x 9½

THE NEBRASKA REVIEW

James Reed, Fiction Editor; Susan
  Aizenberg, Poetry Editor

212 FA
University of Nebraska, Omaha
Omaha, NE 68182-0326
(402) 554-2771
Poetry, fiction.
TNR publishes quality literary
  fiction and poetry, material that
  transcends mere technical profi-
  ciency.
Carolyne Wright, Joseph Geha,
  Joan Joffe-Hall, Elizabeth
  Evans, David Hopes, Vern Rut-
  sala, Cris Mazza, Roger Wein-
  garten, Rosemarie Kinder, Philip
  Dacey, Michael C. White
Unsolicited Manuscripts Received/
  Published per Year: 1,500/6-10
  fiction; 45-50 poetry.
Reading Period: Sept.–May.
Payment: 1 year subscription plus
  contributer's copies.
Reporting Time: 3–5 months
  (longest for poetry.)
Copyright held by magazine; re-

verts to author upon publication.
1972; 2/yr; 500
$9.50/yr; $5.00/ea; 40%
80 pp; 5½ x 8½
Ad Rates: $45/page (3⅝ x 6¼);
$25/½ page (3⅝ x 3)
ISSN: 8755-514X

NEGATIVE CAPABILITY

Sue Brannan Walker, Ron Walker
62 Ridgelawn Dr., East
Mobile, AL 36608
(205) 343-6163

Poetry, fiction, essays, reviews, interviews, photographs, graphics/artwork, original music, bagatelles. Annual poetry & fiction contest: $1,000 award for each.

NEGATIVE CAPABILITY is a creative journal whose emphasis is joy—not merely laughter, though we encourage humor, but the joy that arrives through insight into oneself and others, the world and our all too human condition.

Richard Eberhart, John Brugaletta, Vivian Shipley, Denise Levertov, Marge Piercy, Jimmy Carter, John Updike, Diane Wakoski, Leo Connellan, X. J. Kennedy.

Unsolicited Manuscripts Received/ Published per Year: 4,000/400.

Reading Period: Sept.—May.

Payment: 1 copy.
Reporting Time: 6 weeks.
Copyright held by magazine; reverts to author upon publication.
1981; 3/yr; 1,000
$15/yr ind, $20/yr inst; $5/ea; 40%
180 pp; 5¼ x 8¼
Ad Rates: $100/page (4½ x 8);
$50/½ page (4 x 4); $25/¼ page (4 x 2½)
ISSN: 0277-5166

NEW AMERICAN WRITING

Maxine Chernoff, Paul Hoover
2920 West Pratt
Chicago, IL 60645
(312) 764-1048

Poetry, fiction, essays, plays, graphics.

Nathaniel Mackey, Lyn Hejinian, Charles Simic, Ron Padgett, Bob Perelman, Robert Creeley, John Ashbery, Wanda Coleman.

Unsolicited Manuscripts Received/ Published per Year: 1,500/50.

Reading Period: Sept.–Dec. and Mar.–June.

Payment: $5/page, when available.
Reporting Time: 1–3 months.
Copyright held by OINK! Press, Inc.; reverts to author upon publication.
1971; 2/yr; 5,000
$18/3 issues; $7/ea; libraries and

foreign orders: $24/3 issues,
$9/ea; 40%
150 pp; 5½ x 8½
Ad Rates: $150/page (5 x 8);
$100/½ page (2¼ x 4)
ISSN: 0893-7842
Ingram, SPD, Ubiquity, Total

NEW DELTA REVIEW

Nicola Mason, Catherine Williamson, Editors; Juliette Busby, Poetry Editor; Matt Clark, Fiction Editor
c/o Department of English
Louisiana State University
Baton Rouge, LA 70803-5001
(504) 388-4079

Poetry, fiction, essays, interviews. **NDR** is a literary journal published by the Creative Writing Program at LSU. We are are most interested in new writers and exploring new directions in poetry and fiction. We offer the Eyster Prizes, which honor Warren Eyster, teacher, author, and faculty advisor to **NDR**'s predecessors.

James English, Julie McCracken, Virgil Suarez, Mircea Cartarescu, and an interview with Pulitzer Prizewinner Robert Olen Butler.

Unsolicited Manuscripts Received/ Published per Year: 2,000/45.
Reading Period: year–round.

Payment: in copies; Eyster Prize awarded to 1 poet and 1 fiction writer per issue.
Copyright: First North American; reverts to author upon publication.
1984; 2/yr; 500
$7/yr; $4/ea; 40%
100 pp; 6 x 9
Ad Rates: from other literary magazines.

NEW ENGLAND REVIEW

Stephen Donadio
Middlebury College
Middlebury, VT 05753
(802) 388-3711 ext 5075

Fiction, poetry, essays, reviews, translations, interviews—open to memorable writing of all kinds.

NEW ENGLAND REVIEW has been a mainstay of the American literary community for almost twenty years. Now located at Middlebury College, under new editorship, and newly affiliated with University Press of New England, **NER** is committed to the exploration of all forms of contemporary cultural expression, in the United States and elsewhere. In addition to original literary work in traditional genres, the magazine welcomes speculative and in-

terpretive essays, critical reassessments, statements by visual artists, and letters from abroad. Arnost Lustig, Ann Beattie, Stephen Dunn, Donald Hall, Edward Hirsch, W. D. Wetherell, Miroslav Holub, Samuel F. Pickering.
Reading Period: Sept.–June.
Payment: $10/minimum.
Reporting Time: 5–7 weeks.
Copyright held by author.
1978; 4/yr; 3,000
$23/yr ind, $30/yr inst; $7/ea; 40%
180 pp; 6 x 9
Ad Rates: $300/page (7 x 10); $150/½ page (7 x 5); $100/¼ page (3½ x 5)
ISSN: 0736-2579

NEW HOPE INTERNATIONAL
Gerald England
20 Werneth Ave.,
Gee Cross, Hyde, Cheshire
SK14 SNL ENGLAND
0161-351-1878
Poetry, short fiction, b & w artwork
NHI WRITING publishes poetry from traditional to avant-garde, including translations. **NHI REVIEWS** cover books, mags, cassettes, PC-software, etc.
Lisa Kucharski, B. Z. Niditch, Mary Rudbeck Stanko.

Unsolicited Manuscripts Received/ Published per Year: 5000/150
Payment: in copies only.
Reporting Time: usually within 2–3 months.
Copyright: First British Serial Rights.
1980; 2–6/yr; 1,500
$30/yr; $5/ea ($10 cheque)
36 pp
ISSN: 0260-7958

NEW LAUREL REVIEW
Lee Meitzen Grue
828 Lesseps St.
New Orleans, LA 70117
(504) 947-6001
Poetry, fiction, criticism, essays, reviews, translation, interviews, graphics/artwork, whatever is interesting.
NEW LAUREL REVIEW publishes poetry, fiction, translation, articles; work of sound scholarship which is alive. We hope to continue showing the best writing by nationally accepted writers with that of fresh new talent not seen before.
Enid Shomer, Sue Walker, Martha McFerren, James Nolan, Nahid Rachlin.
Reading Period: Sept.–May.
Reporting Time: varies.
Copyright held by author.
1971; 500

$9/yr ind, $11/yr inst.
125 pp; 6 x 9
ISSN: 0145-8388

NEW LETTERS

James McKinley, Editor; Robert
Stewart, Managing Editor;
Glenda McCrary, Administrative
Assistant
University of Missouri, Kansas
City
Kansas City, MO 64110
(816) 235-1168 or 235-1120

Poetry, fiction, reviews, photographs, graphics/artwork.

NEW LETTERS, an international
literary quarterly, publishes contemporary writing, including
that of well-known writers and
fresh, new talents and interviews with Nobel Laureates and
Pulitzer Prize Winners. Also
publishes photographs and
graphics; notable discoveries of
overlooked gems. e.g., Theodore
Roethke interview, Countee
Cullen memoir, and Richard
Wright, archival material.
Jim Harrison, Jorie Graham, William H. Gass, Tess Gallagher,
Luisa Valenzuela, Margaret Atwood, Thomas Berger, William
Burroughs, Rosellen Brown,
Lisel Mueller, Amiri Baraka,
John Updike, Annie Dillard.
Unsolicited Manuscripts Received/

Published per year: 5,000/100.
Reading Period: Oct. 15–May 15.
Payment: small honorarium and
copies.
Reporting Time: 6 weeks.
Copyright held by magazine; reverts to author upon publication.
1934; 4/yr; 2,500
$17/yr ind, $20/yr inst; $5/ea;
40%–50%
128 pp; 6 x 9
Ad Rates: $150/page (4 x 6⅞);
$100/½ page (4 x 3⅛)
Ingram, Ubiquity

NEW MYTHS: MSS

Robert Mooney
SUNY Binghampton
Box 530
Binghampton, NY 13901
(607) 777-2168

Poetry, fiction, essays, photographs, graphics.
Special emphasis on publishing
the best work of young and
unestablished writers with the
work of well-known writers.
Andrew Hudgins, Dianne Bene-
dict, Gerald Stern, William
Stafford, Linda Pastan.
Payment: whenever funds allow.
Reporting Time: 2–8 weeks.
Copyright reverts to author upon
publication.
1961; 2/yr; 1,000
$8.50/yr ind, $14/yr inst; $5.50/ea

Ad Rates: $500/page; $250/½ page

NEW ORLEANS REVIEW

Ralph Adamo
Box 195
Loyola University
New Orleans, LA 70118
(504) 865-2294

Poetry, short fiction, translations, literary & film criticism, artwork.
Payment: please inquire
Reporting Time: 3 months
1968; 4/yr; 1,000
$30/yr; $10/ea.
100-160 pp; 6 x 9
ISSN: 0028-6400

THE NEW PRESS

Robert Dunn, Editor; Bob Abramson, Publisher
53-35 Hollis Ct. Blvd.
Flushing, NY 11365
(718) 229-6782

Poetry, short stories, essays, line drawings.
A literary quarterly that stresses poetic vision and voice. For the literate mind. Work should be accessible and enjoyable to an intelligent reader.
Joe Malone, Ken Di Maggio, Lawrence Ferlinghetti, Karen Swenson, Ann Chandler.

Unsolicited Manuscripts Received/ Published per Year: 400/80.
Payment: 3 copies; $15 for prose. Poetry, essay, and short story contests.
Reporting Time: 2 months.
Copyright: First time serial rights; reverts to author.
1984; 4/yr; 2,000
$15/yr; $4/ea; 40%
40 pp; 8½ x 11
$100/page; $60/½ page; $40/¼ page; $20/business card
ISSN: 0894-6078
Ubiquity

the new renaissance

Louise T. Reynolds, Harry Jackel, Patricia Michaud, Michal Anne Kucharski
9 Heath Road
Arlington, MA 02174

Fiction, poetry; lead articles; stories & poetry in bilingual translations; reproduction of paintings, sculpture, mixed media, photographs; commentary, graphics, illustrations, essays, reviews.
We offer a forum for idea/opinion pieces on political/sociological pieces, and publish a wide variety of styles, statements, tones, and visions in fiction, poetry and art. Since we take a classicist position, we avoid the

trendy and the fashionable, for the most part, but our range is so broad it includes contradictory statements within a single issue. There is, however, an emphasis on the human condition.

Tom Ruane, Jacqueline Merriam-Paskow, Kurt Kusenberg (Lauren Hahn translator); Joe Bolton translations from Spanish, Rose Rosberg, Norman Nathan, de Andrado (Alexis Leuctin translator), Daniel Bourno (translator of Ryszard Halzer).

Unsolicited Manuscripts Received/Published per Year: 1,000+/30-40.

Reading Period: Sept.—Oct. only.

Payment: After publication.

Reporting Time: 60–20 weeks, poetry; 35–55 weeks, prose. One month for queries. Submissions in Sept. & Oct. only w/$10.00 for 2 back issues or a current issue. EXCEPTIONS: All current subscribers & anyone who has bought one or more issues since April '93.

Copyright held by magazine.

1968; 2/yr; 1,500

$19.50/3 issues; $21/3 issues (CANADA); $23/3 issues (other); $8.50/sample of most recent issue.

144–192 pp; 6 x 9

ISSN: 0028-6575

NEW VIRGINIA REVIEW

Mary Flinn, Editor; Margaret Gibson, Poetry Editor.

1306 East Cary St., 2A

Richmond, VA 23219

(804) 782-1043

Poetry, fiction, essays.

NEW VIRGINIA REVIEW: a trice yearly collection of new poetry, fiction, and essays that strives to publish the best possible work being done by contemporary authors both unknown and widely recognized. Special issues forthcoming. Nature and poetry at the end of the century; New Russian prose in translation.

Richard Bausch, Peter Taylor, Mandy Sayer, Mona Van Duyn, Rachel Hadas.

Unsolicited Manuscripts Received/Published per Year: 6,000+/40.

Payment: $10/printed page, $25 minimum for poems, upon publication.

Copyright held by magazine, and individual writers; reverts to author upon publication.

1979; 3/yr; 3,000

$15/yr; $6/ea; 50% w/no return discount on back issues w/subscriptions.

160–200 pp; 6½ x 10

No ads

ISSN: 0-939233-00-2

NEXT PHASE
Kim Means
33 Court St.
New Haven, CT 06511
(203) 772-1697; fax same
Fiction, commentary, reviews, poetry.

Whether your interest lies in innovative ways to save our planet, social science fiction, or winning poetry, **NEXT PHASE** offers a unique compilation of the best of the small press in a well designed format.
Dr. Timothy Leary, D.F. Lewis, R.T. Smith, Jon Emory.
Unsolicited Manuscripts Received/ Published per Year: 150/20.
Payment: 3 contributors copies.
Reporting Time: 6 weeks.
Copyright reverts to author.
1989; 3/yr; 1,300
$8/yr; $16/2yr
44 pp; 8½ x 11
Ad Rates: $100/page; $60/½ page; $40/¼ page
Fine Print, Ubiquity, Desert Moon, Bear Family, IPD

NIGHT ROSES
Allen T. Billy, Sandra Taylor
P.O. Box 393
Prospect Heights, IL 60070
(708) 392-2435
Poetry, some art.
We like to publish romance poetry, flower poetry, ghost images of past or future and odds and ends of interest.
Genoa, Mary R. De Maine, Ken Stone, Jane Camron.
Unsolicited Manuscripts Received/ Published per Year: 1,500/150.
Reading Period: Sept.–July.
Payment: copy of issue.
Reporting Time: 4–12 weeks.
Write for guidelines before submitting work.
Copyright belongs to authors.
1986; 2–4/yr; 250
$10/3 issues; $4/sample;
$5/Current New issues per copy
44–56 pp; 5⅜ x 8½

NIMROD: International Journal of Prose & Poetry
Francine Ringold
Arts and Humanities Council of Tulsa
2210 South Main
Tulsa, OK 74114
(918) 584-3333
Poetry, fiction, prose, translation, photographs, graphics/artwork, interviews.
NIMROD seeks vigorous writing that is neither wholly of the academy nor of the streets. Fall issues feature the winners and finalists of the Nimrod Hardman Literary Awards Competition and spring issues are thematic.

Past thematic issues include "Arabic Literature," "China Today," "India: A Wealth of Diversity," "from the Soviets," "Oklahoma Indian Markings," "Clap Hands and Sing: Writers of Age," "Australian Literature: Then and Now" and "O! Canada."

Wendy Stevens, Tess Gallagher, Denise Levertov, Gish Jen, Sharon Sakson, Alvin Greenberg, Janette Turner Hospital.

Unsolicited Manuscripts Received/Published per Year: 500-800 fiction and poetry/1%.

Reading Period: year–round.

Payment: $5/page up to $25 plus two copies; also $1,000 to first place winners in our fiction and poetry competition, $500 for second place.

Reporting Time: 3–6 months.

Copyright of entire magazine held by the Arts & Humanities Council of Tulsa. Rights to individual stories revert to authors.

1956; 2/yr; 4,000–4,500

$15.00/yr; $8.00/ea

160 pp; 6 x 9

Ad Rates: $200/page; $100/½ page

ISSN: 0029-053X

96 INC

Vera Gold and Julie Phipps, Editors

P.O. Box 15559

Boston, MA 02215

(617) 267-0543; (617) 267-6725 Fax

Fiction, poetry, interviews, graphics/artwork.

96 INC, the parent organization of the Kenmore Writers Group, was formed to foster the publication of original literary works, with an emphasis on new writers; to sponsor public and private readings; and to train students of high school and other ages.

Payment: 4 copies of magazine and free sucsbription. Modest fee when funds are available.

Copyright reverts to author upon publication.

1992; 2/yr; 3,000

$10/yr; $4/ea; 40%; consignment

50 pp; 8½ x 11

Ad Rates: $100/page (8½ x 11); $75/½ page (4¼ x 5½); $50/¼ page (2⅛ x 2¾)

DeBoer

NIT & WIT

Harrison McCormick, Marie Aguirre

P.O. Box 627

Geneva, IL 60134

(312) 232-9496

Poetry, fiction, essays, reviews, interviews, photographs, graphics/artwork.

NIT & WIT is a full-spectrum
cultural arts magazine with
regular features on art, music,
dance, theatre, film, architecture, photography, reviews, essays, fiction and poetry.
Philip Graham, June Brinder, Gordon Lish, Sharon Sheehe Stark.
Payment: none.
Reporting Time: 2–3 weeks.
Copyright held by author.
1977; 6/yr; 6,000
$12/yr; $2/ea; 40%–50%
68 pp; 8½ x 11
Ad Rates: $750/page (7⅛ x 10);
$390/½ page (4¹¹⁄₁₆ x 7⅜);
$210/¼ page (3½ x 4¹⁵⁄₁₆)

NO ROSES REVIEW
Carolyn Koo, Natalie Kenvin, Jua-
nita Garza
P.O. Box 14258
Chicago, IL 60614
Poetry, fiction, solicited essays.
Progressive, experimental work
encouraged. Fiction 20 pages
double spaced maximum. Poetry
10 pages maximum.
Elaine Equi, David Trinidad,
Caroline Knox, John Traiter,
Susan Wheeler, Rosmarie Wal-
drop, Carolyn Forché.
Payment: in copies.
Reporting Time: 2–3 months.
Copyright reverts to author upon
publication.

1992; 2/yr; 500
$12/yr; $6/ea
96 pp
ISSN in application.

**THE NORTH AMERICAN
REVIEW**
Robley Wilson
University of Northern Iowa
Cedar Falls, IA 50614
(319) 273-6455
Poetry, fiction, criticism, essays,
reviews, graphics/artwork.
Oldest magazine in North America,
publishing fiction and nonfiction,
poetry and reviews. Winner in
1981 and 1983 of National
Magazine Award for fiction.
Nonfiction frequently has
ecological/environmental slant.
Unsolicited Manuscripts Received/
Published per Year: 20,000 poetry, 3,000 prose/30-35 poems,
55-65 prose.
Reading Period: Jan.–Apr. 1, Fiction.
Payment: $10/published page;
50¢/line for poetry, $20 mini-
mum.
Reporting Time: 1–3 months.
Copyright by University of Northern Iowa; reverts to author upon
publication.
1815; 6/yr; 4,700
$18/yr; $4/ea
48+ pp; 8⅛ x 10⅞

Ad Rates: $500/page (7 x 10);
$200/⅓ page (2¼ x 10)
ISSN: 0029-2397
Eastern News

NORTH ATLANTIC REVIEW

John Gill
15 Arbutus Lane
Stony Brook, NY 11790-1408
(516) 751-7886
Poetry, Fiction, Essays.
General fiction and poetry, with a
special section in each issue de-
voted to literary or social issues.
Lewis Turco, Burton Raffel,
Walter Cummins, Richard Eber-
hart, David Ignatow, Archibald
MacLeish, James Dickey, May
Swenson, David Slavitt, Richard
Wilbur.
Unsolicited Manuscripts Received/
Published per Year: 1,600/40.
Reading Period: year–round.
Reporting Time: 4–5 months.
Copyright held by author.
1989; 1/yr; 1,000
$10/yr; 40%
300; 7 x 9½
$200/page; $125/½ page; $75/¼
page
ISSN: 1040-7324

Greenville, NC 27858
(919) 328-4876 or (919) 328-6041
(919) 328-4889 Fax
Articles, essays, interviews, re-
views, photos, w/NC focus.
A magazine of literature, culture,
and history, for serious readers
found as often in bookstores
and libraries as in universities.
Fred Chappell, A.R. Ammons,
Leon Rooke, Janet Lembke,
James Applewhite, Louise
Anderson, Margaret Maron,
Linda Flowers.
Unsolicited Manuscripts Received/
Published per Year: 110/6.
Payment: $50–$500.
Reporting Time: 6 weeks on que-
ries; no unsolicited fiction or
poetry, please.
Copyright: First rights held by
magazine; returned to author on
request.
1992; 2/yr; 1,200 paid
$18/yr; $10.50/ea ppd.;
Returnable/NR 30–40%
200 pp; 7½ x 10
Ad Rates: $200/page; $125/½
page; $75/¼ page
ISSN: 1063-0724
Ebsco, Faxon, Cox, Swets

**NORTH CAROLINA LITER-
ARY REVIEW**

Alex Albright
English Dept., ECU

**NORTH DAKOTA QUAR-
TERLY**

Robert W. Lewis, Editor; William
Borden, Fiction Editor; Jay

Meek, Poetry Editor
University of North Dakota, Box 7209
Grand Forks, ND 58202
(701) 777-3322
Poetry, fiction, criticism, essays, reviews, graphics.
An interdisciplinary journal in the arts and humanities. Recent and forthcoming special issues on Yugoslav culture, Egypt, and Hemingway.
Sherman Paul, Kathleen Woodward, Philip Booth, Donald Hall, Alane Rollings, Naguib Mahfouz, Carol Shields.
Unsolicited Manuscripts Received/ Published per Year: 1,000/125.
Payment: in copies.
Reporting Time: 1–3 months.
Copyright by University of North Dakota.
1909; 4/yr; 1,000
$20/yr; $5/ea; $10 for special issues; 20%
200 pp; 6 x 9
ISSN: 0029-277X

NORTHEAST ARTS

Mr. Leigh Donaldson
J.F.K. Station
P.O. Box 6061
Boston, MA 02114
Poetry, reviews, fiction.
NORTHEAST ARTS is an arts literary journal, featuring original poetry, short fiction, essays, photography, black & white art and reviews.
Otto Laska, S.P. Luttrell, Sebastian Lockwood.
Unsolicited Manuscripts Received/ Published per Year: 2,000/100.
Payment: 2 copies.
Reporting Time: 2–3 months.
Copyright: one-time use, rights revert to creator.
$10/yr; $4.50/ea
26-32 pp; 6½ x 9½
Ad Rates: $75/page (5 x 8); $45/½ page (5 x 4½) or $50/½ page (2½ x 8)

NORTHEAST CORRIDOR

Susan Balée, Editor; Peggy Finn, Fiction Editor; Jeffrey Loo, Janna King, Poetry Editors
Beaver College
450 S. Easton Rd.
Glenside, PA 19038
(215) 572-2963
Short stories, poetry, drama, personal essays, interviews, black & white photos, line art.
NORTHEAST CORRIDOR is a literary magazine focusing on the work of writers and artists in the Northeastern United States. We seek excellent fiction, poetry, plays, essays, black and white line art and photography.

Eleanor Wilner, Glen Weldon, Kermit Moyer, Frederick Morgan, Geoffrey Clark.

Unsolicited Manuscripts Received/ Published per Year: 900/40–60.

Reading Period: Sept.–May.

Payment: $10/per poem; $25/story or essay; $100 for best of each genre in issue.

Reporting Time: 3 months or less.

Copyright held by NEC until publication; then it reverts to author.

1993; 2/yr; 1,000

$20/libraries; $10/ind; $5.00/ea; $3.00

90-150 pp; 6½ x 9

Ad Rates: $200/page

Fine Print

NORTHWEST LITERARY FORUM

Ce Rosenow, Nancy Hune

2012 S. 314th Ste. 158

Federal Way, WA 98003

Haiku, poetry, fiction.

We are a quarterly which integrates haiku and its related forms with poetry and short fiction.

Vincent Tripi, Michael Dylan Welch, Andrew Grossman, Phyllis Walsh, taylor Graham.

Unsolicited Manuscripts Received/ Published per Year: 500/100.

Reading Period: year-round.

Payment: 1 copy of journal.

Reporting Time: 1–2 months.

Copyright reverts to author upon publication.

1992; 4/yr

$15/yr; $4/ea; 60%/40%

28 pp; 8½ x 5½

ISSN: 1062-3353

NORTHWEST REVIEW

John Witte, Hannah Wilson

369 PLC

University of Oregon

Eugene, OR 97403

(503) 346-3957

Poetry, fiction, criticism, essays, reviews, translation, interviews, graphics/artwork.

NORTHWEST REVIEW is a tri-annual publishing poetry, fiction, artwork, interviews, book reviews and comment. We have no other criterion for acceptance than that of excellence. We are devoted to representing the widest possible variety of styles and perspectives (experimental, feminist, political, etc.), unified within a humanist framework. "A publication to which the wise and honest, and literate, may repair!"—William Stafford.

Joyce Carol Oates, Madeline DeFrees, Alan Dugan, Morris Graves, Raymond Carver.

Unsolicited Manuscripts Received/ Published per Year: 4,000/90.
Payment: in copies.
Reporting Time: 8–10 weeks.
Copyright held by magazine; reverts to author upon request.

1957; 3/yr; 1,100
$14/yr; $5/ea; 20%–40%
160 pp; 6 x 9
Ad Rates: $160/page/6 x 9
ISSN: 0029-3423

O

OASIS, a literary magazine

Neal Storrs, Editor & Publisher;
   Eugene Storrs, Assistant Editor
1833 10th Street SW
Largo, FL 34648
(813) 587-9552

Poetry, fiction, essays, translation. First, last and only consideration is quality of writing. Genres, target audiences, don't apply. Strongly interestedin translations. Mailings, Neal Storrs, Bookstores in Tampa Bay area. Want nothing more than to stay on present course.

James Sallis and Susan Medenica.

Payment: $5/poem; $15–$50/prose work.

Reporting Time: no more than ten days.

Copyright: Neal Storrs, reverts to author upon publication.

1992; 6/yr; 150
$25/yr ind; $25/yr inst; $4.95/ea
70 pp; 7 x 10
ISSN: 1064-6299

OBJECT LESSON/ Weighted Anchor Press

Joshua S. Beckman, John C. Horoschak
P. O. Box 1186
Hampshire College
Amherst, MA 01002

Fiction, poetry, one act plays, essays, essays on art, interviews, black and white artwork, artists books, letters.

OBJECT LESSON is open to all styles of writing no length requirements. Annual poetry and fiction contests.

Alice Mattison, Lance Olsen, Harry Brody, Paul Beckman.

Unsolicited Manuscripts Received/ Published per Year: 1,200/50.

Reading Period: year–round.

Payment: in copies.

Reporting Time: 6–8 weeks.

Copyright: bluestone Press, reverts to author on publication.

1990; 2/yr; 300
$10/yr; $5/ea
300 pp; 5½ x 8½, perfect bound
Ad Rates: $50/page (8 x 5);
  $35/½ page (4½ x 5½); trades
  avail.
ISSN: 1061-429X (issued 1–7; 1
  pending issue 8+)

**OBSIDIAN II: Black Literature
In Review**
Gerald Barrax, Joyce Pettis
Box 8105
Department of English
North Carolina State University
Raleigh, NC 27695-8105
(919) 737-3870
Poetry, fiction, criticism, essays,
  reviews.
OBSIDIAN II is a biannual re-
  view for the study and cultiva-
  tion of creative works in En-
  glish by Black writers
  worldwide, with scholarly criti-
  cal studies by all writers on all
  aspects of Black literature, book
  reviews, poetry, short fiction,
  interviews, bibliographies, bib-
  liographical essays, and very
  short plays in English.
Houston A. Baker, Jr., Gayl Jones,
  Wanda Coleman, Raymond R.
  Patterson, Gerald Early.
Payment: none.
Copyright held by Department of
  English, North Carolina State

University; reverts to author
  upon publication.
1986; 2/yr; 500
$12/yr ind, $12/yr inst; $5/ea;
  40%
130 pp; 6 x 9
Ad Rates: $200/page (4½ x 7⅛);
  $100/½ page (4½ x 3½)
ISSN: 0888-4412

ODESSA POETRY REVIEW
Jim Wyzard
RR 1, Box 39
Odessa, MO 64076
Poetry.
Ester Leipen, Rod Kessler, Roch-
  elle Lynn Holt, Marian Park.
Payment: varies with quality of
  work.
Copyright held by Jim Wyzard;
  reverts to author upon publica-
  tion.
1984; 4/yr; 500–700
$16/yr; $4/ea; 40%
150 pp; 5½ x 8½
No ads

**THE OGALALA REVIEW
(formerly EPIPHANY)**
Gordon Grice
P.O. Box 2699
University of Arkansas
Fayetteville, AR 72701
Fiction, poetry, translations, cre-
  ative nonfiction.
TOR specializes in literary fiction,

nonfiction, and poetry.

Alicia Ostriker, R. S. Gwynn, Enid Shomer, David Citino, Trent Busch.

Unsolicited Manuscripts Received/ Published per Year: 2,000/24.

Reading Period: year–round.

Payment: 2 copies, small honorarium when funds permit.

Reporting Time: 1–2 months.

Copyright: One time publishing right—copyright reverts to author.

1990; 2/yr; 400

$10/yr; $5/ea; 10% to bookstores

100 pp; 8½ x 5½

Ad Rates: $100/page (5 x 8); $60/½ page (5 x 3¾)

THE OHIO REVIEW

Wayne Dodd

209 C Ellis Hall

Ohio University

Athens, OH 45701-2979

(614) 593-1900

Poetry, fiction, essays, reviews.

THE OHIO REVIEW publishes the best in contemporary American poetry, fiction, book reviews, and essays.

Marianne Boruch, Bim Ramke, Mary Oliver, Donald Revell, Leonard Kriesel.

Unsolicited Manuscripts Received/ Published per Year: 2,000/20.

Reading Period: Sept.–May 31.

Payment: $1/line (poetry), $5/page (prose).

Reporting Time: 90 days.

Copyright held by magazine; reverts to author upon request.

1971; 3/yr; 2,700

$16/yr, $40/3yrs; $6/ea; 40%

144 pp; 6 x 9

Ad Rates: $175/page (4¼ x 7¼); $100/½ page (4¼ x 3¼)

ISSN: 0360-1013

Ingram, DeBoer, Ubiquity, Michiana News Service

ON THE ISSUES (The Progressive Woman's Quarterly)

Merle Hoffman, Ronni Sandroff

97-77 Queens Blvd.

Forest Hills, NY 11374

(718) 459-1888 ext. 208

Women's issues.

The women's magazine you've been looking for (but never thought you'd find). ON THE ISSUES engages your mind, heart,and principles. It features unexpurgated discussions of points of view too controversial for the mainstream medium. Focuses on feminism today, women's health, relationships, campus politics, ecology, animal rights, global humanism, and women in the arts.

Louise Armstrong, Phyllis Chesler, Andrea Dworkin, Liz Holtzman,

Mary Hunt, Julia Kagan, Cong.
John Lewis, Andrea Peyser, Ar-
lene Raven, Elayne Rapping,
Rep. Pat Schroeder, Anne Mol-
legen Smith, John Stoltenberg,
Alice Vaachs.
Payment: negotiated.
1991; 4/yr
$14.95/yr, add $10/inst; $3.95/ea;
    30%
64 pp; 8⅜ x 10⅞
Ad Rates: $660/page, B/W only
    (color add'l $250).
ISSN: 0895-6014
Eastern News

ONTARIO REVIEW

Raymond J. Smith, Joyce Carol
    Oates
9 Honey Brook Dr.
Princeton, NJ 08540
Poetry, fiction, essays, interviews,
    photographs, graphics.
Maxine Kumin, Albert Goldbarth,
    Russell Banks, Alicia Ostriker,
    Tom Wayman.
Unsolicited Manuscripts Received/
    Published per Year: 1,500/25.
Payment: $10/page.
Reporting Time: 6 weeks.
Copyright held by magazine; re-
    verts to author upon publication.
1974; 2/yr; 1,100
$12/yr; $6/ea; 40%
112 pp; 6 x 9
Ad Rates: $125/page (4¼ x 7);

$75/½ page (4¼ x 3¼); $50/¼
page (2 x 3¼)
ISSN: 0316-4055
Ingram, Ubiquity

ONTHEBUS

Jack Grapes
P.O. Box 481270
Bicentennial Station
Los Angeles, CA 90048
(213) 651-5488
Poetry, fiction, translations, essays,
    interviews, book reviews.
Open to all kinds, experimental to
    neo-narrative to Bohemian-
    language-confessional haiku!
    6-10 poems max, fiction 1,500
    max.
Joyce Carol Oates, Charles
    Bukowski, Ai, David Mura,
    Wanda Coleman, Kate Braver-
    man, Norman Dubie.
Unsolicited Manuscripts Received/
    Published per Year: 3,500/200.
Reading Period: Feb. – May.
Payment: 1 copy.
Reporting Time: 2–6 months.
Copyright reverts to contributors.
1989; 2/yr; 3,200
$28/3 issues; $11/ea; 20-40%
336 pp; 8 ½ x 5 ½
Ad Rates: $300/page (7 ¼ x 4 ¼);
    $200/½ page; $125/¼ page
ISSN: 1043-884X
DeBoer, Bookpeople, SPD, Fine
    Print

ORO MADRE

Loss Pequeño Glazier
P.O. Box 143
Getzville, NY 14068-0143
Poetry, fiction, criticism, reviews, graphics.

ORO MADRE seeks to present writings with attention to details of the poem's status and the uncertain edges of the poetic act; of interest also, electronic poetries and the language of electronic communication; it also focuses on coverage of the small press world through reviews, interviews, and articles on small press activities and trends.
Alejandro Muguia, Jack Hirschman, Robert Anbian.
Reading Period: year–round.
Payment: in copies.
Reporting Time: 2 months.
Copyright held by author.
1981; irreg; 500
$14/yr ind, $20/yr inst; $3.50/ea; 40%
48 pp; 5½ x 8
Ad Rates: $40/page (5 x 7½); $25/½ page (5 x 3¾)

OSIRIS

Andrea and Robert Moorhead
Box 297
Deerfield, MA 01342
(413) 774-4027
Poetry, photographs, graphics/artwork.

OSIRIS is a multi-lingual poetry journal publishing contemporary work in English, French, and German. Poetry in other languages such as Hungarian, Portuguese, and Danish appears in a bilingual format.
Robert Marteau, Madeleine Gagnon, Eugenio de Andrade, Hans Raimund, John Falk.
Unsolicited Manuscripts Received/Published per Year: 150-200/6-8.
Payment: in copies.
Reporting Time: 4 weeks.
Copyright reverts to author upon publication.
1972; 2/yr; 500
$10/yr; $5/ea
40 pp; 6 x 9
Ad Rates: $125/page (5½ x 8½)
ISSN: 0095-019X

OSTENTATIOUS MIND

Patricia D. Coscia
JAF Station Box 7415
New York, NY 10116-4630
Poetry; all types except x-rated.

OSTENTATIOUS MIND is designed to encourage the intense writer, the cutting reality. The staff deals in the truth of life: political, social, and psychological. SASE for submission guidelines.

Payment: 4 copies.

Reporting Time: as soon as possible.

1987

$2/ea

10 pp; 7 x 8

40%, 50% to distributors

225 pp; 7 x 9

Ad Rates: $100/page (7 x 9);
$75/½ page (3½ x 4½)

ISSN: 8756-4696

OTHER VOICES

Lois Hauselman, Sharon Fiffer,
Editors; Ruth Canji, Tina Peano,
Assistant Editors

University of IL at Chicago

Dept. of English (M/C 162)

601 S. Morgan St.

Chicago, IL 60607-7120

(312) 413-2209

Fiction, interviews.

A Prize-winning (IAC), independent market for quality fiction, we are dedicated to original, fresh, diverse stories and novel excerpts. We've won 15 IAC awards in 10 years, plus a CCLM/GE Younger Writers Award in 1988.

David Evanier, Rolaine Hochstein, Edith Pearlman, Stephen Dixon, Karen Karbo.

Unsolicited Manuscripts Received/ Published per Year: 1,000/40-50.

Reading Period: Oct.–April 1.

Payment: gratuity plus copies.

Reporting Time: 10–12 weeks.

Copyright held by magazine; reverts to author upon publication.

1985; 2/yr; 1,500

$20/yr ind, $24/2 yr inst; $7/ea;

OUTERBRIDGE

Charlotte Alexander

112 E. 10th St.

New York, NY 10003

Poetry, fiction.

Craft first. Regular special themes, i.e., urban, rural, Southern. Slight bias to new voices and less published writers. Personal replies. Anti pure polemic. Theme projects: interdisciplinary (biology, physics, music, astronomy, etc.); nature, animals, ecology, environment; broad theme of love and friendship agape to eros.

Stuart Ackerman, Walter McDonald, Candida Lawrence, Thomas Swiss, Tom Lish, Laurie Calhoun, Louise Budde De Lourentis.

Unsolicited Manuscripts Received/ Published per Year: 500+/30+.

Payment: 2 copies.

Reporting Time: 2–2½ months, except July–Aug.

Copyright held by magazine; reverts to author upon publication.

1975; 1/yr; 800

$5/yr; $5/ea

120 pp; 8½ x 5
ISSN: 0739-4969

OWEN WISTER REVIEW

(Editors rotate yearly)
P.O. Box 4238, University Station
University of Wyoming
Laramie, WY 82071
(307) 766-3819

Prose (to 3,000 words), B & W artwork, poetry (no line limit).
Student produced magazine, but publishes a mixture of student and small press authors. Perfectbound, slick paper, high quality printing. Built to last.
Gerald Locklin, Richard Kostelanetz, W.D. Ehrhart, Cathy Lynn, Laurel Speer, Rane Arroyo.
Unsolicited Manuscripts Received/ Published per Year: 500+/75-100.
Reading Period: Sept.–Mar.
Payment: 1 copy, 10% off additional copies.
Reporting Time: 1–4 months. Do not read over the summer.
Copyright reverts to author upon publication.
1978; 2/yr; 500
$15/yr; $7.50/ea; Inquire
approx. 100 pp; digest

THE OXFORD AMERICAN

Marc Smirnoff
114A South Lamar
Oxford, MS 38655

THE OXFORD AMERICAN is a general interest literary magazine originating from the South. We appeal to the intelligent, but non–academic, general reader.
John Grisham, Larry Brown, Eudora Welty, John Updike, Donna Tartt.
Payment: $100–150 per essay, review, story; $60–75 per poem.
Reporting Time: 1–2 months.
Copyright held by magazine, but reverts to author upon publication.
1993; 6/yr; 60,000
$24/yr; $4.50/ea; 40%
128 pp; 8³⁄₁₆ x 10⅞
Ad Rates: $675/page (7½ x 10);
$1800 B/W (7⅛ x 9¹³⁄₁₆);
$1170/½ page (7⅛ x 4¹³⁄₁₆);
$450/⅙ page (2¼ x 4¹³⁄₁₆)
Ingram, Ubiquity, ICD

OYEZ REVIEW

Sarah L. Kisar
Roosevelt University
430 S. Michigan Ave.
Chicago, IL 60605
(312) 341-2017

Poetry, fiction, photographs.
OYEZ REVIEW is an award-winning, university-based magazine in its 27th year of publication. Each issue contains a number of poems and short sto-

ries written by people from various parts of the country and many different walks of life. The writings are diverse in content; all have universal appeal. Ronald Wallace, David Martin, Barry Silesky, John Jacob, Brooke Bergan.

Payment: none.
Reporting Time: 6 months.
Copyright held by magazine; reverts to author upon publication.
1967; 1/yr; 400
$4/ea; 40%
110 pp; 5½ x 8½
No ads

P

THE PACIFIC REVIEW

James Brown, Faculty Editor

Department of English

California State University

5500 University Pkwy.

San Bernardino, CA 92407-2397

(714) 880-5824; (714) 880-5894

Poetry, fiction, essays, plays, translation, interviews.

THE PACIFIC REVIEW is an academic-based journal of the verbal and visual arts, edited by graduate and undergraduate students at CSUSB. An annual publication now in its thirteenth year, **THE PACIFIC REVIEW** attempts to reflect aspects of its unique position in Southern California whenever possible, but without compromising its goal to serve as a vehicle for both emerging and established creative voices—from and about any area.

Unsolicited Manuscripts Received/ Published per Year: 200-300/15.

Reading Period: Sept.–Feb. 1.

Payment: in copies, upon publication.

Copyright held by magazine; reverts to author upon publication.

1983; 1/yr; 750

$6/yr ind, $7/inst; $4/ea; 40%

102 pp; 6 x 9

Ad Rates: $150/page (5 x 7½); $100/½ page (5 x 3¾); $50/¼ page (2½ x 3¾)

PAINTBRUSH: A Journal of Contemporary Multicultural Literature

Ben Bennani

Division of Language and Literature

Northeast Missouri St. University

Kirksville, MO 63501

(816) 785-4185

Poetry, criticism, essays, reviews, interviews, translation, photographs, graphics/artwork.

Publishes serious but innovative poetry, translations from any language—especially neglected ones—interviews and book reviews. The focus is always on quality and novelty.

William Stafford, Richard Eberhart, Colette Inez, Kathleen Spivack, Charles Edward Eaton.

Unsolicited Manuscripts Received/Published per Year: 300/50.

Payment: in copies or $10/page when available.

Reporting Time: 4–6 weeks.

Copyright held by magazine; reverts to author upon publication.

1974; 1/yr; 500

$15/yr ind, $20/yr inst; 40%

200+ pp; 5½ x 8½

Ad Rates: $150/page

ISSN: 0094-1964

is a journal of literary and visual arts associated with the Painted Bride Art Center in Philadelphia. We publish both local and national writers and artists; the emphasis is on quality. We like crafted, articulate writing in any genre.

Naomi Shihab Nye, Eugene Howard, Etheridge Knight, Tina Barr, Robert Bly, Marnie Mueller.

Reading Period: Sept.–June.

Payment: copies and 1 year subscription.

Reporting Time: 2 weeks–2 months.

Copyright reverts to author.

1973; 4/yr; 1,000

$12/yr ind, $16/yr inst; $5/ea; 50%

80 pp; 5 x 8½

Ad Rates: $75/page; $50/½ page; $25/¼ page

PAINTED BRIDE QUARTERLY

Brian Brown, Marion Wrenn, Kathy Volk Miller
230 Vine Street
Philadelphia, PA 19106
(215) 925-9914

Poetry, fiction, criticism, essays, reviews, plays, photographs, graphics/artwork.

PAINTED BRIDE QUARTERLY

PAISLEY MOON PRESS/OPEN UNISON STOP

Michael Spring, P. Notzka
P.O. Box 95463
Seattle, WA 98145

Poems, prose, reviews.

Joyce Odam, Stephen Kessler, Judson Crews, Carolyn Stoloff.

Payment: 1 copy.

Reporting Time: 1 day–3 months.

300

$10/yr; $3/ea
5½ x 8½
No ads

PANDORA
Meg MacDonald
2063 Belford
Holly, MI 48442

Poetry, fiction, graphics/artwork.
Character-oriented science fiction
and fantasy by new and established writers. We emphasize
character intensive fiction rather
than nuts and bolts SF or stock-
plot fantasy.
W. Gregory Stewart, Beckett
Gladney, Deborah Wheeler,
Roger Dutcher.
Payment: 1¢-2¢/word; $10 and up
on illus; $3.50 and up on car-
toons and fillers.
Closed to unsolicited manuscripts
at this time.
Copyright held by author. We buy
First North American serial
rights usually.
1978; 2/yr; 500
$12/2, $6/ea (US); $14/2, $7/ea
(CANADA); $20/2, $10/ea
(overseas); *US funds please!*
112 pp; 5½ x 8½; color cover
ISSN: 0275-519X
Faxon

PANHANDLER
Laurie O'Brien
English Department

University of West Florida
Pensacola, FL 32514-5751
(904) 474-2923

Poetry and short fiction.

THE PANHANDLER is a magazine of contemporary poetry and
fiction. We want poetry and
stories rooted in real experience
in language with a strong collo-
quial flavor. Works that are engaging and readable stand a
better chance with us than
works that are self-consciously
literary. Annual poetry chapbook competition: Winner receives $100 plus 50 copies.
Send SASE for details.
Walter McDonald, Malcolm Glass,
Enid Shomer, David Kirby, Joan
Colby.
Unsolicited Manuscripts Received/
Published per Year: 4,000+/70-
80.
Reading Period: year–round,
slower in summer.
Payment: in copies.
Reporting Time: 2–3 months.
Copyright held by University; reverts to author upon publication.
1976; 2/yr; 500
$10/yr, $18/2yr–both include win-
ning chapbook; 40%
64 pp; 6 x 9
ISSN: 0738-8705
Ebsco

PAPER BAG

M. Brownstein
P. O. Box 268805
Chicago IL 60626-8805
Guidelines included.
Literary arts publication: all forms
of poetry—looking for original
and strong images, black-and-
white illustrations, and short
short fiction (under 500 words).
Claudette Bess, Jean Townes.
Unsolicited Manuscripts Received/
Published per Year: 500/30.
Payment: 1 copy.
Reporting Time: 2 minutes–1
month.
Copyright: no.
1988; 4/yr; 200+.
$10/yr; $2.50/ea
20–30 pp; 5½ x 4¾

THE PAPER SALAd Poetry Journal

R. L. Moore
P.O. Box 520061
Salt Lake City, UT 84152-0061
Poetry.
Digest sized, flat spined about 100
pages about 30 poets, some-
times color cover, annual.
Rich Cronshey, Glenn Parker.
Unsolicited Manuscripts Received/
Published per Year: 500/30+.
Reading Period: year–round.
Payment: 1 copy upon publication.

Reporting Time: about 2 months.
Poets retain copyright.
1990; 1/yr; 400
$7.25/ea
100 pp; digest
Ad Rates: contact me and we'll
work something out.

PARABOLA: The Magazine of Myth & Tradition

Virginia Baron, Ellen Dooling
Draper
656 Broadway
New York, NY 10012
(212) 505-6200
Essays, reviews, interviews, retell-
ings of traditional myths and
stories, photographs, graphics/
artwork.
PARABOLA's focus is on myth
and the world's cultural and
spiritual traditions. Accordingly,
PARABOLA's approach to literature involves an emphasis on
myths, legends, folktales, and
oral transmission. PARABOLA
primarily publishes articles and
interviews which deal with my-
thology, comparative religion, and
contemporary spirituality. Each
issue focuses on a central theme.
P.L. Travers, Peter Brook, Eknath
Easwaran, Frederick Franck,
Robert Lawlor, Rhich Nhat
Hanh, Chinua Achebe.
Payment: sliding scale.

Reporting Time: 6 weeks.
Copyright held by author.
1976; 4/yr; 41,000
$20/yr; $6/ea; 40%
128 pp; 6¾ x 10
Ad Rates: $815/page (5¹⁄₁₆ x
8⁵⁄₁₆); $545/½ page (5¹⁄₁₆ x
4⅛); $310/¼ page (2⁷⁄₁₆ x 4⅛)
ISSN: 0362-1596

THE PARIS REVIEW

George Plimpton, Fiction Editor;
Richard Howard, Poetry Editor
541 E. 72nd St.
New York, NY 10021
Fiction, poetry, literary non-fiction.
Focus on best of emerging and
established poets, writers and
artists. Always on the look-out
for lively newcomers.
Joseph Brodsky, Carolyn Kizer,
Rick Bass, E.L. Doctorow,
Alice Munro, Joanna Scott.
Unsolicited Manuscripts Received/
Published per Year: 20,000/35.
Payment: varies.
Reporting Time: 8–10 weeks.
Copyright held by Paris Review
Inc.; reverts to author upon publi-
cation.
1953; 4/yr; 12,000
$34/yr; $10/ea
304 pp; 5½ x 8¼
Ad Rates: $1,000/page; $700 non-
profit

ISSN: 0031-2037
Random House

PARIS TRANSCONTINENTAL

Claire Larriere
Institut du Monde Anglophone
Sorbonne Nouvelle,5
Rue de L'Ecole de Medecine
75006 Paris, FRANCE
Short stories exclusively.
A forum for writers of excellent
stories whose link is the English
language, wherever spoken.
**PARIS TRANSCONTINEN-
TAL** hopes to introduce the best
among today's authors, wher-
ever they hail from, for non
literatures are evolving which
enrich our common space and
actual understanding.
Stephen Dixon, Jayan Ya Mahap-
atra, Joyce Carol Oates, Albert
Russo, Alan Sillitoe, Michael
Wilding, etc.
Unsolicited Manuscripts Received/
Run per Year: 1000.
Reading Period: Oct.–June.
Payment: 2 copies of issue.
Reporting Time: 2–3 months.
Copyright is in name of individual
authors.
2/yr; 1,000
FF 140/yr; FF 75/ea or $20/yr;
$11/ea, or £14/yr; £8/ea
128 pp

Ad Rates: none
ISSN: 1146-5948

Ad Rates: $250/page (6 x 9¼);
$150/½ page (5 x 4)
ISSN: 0048-3028
Spectacular Diseases (UK)

PARNASSUS

Herbert Leibowitz
41 Union Square West, Room 804
New York, NY 10003
(212) 463-0889

Criticism, essays, poems, reviews, photographs, graphics/artwork.

Devoted to the in-depth analysis of contemporary books of poetry. **PARNASSUS** seeks essays and reviews that are themselves works of art. The ideal reviewer is a poet with his or her own particular point of view. **PARNASSUS** publishes special issues on music, poetry in translation, the long poem, poetry and prose; includes paintings, illustrations and photographs.

Seamus Heaney, Ross Feld, Alice Fulton, William Logan, Helen Vendler, Mary Karr.

Unsolicited Manuscripts Received/ Published per Year: 250–300/1–2.

Payment: $25–$250.

Reporting Time: varies.

Copyright held by Poetry in Review Foundation; reverts to author upon request.

1972; 2/yr; 2,500
$23/yr ind, $44/yr inst; $10/ea
350 pp; 6 x 9¼

PARTING GIFTS

Robert Bixby
3413 Wilshire Dr.
Greensboro, NC 27408

Poetry, fiction.

Unsolicited Manuscripts Received/ Published per Year: 2,000/80-100.

Reading Period: Jan.–May, but Mss. welcome anytime.

Payment: 1 copy.

Copyright held by March Street Press; reverts to author upon publication.

1988; 2/yr; 100
$8/yr; $4/ea; 40%
40 pp; 5½ x 8½
ISSN: 1043-3325

PARTISAN REVIEW

William Phillips, Editor-in-Chief;
Edith Kurzweil, Editor
236 Bay State Rd.
Boston, MA 02215
(617) 353-4260

Essays, criticism, reviews, fiction, poetry, translation, interviews.

PARTISAN REVIEW examines the central issues of contemporary culture and social thought. It publishes critical essays on the arts and politics, new fiction and poetry, and book reviews. Octavio Paz, Cynthia Ozick, Doris Lessing, Joseph Brodsky, Czeslaw Milosz, Donald Revell, George Konrad.

Unsolicited Manuscripts Received/ Published per Year: 1,000/5 (fiction); 1,000/10-15 (poetry).

Reading Period: year–round.

Payment: varies.

Reporting Time: 2 months.

Copyright held by Partisan Review, Inc; reverts to author upon publication.

1937; 4/yr; 8,150

$22/yr ind, $32/yr inst; $7.50/ea; 160 pp; 6 x 9

Ad Rates: $200–$250 page (4¼ x 7⅜); $120/½ page (4¼ x 3½); $75/¼ page (2 x 3½)

ISSN: 0031-2525

Eastern News

PASSAGES NORTH

Michael Barrett, Editor; Conrad Hillberry, Poetry Editor

Kalamazoo College

1200 Academy

Kalamazoo, MI 49007

Fiction, poetry, creative non-fiction, interview, visual art and photography.

PASSAGES NORTH publishes high quality writing and art by established and emerging writers and artists. Perfect bound, semiannual.

Tony Hoagland, Thomas Lux, Jim Daniels, Tess Gallagher, Richard Jackson, Alison Baker, Roger Brown, Mary Whalen.

Payment: copies.

Reporting Time: 6–8 weeks.

Copyright held by magazine; reverts to author upon publication.

1979; 2/yr; 1,000

$10/yr; $18/2 yr; $6/sample copy

Ad Rates: $200/page; $100/½ page; $50/¼ page

ISSN: 0278-0828

PASSAIC REVIEW

Richard Quatrone

Forstmann Library

195 Gregory Avenue

Passaic, NJ 07055

Poetry, fiction, plays, photographs, graphics/artwork.

PASSAIC REVIEW is an independent magazine that publishes the best work submitted to it. Emphasis is on strong, clear, direct writing.

Antler, Ronald Baatz, Amiri Baraka, Allen Ginsberg, Eliot Katz, Wanda Phipps.

Payment: none.

Reporting Time: 1–52 weeks.

Copyright held by magazine; reverts to author upon publication.
1979; 2/yr; 500
$6/yr ind, $10/yr inst; $3.75/ea; 40%
48–54 pp; 5 x 8½
Ad Rates: $80/page (5 x 8½); $40/½ page (2¾ x 4¼); $20/¼ page (1⅜ x 2⅛)
ISSN: 0731-4663

PEMBROKE MAGAZINE

Shelby Stephenson
Box 60, PSU
Pembroke, NC 28372
(919) 521-4214, ext. 433
Poetry, fiction, criticism, reviews, plays, interviews, graphics/artwork.
Open to poetry, fiction, essays, interviews, and artwork.
A.R. Ammons, Fred Chappell, Barbara Guest, Robert Morgan, Betty Adcock.
Payment: none.
Reporting Time: up to 3 months.
Copyright held by magazine; reverts to author upon publication.
1969; 1/yr; 500–800
$5/yr; $5/ea; (surface mail add .50 to each rate)
250 pp; 6 x 9
Ad Rates: $40/page; $25/½ page

THE PENNSYLVANIA REVIEW

Rick Sides, Editor; Maria McLeod, Poetry Editor; Julie Albright, Fiction Editor; Kathleen Veslany, Non-fiction Editor
English Department, 526 CL
University of Pittsburgh
Pittsburgh, PA 15260
(412) 624-6506
Poetry, fiction, criticism, essays, reviews, translations, interviews, graphics/artwork, photos (b&w).
Publishing the finest contemporary fiction, poetry, nonfiction and illustrations, *Choice* calls **THE PENNSYLVANIA REVIEW** a "fine small literary magazine . . . highly recommended".
Cornelius Eady, Dorothy Barresi, Christopher Buckley, Joyce Carol Oates, Linda Pastan.
Unsolicited Manuscripts Received/ Published per year: 800–1,000/20–25.
Payment: in copies.
Reporting Time: 8–12 weeks.
Copyright held by Univ. of Pittsburgh; reverts to author upon publication.
1985; 2/yr; 600; 1994; Vol. 6 #2, forthcoming January 1995 (new tabloid size).
$7/yr; $3.50/ea; 40%
32 pp; 11 x 15
Ad Rates: $180/page (9 x 13);

$90/½ page (6 x 9); $45/¼ page (4 x 6)
ISSN: 8756-5668

PEQUOD

Mark Rudman
N.Y.U. English Dept., 2nd floor
19 University Pl.
New York, NY 10003
Poetry, fiction, criticism, essays, translation.
Past issues of **PEQUOD** have featured Irish, Scandinavian, Russian, Israeli, Ukranian, and British poetry. Recent issues have included a special issue on literature and the visual arts, a focus on the long poem, and two issues on the subject of mourning. A forthcoming issue will focus on the topic of the desert.
Thomas Bernhard, Louise Glück, Donald Hall, Jane Kenyon, Joyce Carol Oates, Charlie Smith, David St. John, John Updike.
Unsolicited Manuscripts Received/ Published per Year: 2,600/varies.
Reading Period: Oct.—Apr.
Payment: some payment to contributors.
Copyright held by magazine.
1974; 2/yr; 1,000–2,000
$12/yr ind, $20/2 yrs ind; $18/yr inst, $34/2 yrs inst; $10/ea

200 pp; 5½ x 8½
Ad Rates: $150/page (5½ x 8½); $200/2 pp
ISSN: 0149-0516
DeBoer

PEREGRINE: The Journal of Amherst Writers & Artists

Pat Schneider
P.O. Box 1076
Amherst MA 01004
(413) 253-3307
Poetry, fiction, cover graphics/artwork.
PEREGRINE is the journal of Amherst Writers & Artists, an organization dedicated to the belief that good writing is honest and unpretentious. We believe literature is related to the speech of home and workplace, and to the meanings discovered in ordinary lives.
Jane Yolen, Barbara Van Noord, Steven Reil.
Unsolicited Manuscripts Received/ Published per Year: 500/15.
Payment: in copies upon publication.
Copyright held by Amherst Writers & Artists Press, Inc.; reverts to author upon publication.
1983; 1/yr; varies
$5 plus $2 postage/ea; 40%
Sample copy $4 postage included
64 pp; 5½ x 8¼

Ad Rates: contact magazine for information
ISSN: 0890-662X

PERMAFROST

c/o English Department
203 Fine Arts Building
University of Alaska
Fairbanks, AK 99775
(907) 474-7193

Poetry, fiction, creative nonfiction, black & white photographs/art.

PERMAFROST seeks to promote excellence in contemporary literature and welcomes submissions in this vein. Although the magazine is regionally based, material need not refer to Alaska. Manuscripts from the lower 48 states, Hawaii, and international submissions (in English) are welcomes. **PERMAFROST** also sponsors the Midnight Sun Poetry Chapbook Contest (entry fee $10) and the Midnight Sun Fiction Contest (entry fee $10) [Chapbook winning manuscript (20–25 pp.) receives 25 copies. Fiction contest winner (10–40 pp) receives $50.]
Reading Period: Aug.–May.
Payment: 2 copies.
Reporting Time: 4 months, 6 months for mss. received in Summer.

Copyright held by author.
1975; 1/yr; 400 journal; 50 chapbook
$7/yr; 40% disc. to booksellers
115 pp; 5 x 8
Ad inquiries welcome.

PIEDMONT LITERARY REVIEW

Gail White
Piedmont Literary Society
1017 Spanish Moss Ln.
Breaux Bridge, LA 70517
(804) 384-2027

Poetry, fiction, graphics/artwork, newsletter.

We publish mainly poetry, short stories; approximately 40 poems, 2 short stories. We need short stories of around 1,500 to 2,000 words. Traditional to free verse—we publish established poets and many first timers.
Wm. Stafford, X.J. Kennedy, Martha Bosworth, Barbara Loots, Judson Jerome.
Unsolicited Manuscripts Received/ Published per Year: 500/75.
Payment: in copies.
Reporting Time: 5 days–3 months.
Copyright held by magazine; reverts to author upon publication.
1976; 4/yr; 300
$12/yr; $3/ea
50 pp; 5½ x 8½
ISSN: 0257-357X

PIG IRON

Jim Villani

P.O. Box 237

Youngstown, OH 44501

(216) 783-1269

Poetry, fiction, essays, translation, interviews, photographs, graphics/artwork.

Special emphasis on popular culture, genres, and new literature in a highly visual and cerebral format. Publishes issues around special themes: recent issues have featured Third World, Humor, Psychological Literature, Viet Nam Era, Surrealism, Science Fiction, Baseball, Labor, the epistolary form. Most recent volume is "Environment: Essence and Issue." Back issues available.

James Bertolino, Warren Woessner, Helen Ruggieri, Claudia Ricci, Ralph Braver, Wayne Hogan, Coco Gordan, Barbara Kasselmann.

Unsolicited Manuscripts Received/ Published per Year: 6,000/85.

Payment: $5/page.

Reporting Time: 3 months.

Copyright held by editors; reverts to author upon publication.

1975; 1/yr; 1,500

$8/1 issue; $15/2 issues

$9.95/ea; 40%

128 pp; 8½ x 11

ISSN: 0362-5214

THE PIKESTAFF FORUM

Robert D. Sutherland, James R. Scrimgeour, James McGowan, Curtis White

P.O. Box 127

Normal, IL 61761

(309) 452-4831

Black and white photographs; line-drawings; small-press book reviews. Poetry, fiction, commentary on contemporary literature and the small-press scene.

A literary magazine eclectic in its tastes, publishing the best poetry and fiction that comes its way; sets a standard in tabloid design and format.

Gayl Teller, Jeff Gundy, Enid Dame, J. W. Rivers, R. Cooperman.

Unsolicited Manuscripts Received/ Published per Year: 2,500/58.

Payment: 3 free copies of issue in which work appears; 50% discount on extras.

Reporting Time: 3 months.

Copyright remains with authors and artists.

1978; 1/yr; 1,000

$12/6 issues; $3/ea

40 pp; tabloid

ISSN: 0192-8716

THE PITTSBURGH QUARTERLY

Frank Correnti, Editor; James Deahl, Canadian Editor; Lyn

Ferlo, Art Editor
36 Haberman Ave.
Pittsburgh, PA 15211-2144
Canadian address: P.O. Box 20
99 Kimberley Ave
London, Ontario, N5Z 5A1
(412) 431-8885
Per issue: short short stories (up to 4,000 words), poetry, interview, reviews, features, (essays, etc).

THE PITTSBURGH QUAR-TERLY is a community writing project which networks (publishes) writers from all parts of the US, Canada, and overseas. We emphasize personal expression and craft over ideology.
Judith R. Robinson, Daryl Palmer, Ellen Smith, Rina Ferrarelli, Bill Ryan Richard Dillon.
Unsolicited Manuscripts Received/ Published per Year: 400/100.
Payment: 2 copies.
Reporting Time: 3 months.
Copyright reverts to author upon publication. Acknowledge **TPQ** in future publication.
1991; 4/yr; 600
$12/yr; $14/overseas; $4/ea; 10 or more 40%
76 pp; 5½ x 8½
Ad Rates: $100/full page (4½ x 7½); $50/½ page; $25/¼ page
ISSN: 1054-6340
Central Wholesale (Pittsburgh PA 15203)

PIVOT
Martin Mitchell
250 Riverside Dr. #23
New York, NY 10025
(212) 222-1408
Poetry.
Now in its 44th year, **PIVOT** publishes the work of both seasoned and new poets. It has a reputation for "firsts" of admirable performance.
Philip Appleman, Eamon Grennan, William Matthews, Grace Schulman, W. D. Snodgrass, Robert Wrigley.
Unsolicited Manuscripts Received/ Published per Year: 500/25.
Reading Period: Jan. 1–June 1.
Payment: in copies.
Reporting Time: 2–4 weeks.
Copyright held by Sibyl Barsky Grucci; reverts to author upon publication.
1951; 1/yr; 1,500–3,000
$5/ea
76 pp; 6 x 9
Ad Rates: $125/page; $70/½ page; $40/¼ page

PLAINS POETRY JOURNAL
Jane Greer
P.O. Box 2337
Bismarck, ND 58502
Poetry, essays.
PLAINS POETRY JOURNAL is a forum for poetry using tradi-

tional poetic conventions: meter, rhyme, alliteration, assonance, painstaking attention to sound. No prosaic, conversational "free verse." No Hallmark verse. Will publish one essay per issue: humorous or serious essays on poetry. Widely published and unpublished poets receive same consideration.

Rhina Espaillat, Jack Butler, Johnny Wink, Gail White, Frederick Feirstein, Frederick Turner.

Unsolicited Manuscripts Received/ Published per Year: 2,000+/100.

Reading Period: year–round.

Payment: 2 copies.

Reporting Time: 1 month.

Copyright held by magazine; reverts to author upon publication.

1982; 2/yr; 500

$9/yr; $18/5 issues; $4.50/ea; negotiable

60 pp; 5½ x 8½

ISSN: 0730-6172

on a revolving basis by professional poets and writers to reflect different and contrasting points of view.

Roselleu Brown, James Welch, Sue Miller, Al Young, Tobias Wolff, Marie Howe, Christopher Tilghman, Alberto Ríos, Carolyn Forché.

Unsolicited Manuscripts Received/ Published per Year: 5,000/200

Reading Period: Aug. 1–March 31.

Reporting Time: 3–5 months.

Copyright reverts to author upon publication.

1971; 3/yr; 6,000

$19/yr ind, $22/yr inst; $8.95/ea; 20%–40%

280 pp; 5½ x 8½

Ad Rates: $300/page (4½ x 7); $200/½ page (4½ x 3¼);

ISSN: 0048-4474

DeBoer, Fine Print, Ingram Periodicals, L-S Distributors

PLOUGHSHARES

DeWitt Henry, Don Lee, David Daniel

Emerson College

100 Beacon St.

Boston, MA 02116

(617) 578-8753

Poetry, fiction, translation.

A magazine of new writing edited

THE PLUM REVIEW

M.Hammer, Christina Daub

P.O. Box 3557

Washington, DC 20007

Poetry, poetry book reviews, interviews.

All-poetry magazine featuring the best in contemporary poetry by both established and emerging poets from around the world.

Joseph Brodsky, Mark Strand,
Marge Piercy, Robert Bly,
Donald Hall, Linda Pastan, Jane
Hirshfield.
Unsolicited Manuscripts Received/
Published per Year:
3,000+/50–60.
Reading Period: Sept.–May.
Payment: 1 copy.
Reporting Time: 1 month.
1991; 2/yr; 1,000
$12/yr; $6/ea
120 pp; 6 x 9 flat-spined
Ad Rates: $200/page; $125/½
page
DeBoer

POEM

Nancy Frey Dillard
English Department
University of Alabama in Hunts-
ville
Huntsville, AL 35899
(205) 895-6320
Poetry.
High quality mature poetry. No
bias as to form or theme. Par-
ticular regard given to less well
known poets.
Charles Edward Eaton, John
Ditsky, Stephen Lang, R.T.
Smith, Alison Reed.
Unsolicited Manuscripts Published
per Year: 100-120.
Payment: in copy.
Reporting Time: 1 month.

Copyright held by Huntsville Literary Association.
1967; 2/yr; 400
$10/yr; $5/ea
70 pp; 4½ x 7½
No ads

POET LORE

Sunil Freeman
Poet Lore, The Writer's Center
4508 Walsh St.
Bethesda, MD 20815
(301) 654-8664
Poetry, criticism, essays, reviews,
translation, graphics/artwork.
POET LORE publishes original
poems of all kinds. The editors
continue to welcome narrative
poetry and original translations
of contemporary world poets.
POET LORE publishes re-
views of poetry collections and
critical essays of contemporary
poetry.
Walter McDonald, Sharon Olds,
Leonard Nathan, Peter Wild,
Albert Goldbarth.
Unsolicited Manuscripts Received/
Published per Year: 1,500/150.
Payment: 2 copies.
Reporting Time: 3 months.
Copyright held by The Writer's
Center; reverts to author upon
publication.
1889; 4/yr; 600

$15/yr ind, $24/yr inst; $4.50/ea;
40%
80 pp; 6 x 9
Ad Rates: $100/page (5½ x 8);
$55/½ page (5½ x 4)
ISSN: 0032-1966
Faxon, Ebsco, McGregor, Boley

POET'S SANCTUARY

Hollee Donavan
P.O. Box 832
Hopkins, MN 55343-0832
Poetry, very short stories, reviews,
visual poetry and more.
POET'S SANCTUARY contains
diversified literature,
social/environmental information and topics, poetry education, interesting facts, humorous
segments, reviews, and a pen
pal section. Artwork compli-
ments material throughout
magazine. Accepts writing subjects mainly of metaphysics,
fantasy/sci-fi, love, leftish politics, but will consider other topics.
Philip White, Janet Kuypers,
Kennon Webber.
Unsolicited Manuscripts Received/
Published per Year: 100.
Payment: 2 copies.
Reporting Time: 2–3 months.
Copyright reverts back to author
upon publication.
1993; 4/yr; appx. 75–100

$10/yr; $5/ea; $3.50/back issues.
75 pp; 8½ x11
Ad Rates: $40/6 x 6; $30/4 x 6;
$20/2 x 6; $10/1 x 6

POETIC SPACE: POETRY
AND FICTION

Don Hildenbrand, Editor; Thomas
Strand, Fiction Editor
P.O. Box 11157
Eugene, OR 97440
Poetry, fiction, reviews, inter-
views, graphics/artwork, theater
and film reviews. Chapbook and
Anthology now available; for
information send SASE.
Patty McDonald, Albert Huffstick-
ler, William Meyer, Crawdad
Nelson, Arthur Winfield Knight,
Spenser Reese, Sesshu Foster.
Unsolicited Manuscripts Received/
Published per Year: 500+/50.
$10/yr, $18/2 yr; $3/ea, $4/back
issues.

POETICS JOURNAL

Lyn Hejinian, Barrett Watten
2639 Russell St.
Berkeley, CA 94705
(510) 548-1817
Criticism, essays, reviews.
POETICS JOURNAL is an ir-
regularly published journal of
contemporary poetics by poets
and prose writers as well as by

other artists, critics, linguists, and political theorists. It features essays, articles, and investigatory reviews. Individual issues focus on topics including "close reading", "poetry and philosophy", "women and modernism", "non-narrative", etc. Ron Silliman, George Lakoff, Rae Armantrout, Kofi Natambu, Leslie Scalapino.
Unsolicited Manuscripts Received/ Published per Year: 40-50/3.
Payment: in copies.
Reporting Time: 2–4 weeks.
Copyright held by author.
1982; irreg.; 600
$10/ea; 25%–40%
144 pp; 6 x 9
ISSN: 0731-5236
SPD, Sun & Moon

POETPOURRI

Comstock Writer's Group; Kathleen Bryce Niles, Coordinator; Jennifer B. MacPherson, President
907 Comstock Ave.
Syracuse, NY 13210
(315) 475-0339
Poetry only.
Perfect-bound 100 pp, put out twice yearly. We accept poetry on the basis of quality, not reputation. We do not accept porno, sentimental, greeting card verse and very few haikus or religious verse. Well crafted poetry, free or formal, written in understandable, grammatically correct English—metaphor, fresh, vivid imagery enjoyed.
Gayle Elen Harvey, Robt. Cooperman, R. Nikolas Macioci, Kathryn Howd Machan, Michael Bugeja.
Unsolicited Manuscripts Received/ Published per Year: thousands/300.
Payment: copy, prize money.
Reporting Time: usually 2–4 weeks, with comments.
Copyright reverts to author.
1986; 2/yr; 500
$8/yr; $15/2 yrs; $4/ea
75–100 pp; 5½ x 8½

POETRY

Joseph Parisi
60 West Walton St.
Chicago, IL 60610
(312) 280-4870
Poetry, reviews, essays.
For over 80 years **POETRY** has been the most widely read monthly of verse. From Auden to Ashbery, Pound to Pinsky, Stevens to Soto—voices famous and new.
Adrienne Rich, A.R. Ammons, Richard Kenney, J.D. McClatchy, Sharon Olds.

Unsolicited Manuscripts Received/
Published per Year:
75,000/300±.
Reading Period: year–round.
Payment: $2/line for verse;
$20/page of prose.
Reporting Time: 8–10 weeks.
Copyright held by Modern Poetry
Association; reverts to author
upon request.
1912; 12/yr; 7,600
$25/yr ind, $27/yr inst; $2.50/ea
64 pp; 5½ x 9
Ad Rates: $280/page (3¾ x 7);
$174/½ page (3¾ x 3½);
$111/¼ page (1¾ x 3½)
ISSN: 0032-2032
DeBoer, Ingram, Fine Print, Mi-
chiana News Service, Ubiquity

POETRY CANADA

Barry Dempster, Poetry Editor;
Bob Hilderley, Prose Editor
P.O. Box 1061, 221 King St. E.
Kingston, Ontario K7L 4Y5
CANADA
(613) 548-8429 Fax: (613) 548-
1556
Poetry essays on poetry, reviews
of poetry books.
Bill Bissett, Maggie Helwig,
Daniel David Moses.
Unsolicited Manuscripts Received/
Published per Year: 2,400/20.
Payment: after publication.
Reporting Time: 4 months.

Copyright: We retain first North
American Serial Rights.
1980; 4/yr; 700
$16/4; $4.55/ea
36 pp; tabloid
Ad Rates: available upon request.
ISSN: 0709-3373

POETRY EAST

Richard Jones
802 W. Belden
English Department
DePaul University
Chicago, IL 60614
(312) 362-5114
Poetry, translations, fiction, art,
interviews, reviews.
POETRY EAST publishes issues
dedicated to particular poets or
topics. We are also interested in
reading essays on poetics, the
relationship between art and the
world. We are also looking for
translations and ideas for feature/
symposia.
Gerald Stern, Ruth Stone, Jack
Grapes.
Unsolicited Manuscripts Received/
Published per Year:
5,000/200–300.
Payment: in copies, honoraria.
Reporting Time: 3 months.
Copyright reverts to author, but
we reserve the right to include
work in anthologies.
1980; 2/yr; 1,500

$12; $8
200 pp; 5½ x 8½
Ad Rates: $100/page; $50/½ page
ISSN: 0197-4009
DeBoer, Fine Print

POETRY FLASH

Joyce Jenkins, Editor; Richard
Silberg, Associate Editor
P.O. Box 4172
Berkeley, CA 94704
(510) 525-5476

Criticism, essays, reviews, interviews, photographs, poetry.

POETRY FLASH, A Poetry Review and Literary Calendar,
publishes the most complete
literary calendar of the West
available. Also reviews of
books, magazines, readings, and
events, as well as interviews,
occasional essays, photos, general commentary and information on submissions and publications for poets.

Keith Abbott, Marilyn Chin, Cat-
alina Cariaga, Kathleen Fraser,
Jack Marshall, Jack Foley,
Dorianne Laux, Tony Barnstone.

Unsolicited Manuscripts Received/
Published per Year: 1,500/50.

Reading period: year–round.

Payment: subscription to $25; $50
to $100 maximum.

Reporting Time: 3 months.

Copyright held by author.

1972; 12/yr; 20,000; free to public
places
$15/yr ind, $16/yr inst
24–36 pp; 11½ x 15
Ad Rates: $500/page (10 x 13¾);
$250/½ page (10 x 7); $125/¼
page (6½ x 5) or $130/5 x 7
ISSN: 0737-4747

THE POETRY MISCELLANY

Richard Jackson, Michael Panori
University of Tennessee at Chatta-
nooga
Department of English
Chattanooga, TN 37402
(615) 624-7279 or 755-4629

Poetry, essays, reviews, translation, interviews.

We are very much a miscellany in
the traditional sense of that
word; we publish a variety of
"types" of poetry.

John Ashbery, Marvin Bell, Carolyn Forché, Tomaz Salamun,
Mark Strand.

Payment: none.

Reporting Time: 6 weeks.

Copyright held by magazine; reverts
to author upon publication.

1971; 2/yr; 1,100
$3/yr ind; $2/yr inst; $3/ea
20 pp; tabloid
Ad Rates: $100/page (5 x 8);
$65/½ page (5 x 4½); $40/¼
page (5 x 2)

POETRY MOTEL
Ed Gooder Eva Preston-Hart, Bud
  Backen, Patrick McKinnon
1619 Jefferson
Duluth, MN 55812
Poetry.
General poetry magazine open to
  all from "beginners" to "pros."
Todd Moore, Linda Wing, Robert
  Peters.
Unsolicited Manuscripts Received/
  Published per Year: 1,000/100
Reading Period: year–round.
Payment: 1 copy.
Reporting Time: 1 month.
Copyright: yes.
1984; varies; 1,000
$15.95/3 issues; $5.95/ea; $49.00
  lifetime
52 pp; 8 x 7
No ads

**POETRY NEW YORK: A Jour-
nal of Poetry and Translation**
Burt Kimmelman, Tod Thilleman,
  Emmy Hunter
P.O. Box 3184
Church St. Station
New York, NY 10008
Poetry, translations of poetry, art-
  work.
About 9 x 6, perfect bound, about
  80 pp.
Bonnefoy, Bronk, Creeley, Di Prima,
  Heller, Mac Low, Rothenberg.
Unsolicited Manuscripts Received

4 poems max./Published per
  Year: 400/5–10.
Reading Period: Spring
Payment: 1 copy.
Reporting Time: 4 months or
  more.
Copyright belongs to author.
1985; 1/yr; 1,500
$5/ea; 500
80 pp; 9 x 6
Ad Rates: swap ads
DeBoer

**POETRY PROJECT NEWS-
LETTER**
Gillian McCain
The Poetry Project
St. Mark's Church
131 E. 10th St.
New York, NY 10003
(212) 674-0910
Poetry, criticism, essays, reviews,
  listings.
Bernadette Mayer, Anselm Hollo,
  Robert Creeley, Kofi Natambu,
  Paul Violi, James Schuyler,
  Nicole Brossard.
Reading Period: Sept.–May.
Payment: none.
Reporting Time: 4 weeks.
Copyright held by author.
1967; 4/yr; 4,000
$20/yr
24 pp; 8½ x 11
Ad Rates: $200/page (7 x 10);
  $130/½ page (7 x 5 or 3½ x

10); $100/⅓ page (3½ x 5 or 7 x 2½); $60/⅙ page (3½ x 2½); $40/¹⁄₁₂ page; Discounts for nonprofits.

POETS ON

Ruth Daigon

29 Loring Ave.

Mill Valley, CA 94941

(415) 381-2824

Poetry.

POETS ON is a semi-annual poetry magazine. Theme-oriented, exploring basic human concerns through insightful, significant, well-crafted poetry. We publish recognized poets as well as unknown poets.

Sue Walker, Michael Bugeja, Marge Piercy, Lyn Lifshin, Barbara Crooker, James Broughton.

Unsolicited Manuscripts Received/ Published per Year: 5,000+/85.

Reading Period: Sept.–Nov. 30, Feb.–April 30.

Payment: in copies.

Reporting Time: 2–3 months.

Copyright reverts to author.

1977; 2/yr; 500

$8/yr; $5/ea

48 pp; 5½ x 8½

THE PORTABLE LOWER EAST SIDE

Kurt Hollander, Arthur Nersesian

P. O. Box 30323

New York, NY 10011

Fiction, poetry, photography, essays.

PORTABLE LOWER EAST SIDE is a literary magazine involved with New York City. Strong emphasis on ethnic and cultural diversity, and on social issues. Latest issue: "Queer City." Forthcoming: Drugs.

Hubert Selby, Margaret Randall, Luisa Valenzuela, Willie Colon, Edward Limonov.

Payment: in copies and small sums.

Reporting Time: 2 months.

Copyright reverts to author.

1984; 2/yr; 2,000.

$11/yr ind, $20/yr inst; $7/ea; 40%

175 pp; 5½ x 7

Ad Rates: $100/page; $75/½ page

SPD, Inland, DeBoer

PORTLAND REVIEW

Kala Rounds

P.O. Box 751

Portland, OR 97207

(503) 725-4468

Fiction, poetry, essays, plays, photographs, graphics/artwork.

The **PORTLAND REVIEW** is the biannual Arts and Literature Magazine of Portland State University. It draws material mainly from the Pacific Northwest, but is open to submissions from outside the region.

Unsolicited Manuscripts Received/
Published per Year: 700/100.
Payment: 1 copy.
Reporting Time: 1–2 months.
Copyright held by author.
1953; 2/yr; 1,000
$10/yr; $5/ea + $1 postage
80 pp; 9 x 12

POTATO EYES
Roy Zarucchi, Carolyn Page
Nightshade Press, P.O. Box 76
Troy, ME 04987
(207) 948-3427
Canadian and US poetry, short
stories, reviews of poetry, black
and white art, contemporary
essays. Now guest edited by
Parks Lanier, Redford University English professor. Send
SASE to Prof. Lanier for
themes but all poetry & short
fiction is welcome. Submissions
to: English Box 6935, Radford
Univ., Radford, VA 24142-6935.
A semi-annual literary arts journal
focusing on poetry, short fiction
and art work from/about the
Appalachians from Alabama to
Quebec. This is a primary, but
not exclusive focus. Nightshade
Press, of which **POTATO
EYES** is an imprint, also publishes a NIGHTSHADE
NIGHTSTAND READER
which contains short stories, as

well as single author short story
collections. Send those submis-
sions to Maine address, c/o
Carolyn Page.
Earl Braggs, Barbara Presnell,
Elizabeth Cohen, Jack Coule-
han, M.D., Ina Cofelt, Edward
M. Holmes, and L.L. Harper.
Unsolicited Manuscripts Received/
Published per Year: 1,600/200+.
Reading Period: year–round.
Payment: in copies.
Reporting Time: 8 weeks.
Copyright held by publisher, re-
verts to author upon publication.
1989; 2/yr; 800
$11/yr; $7.95/ea; 40%
104 pp; 5½ x 8½
ISSN: 1041-9926

POTOMAC REVIEW
Jack Harrison
P.O. Box 134
McLean, VA 22101
(703) 556-0578
Fiction, poetry, literary essays and
criticism.
A mainstream quarterly literary
journal.
Hilary Tham, Richard Peabody,
Karen Loeb, Joan Austin Geier,
Daniel Sklar.
Unsolicited Manuscripts Received/
Published per Year: 2,000/100.
Reading Period: year–round.
Payment: 1 copy.

Reporting Time: 60 days.
Copyright held by author.
1993; 4/yr; 350
$15/yr; $4/ea; 40%
80–100 pp; 5½ x 8½
ISSN: 1073-1989

POTPOURRI

Polly W. Swafford, Senior Editor;
Pat Anthony, Terry Hoyland,
Poetry Editors
P.O. Box 8278
Prairie Village, KS 66208
(913) 642-1503

Fiction, nonfiction, poetry.

POTPOURRI is a not-for-profit,
bimonthly literary magazine.
POTPOURRI publishes a
broad genre of short stories,
poetry, adventure, travel, essays
by both professional and novice
writers.
David Ray, Paltiann Rogers,
Lance Olsen, Lloyd van Brunt.
Unsolicited Manuscripts Received/
Published per Year: 2,700/900.
Reading Period: year-round.
Payment: in copies (2).
Reporting Time: 8–12 weeks.
Copyright: yes.
1989; 6/yr; 3,000
$15/yr; $3.95/sample copy, $1.50
postage and handling
70 pp; 8 x 10 magazine
Ad Rates: Contact publisher for
different rates/sizes.

POULTRY, A Magazine of Voice

Jack Flavin, Brendan Galvin,
George Garrett
P.O. Box 4413
Springfield, MA 01101
(413) 732-0435

Parodies, satire, put-ons, put-
downs of contemporary poetry,
lit & litbiz.
David R. Slavitt, Douglas A. Pow-
ell, Joyce Lamers, Jay Blumen-
thal, Lyn Lifshin, R. S. Gwynn,
Rachel Loden.
Unsolicited Manuscripts Received/
Published per Year: 500/80.
Payment: 10 free copies.
Reporting Time: 2–3 months.
Copyright: first publishing rights.
1979; 2–3/yr; 1,400
$5/yr; $2/ea

PRAIRIE FIRE

Andris Taskans, Managing Editor
423-100 Arthur St.
Winnipeg, Manitoba, R3B 1H3
CANADA
(204) 943-9066

Fiction, poetry, essays, book reviews.
A Canadian magazine with a western perspective, featuring new
writing and special issues on
topics such as ethnic writing,
women's writing, genre writing
and more.
Sandra Birdsell, Carol Shields.

Unsolicited Manuscripts Received/
Published per Year: 1,200/120
Reporting Time: 3–4 months.
Copyright reverts to author upon
publication.
1978; 4/yr; 1,200
$24/yr; $8.95/ea; 30%
128 pp; 6 x 9
ISSN: 0821-1124
Canadian Magazine Publishers
Association

**PRAIRIE JOURNAL/of Cana-
dian Literature**
Prairie Journal Trust
P.O. Box 61203, Brentwood P.O.
Calgary, Alberta,
T2L 2K6 CANADA
Short fiction, poetry, review, es-
says, drama.
Literary small press publication.
No US stamps (submissions will
not be read or returned without
sufficient Canadian postage for
return.)
Fred Cogswell, Lorna Crozier,
Mick Burrs, Robin Mathews,
Bruce Hunter, John V. Hicks,
Shaunt Basmajian, George Am-
abile, Gary Hyland, Glen Sores-
tad, Peter Baltensperger, Dennis
Cooley.
Unsolicited Manuscripts Received/
Published per Year: 200/20.
Payment: Honouraria.
Reporting Time: 3–6 weeks.

Copyright for author.
1983; 2/yr; 500
$6/yr; $3/ea; 40%
60 pp; 7½ x 8
Ad Rates: negotiable
ISSN: 0827-2921

PRAIRIE SCHOONER
Hilda Raz
201 Andrews Hall
University of Nebraska
Lincoln, NE 68588-0334
(402) 472-0911
Poetry, fiction, essays, reviews,
translation.
PRAIRIE SCHOONER, a literary quarterly, publishes the best
writing available from begin-
ning and established writers:
short stories, poems, interviews,
imaginative essays of general
interest, and reviews of current
books of poetry and fiction.
Scholarly articles requiring foot-
note references are generally not
published by **PRAIRIE
SCHOONER**.
Maxine Kumin, Dave Smith, Gary
Soto, Julia Alvarez, Michelle
Carter, Greg Johnson, Toi Derricotte.
Unsolicited Manuscripts Received/
Published per Year: 4,800/120.
Reading Period: Sept.–May.
Payment: 12 annual writing prizes

and grant funds, when available; copies also.

Reporting Time: 3 months.

Copyright held by magazine; reverts to author upon request.

1927; 4/yr; 3,100

$20/yr ind, $22/yr inst; $6.45/ea; 40%

176 pp; 6 x 9

Ad Rates: $150/page (4¾ x 7½)

ISSN: 0032-6682

Ingram

PRIMAVERA

Editorial Board

Box #37-7547

Chicago, IL 60637

(312) 324-5920

Poetry, fiction, photographs, graphics/artwork.

PRIMAVERA focuses on the experiences of women; publishes both established and unknown writers. Literary quality is the most important consideration.

Lynne H. DeCourcy, S.J. Hall, Doris Lynch, Pamela Gemin.

Unsolicited Manuscripts Received/ Published per Year: 1,000/25–30.

Payment: in copies.

Reporting Time: 2 weeks–3 months.

Copyright held by magazine; reverts to author upon publication.

1975; 1/yr; 1,000

$9/yr; $9/ea

5½ x 8½

No ads

ISSN: 0364-7609

PROLIFIC WRITER'S MAGA-ZINE (and Press Release Market)

Brian S.Konradt

P.O. Box 554

Oradell, NJ 07649, Dept. LM

(201) 262-3277 (voice);

Konradb@iia.org (e-mail)

Poems, short stories, interviews, how-to, news, markets.

A literary trade magazine focusing on print media in both the paper and electronic environment.

David Colozzi, Merry Harris, Kim Tobias.

Unsolicited Manuscripts Received/ Published per Year: 300/140.

Reading Period: Jan.–Dec.

Payment: 0–$40; one contributor's copy.

Reporting Time: 1 month; queries 2–4 weeks.

Copyright held by BSK Communications and Associates.

1992; 4–6/yr; 2,000+

$12/yr; $3.50/ea; $3.00

20–40 pp; 8½ x 11

Ad rates: $30/3 x 5; $40/5 x 7; $60/7 x 5½; $95/8½ x 11

BSK

PROSODIA: A New College of California Poetics Journal

Leslie Davis, Cliff Gassoway, Renee Gladman, Hoa Nguyen, Dale Smith

c/o Poetics Program

New College of California

766 Valencia St.

San Francisco, CA 94110

(415) 626-0884, FAX (415) 626-5541

Poetry, and poetic prose.

PROSODIA is produced every Spring by students of the Poetics Program. Each year, a theme is chosen. The 1994 theme was "Peripheral Vision." The 1995 theme is "Birthmarks."

Will Alexander, David Meltzer, Harryette Mullen, Leslie Scalapino, Anne Waldman.

Reading Period: January–April.

Payment: 2 copies.

Reporting Time: 2 months.

Copyright held by Prosodia.

1990; 1/yr; 750

$7/ea; 2–4 10%, 5–9 20%, 10+ 40%

100 pp; 9 x 6

Ad Rates: $125/full page; $65/½ page; $25/¼ page

Small Press Distribution

THE PROSPECT REVIEW

Peter A. Koufos

557 10th St.

Brooklyn, NY 11215

(718) 788-5709

Poetry, fiction.

TPR is a literary journal committed to daring; bridging a gap between the unacknowledged poet and writer with those in academia for cultural unity.

E. Ethelbert Miller, Richard Burgin, Jana Harris, Gina Bergamino.

Unsolicited Manuscripts Received/ Published per Year: many/20.

Payment: copies.

Reporting Time: on or near issue release date.

Copyright reverts to authors upon publication.

1990; 2/yr

$12/yr; $6/ea

86 pp; 6 x 8

Ad Rates: Available on request

ISSN: 1049-0426

DeBoer

PROVINCETOWN ARTS

Christopher Busa

650 Commercial Street

Provincetown, MA 02657

(508) 487-3167

Poetry, fiction, reviews, essays, translation, interviews, photographs, graphics/artwork.

The documentary voice of the artists and writers who visit Cape Cod, **PROVINCETOWN ARTS** focuses on the phenon-

menon of the art colony, not as geographical locus, but as a point of view. A large proportion of this annual book-length magazine emphasizes visual art, exploring the relation of visual art to language.
Alan Dugan, Stanley Kunitz, Susan Mitchell, Mark Doty, Cyrus Cassells, Henri Cole.
Unsolicited Manuscripts Received/ Published per Year: 1,200/varies.
Reading Period: Aug.–Feb.
Payment: $25–$125 per poem; $125–300 per story (fiction & nonfiction).
Reporting Time: 2–4 months.
Copyright: Provincetown Arts, Inc.
1985; 1/yr; 8,500
$10/yr; $6.50/sample; 40%
184 pp; 9 x 12
Ad Rates: $950/page; $550/½ page; $400/⅓ page
Ingram, IPD, New England Circulation Assoc.

PUCK: THE UNOFFICIAL JOURNAL OF THE IRREPRESSIBLE

Brian Clark, Violet Riverrun
47 Noe St. #4
San Francisco, CA 94114-1017
(415) 255-9765; Internet = bcclark@igc.apc.org
Fiction, essays, reviews, graphics, poetry.
A radical reinterpretation of consensus reality. Color covers, 80 pages, 8½ x 11, printed offset, appearing thrice a year.
Dan Pearlman, Paul DiFilippo, Lance Olsen
Unsolicited Manuscripts Received/ Published per Year: 1,000's/ dozens.
Payment: copies and honararium
Reporting Time: 2 weeks–2 months.
Copyright: yes.
1984; 3/yr; 5,000
$17/yr; $6.50/ea; 40%–55%
80 pp; 8½ x 11
Ad Rates: Write, call, or e-mail for rates
ISSN: 1071-7633
Fine Print, Desert Moon, Ubiquity, Bookpeople, Inland, IDP, AK, Tower

PUCKERBRUSH REVIEW

Constance Hunting
76 Main St.
Orono, ME 04473
(207) 581-3832
Fiction, poetry, reviews, criticism, interviews, essays, graphics/artwork, photographs.
The special focus is on Maine literature and literary figures. The intent is to publish fiction, po-

etry and reviews by contemporary Maine writers. The purpose is both to reveal and to encourage the literary energy in this isolated state. "Puckerbrush" = new growth.

Deborah Pease, James Laughlin, Sonya Dorman, Farnham Blair, Sanford Phippen.

Unsolicited Manuscripts Received/ Published per Year: 200/35.

Payment: in copies.

Copyright held by magazine; reverts to author upon publication.

1978; 2/yr; 450

$8/yr; $4/ea; 40%

75 pp; 8½ x 11

Ad Rates: inquire

PUERTO DEL SOL

Kathleene West, Poetry; Antonya Nelson, Kevin McIlvoy, Fiction; Chris Burnham, Essay

Box 30001, Dept. 3E

New Mexico State University

Las Cruces, NM 88003-9984

(505) 646-2345

Poetry, fiction, novel sections, criticism, essays, reviews, translation, interviews, photographs, graphics/artwork.

Though our emphasis is on Southwest writers, forty percent of each issue is the poetry, short fiction, artwork, etc. of artists from all over the United States.

Marilyn Hacker, Alison Joseph, Virgil Suarez, Dagoberto Gilb, Judith Ortiz Cofer, Ricardo Aguilar Melantzón, José Antonio Burciaga, Christopher McIlroy.

Unsolicited Manuscripts Received/ Published per Year: 1,000/25 fiction, 35-45 poetry, 5-10 essay.

Reading Period: Sept.–Apr. 1.

Payment: copies.

Reporting Time: 12–20 weeks.

Copyright held by magazine; reverts to author upon publication.

1960; 2/yr; 1,400

$10/yr ind, $10/yr inst; $8/ea; 40%

250 pp; 6 x 9

Ad Rates: $150/page; $90/½ page; $60/¼ page

ISSN: 0738-517X

Q

QUARRY WEST

Kenneth Weisner
c/o Porter College
University of California
Santa Cruz, CA 95064
(408) 459-2155; (408) 459-2951
(messages)
Poetry, fiction, essays, graphics/
artwork.

QUARRY WEST combines quality design, graphics, production with about 95 pages of poetry and fiction, plus essays and reviews. We value intensity of voice and variety in form, content, intent. "A controversy of poets." We do symposiums, also: #22, Rexroth; #25, Neruda; #29/30, Dissident Song: Contemporary Asian American Anthology.
Marilyn Chin, Francisco X. Alarcón, Bill Knott, Lucille Clifton, Bruce Weigl.

Unsolicited Manuscripts Received/
Published per Year: 800/20.
Payment: 2 contributor's copies.
Copyright held by magazine; reverts to author upon request.
1971; 2/yr; 1,000
$15/yr; $10/ea; $3.50/back issue;
40%
110 pp; 6¾ x 8¼
Ad Rates: inquire
ISSN: 0736-4628

THE QUARTERLY

Gordon Lish
650 Madison Ave.
Suite 2600
New York, NY 10021
(212) 888-4769
Fiction, poetry, essay, humor.
A wide-open venue with particular hospitality for the unaffiliated. Fastest, fairest readings.
Unsolicited Manuscripts Received/

Published per Year: 25,000/200.
Reading Period: year–round.
Payment: author copies.
Copyright held by magazine; re-
verts to author upon publication.
1987; 4/yr; 15,000
Subscription information available
upon request.

QUARTERLY REVIEW OF LITERATURE

Contemporary Poetry Series
Theodore and Renee Weiss
26 Haslet Ave.
Princeton, NJ 08540
Poetry.
QRL, a new concept in poetry,
publishes 4 to 6 prize-winning
books of poetry in each volume,
chosen through international
competition. Called "the most
significant event in years" and
"the best bargain in poetry" and
applauded as "brilliant." Each
issue includes: complete books
of poetry, long poems, poetic
plays,
a book of poetry translation,
plus introductory essays, photographs, and biographies of each
author.
Wislava Szymborska, David Schu-
bert, Nancy Esposito, Larry
Kramer, Julia Mishkin.
Reading Period: May and Nov.
Payment: $1,000 plus 100 copies

per winning manuscript. Please
write for more information, with
SASE.
Reporting Time: 2 months or less.
Copyright held by magazine.
1943; 1/yr; 3–5,000
$20/2 volumes ind paper, $20/cloth
volume inst; $10/ea; 10%
350 pp; 5½ x 8½
Ad Rates: $300/page; $175/½
page
ISSN: 0033-5819

QUARTERLY WEST

M. L. Williams and Lawrence
Coates
317 Olpin Union
University of Utah
Salt Lake City, UT 84112
(801) 581-3938
Fiction, poetry, reviews, translation.
We try to publish the best in
poetry and fiction, both mainstream and experimental. We
conduct a biennial novella competition and also publish reviews and translations. We're
not a western genre magazine.
Biennial Novella Competition;
send S.A.S.E. for details. We
accept multiple submissions
(just tell us, please).
Andre Dubus, Francine Prose, Ron
Carlson, Marvin Bell, Stephen
Dobyns, William Stafford,

Philip Levine, C.E. Poverman, Antonya Nelson.
Unsolicited Manuscripts Received/ Published per Year: 1,000+/40.
Reading Period: year–round.
Payment: fiction $25–$50; poems and reviews $15–$50 each + 2 copies and 1 yr sub.
Reporting Time: 4–12 weeks.
Copyright held by magazine; reverts to author upon request.
1976; 2/yr; 1,000
$11/yr; $6.50/ea; 25%–40%
200 pp; 6 x 9
Ad Rates: $150/page (4⅜ x 7⅞); $85/½ page (4⅜ x 4)
ISSN: 0194-4231

Houston, TX 77098
(713) 529-7944
Poetry, fiction, criticism, essays, translation, interviews.
Social criticism/satire/mucking around.
D. A. Levy, Pablo Neruda, Tuli Kupferberg, Steve Kowitt, Curt Johnson.
Payment: in copies.
Reporting Time: 6 months.
Copyright held by author.
1965; 12/yr; 300
$15/yr; $2/ea
40–100 pp; 4 x 5–11 x 17

QUIXOTE
Morris Edelson, Melissa Bondy
1812 Marshall

R

RACCOON

David Spicer
P.O. Box 111327
Memphis, TN 38111-1327
Poetry, fiction, criticism, essays, reviews, translation, interviews, photographs.
A journal of contemporary literature, with poetry, fiction, essay.
Maurya Simon, Pattiann Rogers, David Romtvedt, Jay Meek, Frank Russell.
Payment: poetry–1 year subscription; prose–$50 and 1 copy.
Reporting Time: 6 weeks–3 months.
Copyright reverts to author upon publication.
1977; 3/yr; 500
$12.50/yr; $5/ea; 40%
ISSN: 0148-0162
SPD, Ebsco, Faxon

RAG MAG/Black Hat Press

Beverly Voldseth
Box 12
Goodhue, MN 55027
(612) 923-4590
Poetry, fiction, essays, reviews, plays, photographs, graphics/artwork.
Small ecletic lit mag.
Kevin Rolly, Karen Sosnoski, Todd Ryan Boss, Carla Bertola.
Unsolicited Manuscripts Received/Published per Year: 800/80.
Reading Period: Jan.–Mar.
Payment: in copies.
Reporting Time: 1 week–2 months.
Copyright held by magazine; reverts to author upon publication.
1982; 2/yr; 250
$10/yr. $6/ea
112 pp; 6 x 9
Ad Rates: $35/page (4 x 7⅜); $20/½ page (4 x 3½); $10/¼

page (4 x 1¾); will exchange ads
ISSN: 0742-2768

RAMBUNCTIOUS REVIEW

M. Alberts, N. Lennon, R. Goldman, E. Hausler
1221 West Pratt Boulevard
Chicago, IL 60626

Poetry, fiction, photographs, graphics/artwork.

We are an annual literary arts magazine devoted to the publication of new and established writers and artists. We sponsor annual poetry and fiction contests and theme issues. Our next issue is focused on "Secrets."

Elizabeth Eddy, Richard Calisch, Hugh Fox, Richard Kostelanetz.

Unsolicited Manuscripts Received/ Published per Year: 1,000/15.
Reading Period: Sept. 1 – May 31.
Payment: 2 issues.
Copyright held by magazine; reverts to author upon publication.
1982; 1/yr; 450
$12/3 issues; $4/sample
48 pp; 7 x 10
No ads
Ingram

RANT

Alfred Vitale
P.O. Box 6872

Yorkville Station
New York, NY 10128

Short fiction, poetry, prose, artwork.

RANT is a hybrid of Zine and Literary Journal . . . unconventional . . . jarring and outspoken writing without pretense . . . features voices that challenge any and all established institutions.

Hal Sirowitz, Gina Grega, Charles Bukowski, Ron Kolm, Arthur Nersesian, Cheryl Townsend, C. F. Roberts, Robert Anton Wilson, Tuli Kupferberg.

Unsolicited Manuscripts Received/ Published per Year: 3,000/150.
Payment: copies.
Reporting Time: 1–3 months, but generally within 1 month.
Copyright: to author.
1993; 3/yr; 1,000
$16/4 issues; $3.95/ea
80 pp; 8½ x 5½
Ad Rates: $100/page; $60/½ page (4 x 5); $40/all other
ISSN: 1068-9419
Ubiquity, Desert Moon

RARITAN

R. Poirier, Editor; Suzanne K. Hyman, Managing Editor
31 Mine St.
New Brunswick, NJ 08903
(908) 932-7887 or 7852

Criticism, essays, reviews, poetry, fiction. A comprehensive critique of contemporary culture. Stanley Cavell, Clifford Geertz, Vicki Hearne, Edward W. Said. Unsolicited Manuscripts Received/ Published per Year: 250/7. Payment: $100/article. Reporting Time: 2 months. Copyright reverts to author in 6 months.
1981; 4/yr; 3,500
$16/yr, $26/2 yrs ind, $20/yr, $30/2 yrs inst; $5/ea; $6/back issues; 40%–50%
160 pp; 6 x 9
Ad Rates: $275/page (4½ x 7½)
ISSN: 0275-1607
DeBoer, Ingram

THE RAVEN CHRONICLES
Kathleen Alcala, Phoebe Bosché, Phil Red-Eagle, Annie Hansen, Arthur Tules, Jim Maloney, John Olson, Jody Aliesan
P.O. Box 95918
Seattle, WA 98145
(206) 343-0249:
Fax (206) 543-1104
Poetry, essays, interviews, fiction, reviews, artwork (b/w), cartoons.
TRC is designed to promote multicultural & transcultural arts and literature. We provide a forum for critical discussion of multi-cultural art forms.
Sherman Alexie, Charles Johnson, Elizabeth Woody, David Whited, Carter Revard. Unsolicited Manuscripts Received/ Published per Year: 1200/100. Reading Peroid: January through November. Payment: 2 copies of issue and $10–40 (varies with each issue). Reporting Time: 3–6 months. Copyright held by author/artists: though we copyright work in each issue.
1990; 3/yr; 3,500
$15/yr U.S.; $20/yr foreign; $3 to $4.50, 50%
48 to 64 pp; 8½ x 11
Ad Rates: (call for information; will barter) Business Card Size: $25; ½ page; $150; Full page; $350.
ISSN: 1066-1883
Small Changes in Pacific Northwest

RED BASS
Jay Murphy
105 W. 28th St.
New York, NY 10001
(212) 239-7470
Poetry, essays, graphics/artwork, criticism, reviews, translation, interviews, fiction, plays, photographs.

RED BASS illuminates the interface between art and politics in a series of thematic book/ magazines, usually of a crosscultural, interdisciplinary nature. Robert C. Morgan, Luisa Valenzuela, James Purdy, Carolee Schneemann, Etel Adnan.
Unsolicited Manuscripts Received/ Published per Year: We are not accepting unsolicited manuscripts.
Payment: in copies, sometimes in cash as funds allow.
Reporting Time: 3 months.
Copyright held by magazine; reverts to author upon publication.
1981; 2/yr; 3,000
$20/3 issues; $35 inst & overseas; $7.50–$10 ea; 40%
150 pp; 8½ x 11
Ad Rates: $300/page; $175/½ page; $75/⅓ page (4 x 5¼)
ISSN: 0883-0126
Ubiquity, Fine Print, Last Gasp, Armadillo, DeBoer, Desert Moon, Central Books (UK)

THE RED CEDAR REVIEW
Laura Klynstra, Tom Bissell
Department of English
17C Morrill Hall
Michigan State University
East Lansing, MI 48824
(517) 355-9656
Poetry, fiction.

We recommend reading past issues before submission. We publish the highest quality of fiction and poetry from our submissions; we seek no particular style or form. Tend to the conventions of English; i.e. use good grammar, write clean prose. Please include SASE for response.
Jim Harrison, Margaret Atwood, tom Paine, Jim Cash, Stuart Dybeck, Diane Wakoski.
Unsolicited Manuscripts Received/ Published per Year: 300/25.
Reading Period: year–round.
$10/yr; $5/ea; $2/sample, 40%
Faxon, Ebsco

RE*MAP MAGAZINE
Todd Baron
8270 Willoughby Ave.
Los Angeles, CA 90046

RENEGADE
Michael Nowicki, Miriam Jones, Larry Snell
P.O. Box 314
Bloomfield Hills, MI 48303
Poems, essays, short stories, plays.
Open literary magazine.
Unsolicited Manuscripts Received/ Published per Year: 500/10–20.
Payment: contributor's copy.

Reporting Time: 2 weeks–6
months.
1989; 2/yr; 100
$9.90/yr; $5/ea
24 pp; 11 x 8½
Ad Rates: free

REPRESENTATIONS

Stephen Greenblatt, Carla Hesse,
Co-Chairs; Editorial Board
English Department
University of California
Berkeley, CA 94720
(510) 642-4671
Criticism, essays, translations.
REPRESENTATIONS publishes
critical essays on interdisciplinary topics; disciplines included
are literature, political theory,
art history, and anthropology,
and roughly 50 percent of the
work published is literary criticism. Of the balance, literary
methodology is a substantial
influence in essays in other
fields such as history, political
theory, anthropology, etc.
Unsolicited Manuscripts Received/
Published per Year; 400/28
Payment: none.
Reporting Time: 6–8 weeks.
Copyright held by University of
California Press.
1983; 4/yr; 2,200
$36/yr ind; $67/yr inst; $24/yr
student

152 pp; 7 x 9¾
Ad Rates: $285/page
ISSN: 0734-6018
DeBoer

RESONANCE
Evan and Patty Pritchard
P.O. Box 215
Beacon, NY 12508
(914) 838-1217
Essays, graphics/artwork, poetry,
review, photographs, fiction,
interviews, music and humor.
RESONANCE is a journal of all
forms of creative expression
inspired by personal spiritual
experience. It strives to create a
popular forum for communication between artists, scientists
and the spiritual community,
however it does not promote or
denigrate any other organiza-
tions, spiritual, educational or
otherwise. It is a forum for individual spiritual insight.
Heather Hughes-Calero, Susan
Hanniford Crowley. Interviews
with Chris Williamson,
Madeleine L'Engle, Arun Gan-
dhi, Pete Seeger, David Lanz,
Joan Houston, others.
Unsolicited Manuscripts Received/
Published per Year: 700/10.
Payment: 1 copy.
Reporting Time: 8 weeks.
Copyright held by Evan and Patty

Pritchard—compilation only; reverts to author upon publication.

1987; 3/yr; 2,000

$10/yr; $3/ea; 40%

52 pp; 8½ x 11

$100/½ page; $50/¼ page; $25/⅛ page

Ubiquity, Homing Pigeon, Armadillo, L-S Distributors, Book Tech, New Leaf

RESPONSE: A Contemporary Jewish Review

Yigal Schleifer, David R. Adler, Michael R. Steinberg

27 W. 20 St. 9th fl.

New York, NY 10011

(212) 620-0350

Fax (212) 929-3459

Unsolicited Manuscripts Received/ Published per Year: 200-300/15.

REVERSE

Jan McLaughlin and Bruce Weber

19 W. 73rd St. #3A

New York, NY 10023

(212) 787-4056

Essays, poetry.

Devoted almost exclusively to essays by poets focusing on issues relevant to poetry. Themes of revent issues: censorship of literature; state of poetry in Florida; forgotten poets. Plan-

ning an issue on problems in translation. Includes avante-garde and academic points of view. Often deals with controversial subjects. A poetry journal that thinks.

Carolyn Forché, Barbara Holley, Yvonne Sapia, Jan McLaughlin, Bruce Weber, Lenny Della–Roca.

Payment: $20 upon publication.

Reporting Time: 3–4 months.

Copyright held by author.

1988; 2/yr; 300

$6/yr; $3.50/ea; 40%

16 pp; 8½ x 11

Ad Rates: $50/¼ page; $25/⅛ page

REVIEW

Alfred J. Mac Adam, Daniel Shapiro, Editors

Americas Society

680 Park Ave.

New York, NY 10021

(212) 249-8950

Fiction, poetry, criticism, essays, reviews, translations, interviews, articles on visual arts and music.

REVIEW presents the best of Latin American literature in English translation. It contains a review section as well as major articles on the Latin American visual and performing arts.

Unsolicited Manuscripts Received/

Published per Year: 75–100/5.
Payment: $100 and up.
Copyright held by the Americas
Society (present); Center for
Inter-American Relations (back
issues).
1967; 2/yr; 5,000
$16/yr ind, $25/yr inst; $9/ea
100 pp; 8½ x 11
Ad Rates: $700/page (7¾ x 9¾);
$400/½ page (5 x 7)
Total, Ingram, Inland

**REVIEW OF CONTEMPO-
RARY FICTION**
John O'Brien, Steven Moore
Campus Box 4241 Illinois State
University
Normal, IL 61790-4241
Criticism, essays, reviews, transla-
tion, interviews.
Each issue is devoted to criticism
on one or two contemporary
novelists.
Upcoming issues are devoted to
Stanley Elkin, Raymond Que-
neau, Edmund White.
Gilbert Sorrentino, Robert Creeley,
Paul Metcalf, Carlos Fuentes,
Toby Olson.
All manuscripts are by invitation
only.
Reporting Time: 2 weeks.
Copyright held by magazine; re-
verts to author upon publication.
1981; 3/yr; 2,800

$17/yr ind, $24/yr inst; $8/ea;
10%–40%
200 pp; 6 x 9
Ad Rates: $150/page (5 x 7½)
ISSN: 0276-0045
DeBoer, Inland, SPD

RFD
Short Mountain Collective
P.O. Box 68
Liberty, TN 37095
(615) 536-5176
Poetry, fiction, essays, reviews,
interviews, photographs,
graphics/artwork.
RFD focuses on rural gay men in
related areas of human growth
and consciousness and is an
open forum for new ideas, radical views and controversial issues. The scope includes articles
on alternative lifestyles, home-
steading skills, collectives, gar-
dening, cooking, contact letters,
poetry, fiction, prisoner section,
book reviews and graphics.
Harry Hay, Bru Dye, Louise Hay,
Robin Walden, Jan Nathen
Long.
Unsolicited Manuscripts Received/
Published per Year: 50/20.
Payment: 1 copy of issue published in.
Reporting Time: 1–6 months.
Copyright held by author.
1974; 4/yr; 3,700

$25/yr ind 1st class, $18/yr ind 2nd class; $20/yr inst; $5/ea; 40%

80 pp; 8½ x 11

Ad Rates: $350/page (8½ x 11); $185/½ page (4¼ x 11 or 8½ x 5½); $98/¼ page (4¼ x 5½12)

ISSN: 0149-709X

RHINO

1808 N Larrabee St.

Chicago, IL 60614

Send 3–5 poems to **RHINO** at either address. Please no sentimental verse. Strong free verse with fresh images!

Unsolicited Manuscripts Received/ Published per Year: 500+/70.

Reading Period: year–round.

Payment: 1 copy.

Copyright held by author.

1976; 1/yr; 500

$6 + $1.05 postage/ea; back issues are $3/ea plus postage; 40%

90+ pp; 5½ x 8⅜

No ads

RIVER CITY (formerly MEMPHIS STATE REVIEW)

Paul Naylor

English Department

The University of Memphis

Memphis, TN 38152

(901) 678-4509

Poetry, fiction, essays, interviews.

No novel excerpts.

The magazine sponsors the River City Writing Awards in fiction: 1st prize $2,000; 2nd prize $500; 3rd prize $300. Send SASE for details.

Fred Busch, Marvin Bell, Mona Van Duyn, Pattiann Rogers, Luisa Valenzuela, John Updike.

Unsolicited Manuscripts Received/ Published per Year: 1,000/40.

Reading Period: Sept.–May.

Payment: varies.

Reporting Time: 1 month.

Copyright reverts to author.

1980; 2/yr; 1,000

$12/yr; $7/ea

100 pp; 7 x 10

Ad Rates: $40/page

RIVER OAK REVIEW

Etta L. Worthington

P.O. Box 3127

Oak Park, IL 60303

(708) 848-2184

(708) 848-9729 (Fax)

Short fiction, creative nonfiction, poetry.

Rooted in the innovativeliterary tradition of the Midwest, we seek to publish work that is compelling accessible, and important, produced by established and emerging writers.

Eric Pankey, Kathleen Norris, Anne Calcagno, Ronald Wal-

lace, Mary Swander.
Unsolicited Manuscripts Received/
Published per Year: 4,800/42.
Reading Period: year-round.
Payment: copies; miminal payment
if grant money available.
Reporting Time: approx. 3
months.
Copyright held by magazine,
rights revert to author.
1993; 2/yr; 450
$12/yr, $6/ea; 40%
96 pp; 6 x 9, perfect bound
Ad rates: $200/full page; $100/½
page
ISSN: 1074-3693
Literati

Unsolicited Manuscripts Received/
Published per Year: 1,500+/50-60.
Reading Period: Sept. and Oct.
Payment: $8/page for literature:
$10/page for photographs or
drawings.
Copyright held by Big River As-
sociation; reverts to author upon
publication.
1975; 3/yr; 1,000
$20/yr ind, $28/yr inst; $7/ea; 33%
112 pp; 5½ x 8½
Exchange ads
ISSN: 0149-8851
Ingram

RIVER STYX

Jennifer Tabin, Quincy Troupe,
Michael Castro
3207 Washington
St. Louis, MO 63103-1218
(314) 361-0043
Poetry, fiction, interviews, photographs, graphics/artwork.
RIVER STYX is a multicultural
journal of poetry, prose and
graphic arts publishing works
by both established and up and
coming writers and artists, significant for their originality,
quality, and craftsmanship.
Sharon Olds, Grace Paley, Derek
Walcott, Marilyn Hacker,
Howard Nemerov.

RIVERWIND

C. A. Dubielak, Audrey Naffziger
Hocking College
Nelsonville, OH 45768
(614) 753-3591 ext 2375
Poetry, fiction, nonfiction.
RIVERWIND is more interested
in publishing the new poet, the
good poet, the challenging, the
true as opposed to the well-
established and/or predictable.
Quality, please. Beginning with
our 1993 edition, the focus of
Riverwind will be on Appalachian Writers (Ohio, W. Virginia, Kentucky, etc.), themes,
characters and concerns.
Simon Percik, James Riley.
Unsolicited Manuscripts Received/

Published per Year: 200/30-50.
Payment: copies.
Reporting Time: 4 weeks–3
months. No summer submis-
sions.
Copyright held by author.
1982; 1/yr; 400
$2.50/yr; $2.50/ea; 60%
80 pp; 6 x 9

ROCKET LITERARY QUARTERLY

Eileen Murphy, Printing and Mar-
keting; Darren Johnson, Editor
P.O. Box 672
Water Mill, NY 11976
(516) 287-4233
Poetry, fiction.
The **ROCKET** wants quality writing with innovative voices;
voices that will take the reader
into the next century, at least,
not sci-fi, but new ways to express meaning. To grow larger
with each season.
Leslie Scalapino, Ana Christy,
Darren Johnson.
Payment: free subscription for poets. 1¢ a word for fiction.
Reporting Time: 1–4 weeks.
Copyright held by Rocket Inc.
reverts to author upon publication.
1993; 4/yr; 300–500

$9.95/yr ind; $8.95/yr
inst;$1.50/ea; 40%
25 pp; 4¼ x 11
Ad rates: $75/full page (4 x
11);$45/½ page (4 x 5½).

ROSEBUD™

Rod Clark
Box 459
Cambridge, WI 53523
(608) 423-9609
Short stories, poems, non-fiction
narrative, articles.
Each issue features five rotating
themes, such as "En Route" and
"Mothers Daughters, Wives."
Stories, articles, profiles and
poems . . . of love, alienation,
travel, humor, nostalgia and un-
expected revelation.
Unsolicited Manuscripts Received/
Published per Year: 4,000/80.
Reading Period: year-round.
Payment: $45 per piece, plus 3
additional awards $150 each.
Reporting Time: 10 weeks.
Copyright returned to the writer.
1993; 4/yr; 7,000
$14/yr; $25/2yr; $5.50/ea; 20%
120 pp; 7⅝ x 10¼
Ad Rates: $500/page (x4 $350);
$300/½ page (4x $20)
ISSN: 1072-1681
Eastern News, institutional sub-
scriptions EBSCO, FAXON

S

SAGUARO
Charles Tatum
315 Douglass Bldg
The University of Arizona
Tucson, AZ 85721
(602) 621-7551
Fiction, poetry, essays, autobiography and biography, no reviews.
Bilingual (Eng/Span) magazine dedicated to writing by and about Chicano/Latinos.
SAGUARO seeks works by both established and unknown writers.
Bernice Zamora, Sandra Cisneros, Joel Huerta, Carmen Tafolla, Maria Herrera-Sobek, Max Aguilera-Hellweg.
Unsolicited Manuscripts Received/ Published per Year: 200/20.
Payment: in copies.
Reporting Time: variable.
Copyright held by Mexican American Studies & Research Center; reverts to author upon publication.
1984; 1/yr; 500
$10/2 issues; $6/ea; 20–40%
100 pp; 6 x 9
No ads
ISSN: 0885-5013

SAIL Studies in American Indian Literatures
Joseph Bruchac, Poetry/Fiction Editor; Robert M. Nelson, Production Editor
California State University
Dept. of English
CSU Fullerton
Fullerton, CA 92634
(714) 449-7039 (daytime)
(714) 525-4841 (evening)
Poetry, fiction, criticism, essays, reviews, translation, interviews, letters, announcements, contrib-

uting notes, scholarly articles and reviews.
SAIL is the only peridical focusing exclusively on literature *by* American Indian authors. **SAIL** publishes poetry, fiction, interviews, autobiography and other nonfiction; also translations/transcriptions of oral texts and performances, as well as reviews and scholarship. We plan to publish proceedings and creative work from "Returning the Gift," a convocation of North American Indian writers, in 1992. We are seeking funds to expand publication of translations and original-language texts, and to permit printing of graphics and half-tones.

Joseph Bruchac, Maurice Kenny, Lance Henson, Charlotte De-Clue, Karoniaktatie.

Copyright held by Sail, reverts to author upon publication.

1989; 4/yr; 350

$12/yr ind, $16/yr inst

50 pp; 5½ x 8½

(518) 584-5000, ext 2302

Poetry, fiction, criticism, essays, reviews, translation, interviews.

SALMAGUNDI is an international quarterly of the humanities and social sciences publishing essays and book reviews on literature, contemporary politics, film, dance, and current ideas. General issues also feature original fiction, poetry, photographs and interviews.

George Steiner, Conor Cruise O'Brien, Nadine Gordimer, Christopher Lasch, Susan Sontag, Seamus Heaney.

Unsolicited Manuscripts Received/Published per Year: 2,000/15-20.

Payment: none.

Reporting Time: 1–5 months.

Copyright held by Skidmore; reverts to author upon publication.

1965; 4/yr; 5,600

$18/yr ind, $25/yr inst; $7/ea

160–230 pp; 8½ x 5½

Ad Rates: $150/page (4 x 7); $85/½ page (4 x 3½)

DeBoer

SALMAGUNDI

Robert and Peggy Boyers, Editors; Thomas S.W. Lewis, Associate Editor, Marc Woodworth, Assistant Editor

Skidmore College

Saratoga Springs, NY 12866

SALTHOUSE
A Geopoetics Journal

DeWitt Clinton

800 W. Main

Department of English

University of Wisconsin

Whitewater, WI 53190
(414) 472-1036

Poetry, fiction, reviews.
Interest is in poetry, fiction and reviews/criticism which is influenced by a sense of anthropology, geography or history. No immediate plans for publishing future issues. Back issues are available. Ask for a catalog.
ISSN: 0737-5506

Reporting Time: 4–5 weeks.
Copyright held by author, although magazine asks for one time North American Serial Rights.
1991; 12/yr; 700
$23/yr ind and inst; $3/ea
36 pp; 8½ x 11
Ad Rates: $375/page (7 x 9½); $300/½ page (3¼ x 9½ or 7 x 4); $200/¼ page (3¼ x 4½)
ISSN: 1054-6774

SAN DIEGO WRITERS' MONTHLY

Charles Harrington Elster, Michael T. McCarthy
3910 Chaman St., Suite D
San Diego, CA 92110
(619) 226-0896;
Fax (619) 223-0226

Quincy Troupe, William Murray, Elizabeth George, Joseph Wambaugh, Raymond Feist.
As San Diego's only monthly literary magazine, our goal is to inform, represent, and entertain while promoting writing from all San Diegans, established and aspiring. Our publication crosses all genres and includes a variety of columns, interviews, essays, features, reviews, fiction and poetry written chiefly by county residents.
Payment: $5/poem, $10–25 for fiction/nonfiction.

SAN FERNANDO POETRY JOURNAL

Richard Cloke, Editor; Shirley Rodecker, Managing Editor; Lori C. Smith, Pub. Editor
Kent Publications, Inc.
18301 Halsted St.
Northridge, CA 91325
(818) 349-2080
Poetry.
Seeks to fuse diverse elements of contemporaneity, ranging from evocation of scientific and technical advances–cosmology, subatomic inner space–cyber-punk S.F.–with a pronounced interest in poetry of social protest which illuminates the ills of our time, with special emphasis on ecology.
Stan Proper, C.J. Roner, Paul Weinman, Jack Bernier.
Unsolicited Manuscripts Received/

Published per Year: 7-800/2-500.

Payment: in copies, discounts on subs.

Reporting Time: 2–3 weeks.

Copyright reverts to author.

1978; 4/yr; 500

$10/yr; $3/ea; 20%–30%

100 pp; 5½ x 8½

Ad Rates: $50/page (4½ x 7); $25/½ page (4½ x 3½)

ISSN: 0196-2884

SAN FRANCISCO REVIEW OF BOOKS

Donald Paul

2909 McClure St.

Oakland, CA 94609

(510) 286-2020; Fax (510) 286-0220

Reviews, interviews, and profiles of literary works and persons.

Commentary, debates, and essays on everything from baseball to Buddhism, thrillers to post-modernism.

Unsolicited Manuscripts Received/ Published per Year: 100/15%

Payment: negotiable.

Copyright held by magazine.

1975; 6/yr; 8,000

$16/yr; $3/ea; 35-50%

48 pp; 8½ x 11

Ad Rates: Full page b/w $995

ISSN: 0194-0724

Eastern News

SANDHILLS REVIEW
(formerly St. Andrews Review)

Stephen E. Smith, Editor

Sandhills Community College

2200 Airport Rd.

Pinehurst, NC 28374

Publishes fiction, poetry and essays of highest quality from both established writers and promising new authors from all over the U.S. and abroad.

Fred Chappell, Hiroaki Sato, Soichi Furuta, Yukio Mishima, Desmond Egan.

Unsolicited Manuscripts Received/ Published per Year: 800/50.

Payment: 1 copy.

Copyright held by magazine; reverts to author upon publication.

1972; 2/yr; 500

$8/ea; 30%

100 pp; 6 x 9

Ad Rates: $200/page (5 x 7); $100/½ page (2½ x 3½); $50/¼ page (1¼ x 1¾)

ISSN: 1061-3579

SANTA BARBARA REVIEW

Patricia Stockton Leddy

1309-A State Street

Santa Barbara, CA 93101

(805) 965-3049

Essays, poetry, fiction, non-fiction, B/W art.

SBR is a semi-annual literary art

journal which provides a forum for artists, writing fiction, essay poetry and translations. **SBR** seeks work for its entertainment and informative values.

Chana Bloch, John Sauford, Tess Gallagher, Stephen Ratcliffe, Marilyn Chaubler.
Reading Period: year-round.
Payment: 2 copies.
Reporting Time: 2–3 months.
Copyright held by Santa Barbara Review
1993; 2/yr
$10/yr; $6/ea; 40%
128–160 pp; 6 x 9
Ad Rates: $60/page; $30/½ page
ISSN: 1068-8617
Ingram Periodicals, Ubiquity Dist., Fine Print, Armadillo

SANTA FE LITERARY REVIEW

Colleen Rae
P.O. Box 8018
Santa Fe, NM 87504-8018
(505) 989-7641
Fiction, poetry, art/graphics, essays.

The goal of the **SANTA FE LITERARY REVIEW** is to explore art as it can be rather than as it "should" be, which requires a firm knowledge of what has been.

Richard Goldstein, Steven Counsell, Nedra Westwater, Patricia Hinnebusch, Lisa Greenleaf.
Payment: 5 copies and a 1 year subscription
Reporting Time: 6 weeks.
Copyright held by Colleen Rae/ Haven Hill Press; reverts to author upon publication.
1991; 4/yr; 1,000
$18/yr; $5/ea; 40%
96 pp; 6 x 9
Ad Rates: $100/page (4 x 7)
ISSN: 1055-8446

THE SANTA MONICA REVIEW

Lee Montgomery
1900 Pico Blvd.
Santa Monica, CA 90405
Fiction, poetry, essays.
Guy Davenport, Charles Baxter, Barry Hannah, Peter Handke, Amy Gerstler, Alicia Ostriker.
Unsolicited Manuscripts Received/ Published per Year: 2,000/4-6.
Reading Period: year–round.
Payment: copies.
Reporting Time: 1–3 months.
Copyright: first serial rights only.
1988; 2/yr; 1,200
$12/yr; $7/ea
128+ pp; 8 x 5
Ad Rates: vary
ISSN: 0899-9848
Armadillo, DeBoer, Fine Print, Ubiquity

SCARLET

Douglas Oliver / Alice Notley

all mss.—61 rue Lepic

75018, Paris, FRANCE

Inquiries only—Notley/Oliver

898 Union St.

Brooklyn, NY 11215

(718) 789-2846

mss. will not be forwarded.

Poetry, prose, drawings.

SCARLET is a poetry magazine
which emphasizes political and
spiritual content and is dedicated to the idea that poetry
shouldn't be boring.

Amiri Baraka, Denise Riley,
Leslie Scalapino.

Unsolicited Manuscripts Received/
Published per Year: about
100/about 10.

Payment: 3 copies.

Reporting Time: varies.

Copyright reverts to author.

1990; 4/yr; 500

$14/yr; $2/sample

24 pp; 8½ x 11

SCREENS AND TASTED PARALLELS

Terrel D. Hale

12714 Barbara St.

Silver Spring, MD 20906

(301) 949-6825

Poetry, some reviews.

Dedicated to providing a forum
for a variety of alternative poetries and poetics, some prose,
mostly poetry.

Arkadii Dragomoschenko, Guido
Zlatkes, Johanna Drucker, Maggie O'Sullivan, Saul Yurkievich.

Unsolicited Manuscripts Received/
Published per Year: 50/10.

Payment: none.

Reporting Time: 3-5 months.

Copyright reverts back to poets.

1989; 1/yr; 800+

$10/yr; $6/sample

239 pp; 8½ x 11

ISSN: 1042-9786

SPD, Spectacular Diseases (UK)

THE SEATTLE REVIEW

Donna Gerstenberger

Padelford Hall, GN-30

University of Washington

Seattle, WA 98195

(206) 543-9865, 543-2690

Poetry, fiction, essays, interviews
with writers.

THE SEATTLE REVIEW is a
journal of poetry and prose published twice yearly. We try to
achieve a balance in our pages
between the work of nationally-
known writers and that of
younger writers of promise.

Rita Dove, W.P. Kinsella, Ursula
Le Guin, William Stafford,
Frances McCue, Jane McCaf-
ferty.

Unsolicited Manuscripts Received/

Published per Year: 2,000-2,500/8-12 fiction, 80 poems, 2 essays, 1-2 interviews.
Reading Period: Sept.–May.
Payment: varies.
Reporting Time: 3–6 months.
Copyright held by magazine; reverts to author upon publication.
$9/yr, $16/2 yrs; $5/ea
100 pp; 6 x 9
Ad Rates: $160/page (5 x 7); $90/½ page (5 x 4½)
ISSN: 0147-6629

SEEMS

Karl Elder
Lakeland College
Box 359
Sheboygan, WI 53082-0359
(414) 565-3871
Poetry, fiction, essays.
Jeffrey Baker, John Birchler, M.J. Echelberger, Chris Halla, Robert Nagler.
Unsolicited Manuscripts Received/ Published per Year: 1,000/25.
Payment: 1 copy.
Reporting Time: 1–3 months.
Copyright held by Karl Elder; reverts to author upon publication.
1971; irreg; 350
$16/4 issues; $4/ea
40 pp; 8½ x 7
ISSN: 0095-1730

SEMIOTEXT(E)/AUTONO-MEDIA

Sylvère Lotringer, Jim Fleming
P.O. Box 568
Brooklyn, NY 11211
(718) 963-2603 (phone/Fax)
Fiction, criticism, essays, translation, interview, photographs.
Contemporary radical cultural politics, "movement" literatures. Also sponsors "Foreign Agents," and "Native Agents" small book series promoting contemporary radical politics and culture, philosophy and human sciences, and literature.
Michel Foucault, Roland Barthes, Felix Guattari, Jean Baudrillard, Gilles Deleuze, Kathy Acker, William Burroughs.
Unsolicited Manuscripts Received/ Published per Year: 350/20.
Payment: none.
Reporting Time: 3 months.
Copyright reverts to author upon publication.
1974; irreg; 8,000
$18/3 issues ind, $36/3 issues inst; $10/ea; 40%
320 pp; 7 x 9
ISSN: 0093-5779

SENECA REVIEW

Deborah Tall
Hobart and William Smith Colleges

Geneva, NY 14456
(315) 781-3364
Poetry, criticism, translation, interviews.
Twice a year the **SENECA REVIEW** publishes poetry and prose about poetry, with a special interest in translation.
Eavan Boland, Rita Dove, Yusy Komunyakaa, Jorie Graham, Rosanna Warren.
Unsolicited Manuscripts Received/ Published per Year: 5,000 poems/70 poems.
Reading Period: Sept.–May 1.
Payment: 2 copies.
Reporting Time: 6–10 weeks.
Copyright held by Hobart and William Smith Colleges; reverts to author upon publication.
1970; 2/yr; 1,000
$8/yr, $15/2 yrs; $5/ea; 40%
90 pp; 5½ x 8½
Ad Rates: $75/page (5 x 8)
ISSN: 0037-2145
Small Press Traffic

SENSATIONS MAGAZINE
David Messineo
2 Radio Ave. A5
Secaucus, NJ 07094
Poetry, fiction, photographs, graphics/artwork.
Unsolicited Manuscripts Received/ Published per Year: 200/30.
Reading Period: Mar. and Sept.

Payment: $125/poem; $50/story.
Reporting Time: 1 month after deadline.
Copyright held by author.
1987; 1/yr; 150
$12/sample (send SASE for info)
100 pp; 8½ x 11
Ad Rates: $100/page; $50/½ page; $25/¼ page

SENSITIVE SKIN
Buddy Kold, Christian X. Hunter
P.O. Box 20344
New York, NY 10009
(212) 477-9687
Fiction.
On the edge fiction from new and established writers—makes reading as fun and easy as watching TV!
Darius James, Emily XYZ, Patrick McGrath, John Giorno, Eileen Myles.
Unsolicited Manuscripts Received/ Published per Year: 500/25.
Reading Period: year-round.
Payment: 2 copies.
Reporting Time: 3 months max.
Copyright held by authors.
1993; 2/yr; 1,000
$12/3 issues; $6/ea; 30%
48 pp; 8½ x 11
Ad Rates: $200/page (7 x 9¾); $125/½ page (7 x 4¾); $75/¼ page (3¼ x 4¾)

ISSN: 1073-1865

DeBoer, Ubiquity, Desert Moon

SEQUOIA

Carlos Rodriguez

Storke Publications Building

Stanford, CA 94305

(415) 362-3420

Poetry, fiction, photographs, art.

We have no set guidelines, nor do we accept simultaneous submissions.

Rita Dove, Seamus Heaney, Susan Howe, Janet Lewis, James Merrill.

Unsolicited Manuscripts Received/ Published per Year: 2,000/80.

Reading Period: Oct.–May.

Payment: in copies.

Reporting Time: 2 months.

Author retains rights.

1892; 2/yr; 500

$10/yr; $5/ea

80–105 pp; 5½ x 8

Ad Rates: $100/page; $60/½ page

L–S Distributors

THE SEWANEE REVIEW

George Core

University of the South

Sewanee, TN 37375

(615) 598-1245

Poetry, fiction, criticism, essays, reviews.

America's oldest literary quarterly publishes original fiction, poetry, essays on literary and related subjects, book reviews and book notices for well-educated readers who appreciate good American and English literature.

Hayden Carruth, Louis D. Rubin, Jr., George Garrett, Donald Davie, Malcolm Cowley, L.C. Knights.

Payment: $10–$12/printed page; 60¢/line for poetry.

Reporting Time: 4 weeks.

Copyright held by author.

1892; 4/yr; 3,500

$15/yr ind, $20/yr inst; $6/ea

192 pp; 6 x 9

Ad Rates: $175/page (4¼ x 7); $110/½ page (4¼ x 3⅜); $80/¼ page

ISSN: 0037-3052

SHENANDOAH

Dabney Stuart, Editor; Lynn Williams, Managing Editor

Troubadour Theater

2nd Floor

Washington & Lee University

Lexington, VA 24450

(703) 463-8765

Poetry, fiction, essays, translations, photographs.

Consider work from both new and established writers. Annual prizes in fiction, poetry and the essay.

Seamus Heaney, Northrop Frye,

Robert Wrigley, Lisa Sandlin,
Shelby Hearon.
Unsolicited Manuscripts Received/
Published per Year: 3,640/less
than 1%.
Reading Period: Sept.—May.
Payment: $2.50/line poetry,
$25/page fiction.
Reporting Time: 2–4 weeks.
Copyright held by magazine; reverts
to author upon publication.
1950; 4/yr; 2,100
$11/yr; $3.50/ea; 50%
130 pp; 6 x 9
Ad Rates: $200/page (4½ x 7).
ISSN: 0037-3583
Armadillo, Fine Print, Ubiquity

SHOOTING STAR REVIEW
Sandra Gould Ford
7123 Race St.
Pittsburgh, PA 15208
(412) 731-7464
Poetry, fiction, essays, reviews,
photographs, graphics/artwork.
SHOOTING STAR REVIEW is
an award-winning illustrated
quarterly that uses the arts to
explore the Black experience.
Guidelines available with
SASE. Sample copy ($3) is sent
with next bulk mailing unless 9
x 12 envelope w/$1.21 postage
included.
Kristin Hunter, Dennis Brutus,
Reginald McKnight, Jerry Ward,

Toi Derricote, Doris Jean Austin, Marita Golden.
Unsolicited Manuscripts Received/
Published per Year: 600/60.
Payment: $20/fiction; $10 and
up/essays; $4/poems.
Copyright held by magazine; reverts to author upon publication.
1987; 4/yr; 1,500
$12/yr ind, $15/yr inst; $3/ea;
20% consignment, 50% outright
purchase
32 pp; 8½ x 11
Ad Rates: $300/page; $150/½
page; $75/¼ page
ISSN: 0892-1407

SHORT FICTION BY WOMEN
Rachel Whalen
Box 1254, Old Chelsea Station
New York, NY 10011
All fiction: short stories, short
novels, novel excerpts; 100%
original.
Our goals are to encourage woman
writers and to give readers an
enjoyable, superbly written maga-
zine.
Joan Frank, Edwidge Danticat,
Opal Palmer Adisa, Kat Meads.
Unsolicited Manuscripts Received/
Published per Year: 3,000/30.
SASE for guidelines.
Payment: depends on length and
budget.
Reporting Time: 1 month.

Copyright: first serial rights only.
1991; 2/yr; 2,500
$18/yr; $9/ea
160–224 pp; 5½ x 8½

SIBYL-CHILD

Nancy Arbuthnot, Saundra Maley
709 Dahlia St. NW
Washington, DC 20012
(202) 723-5468

Established in 1974, **SIBYL-CHILD** is out of print. Back issues of chapbooks—fiction, poetry, translations—available at $2/ea.

Doris Mozer, David Hall, Ann Slayton, Peter Van Egmond, William Griffiths, Nan Fry.
5½ x 8
ISSN: 0161-715X

SIDEWALKS

Tom Heie
Box 321
Champlin, MN 55316
(612) 421-3512

Poetry, short prose (fiction, memoir, essay), graphics.

A magazine for emerging and established writers of poetry and prose.

Michael Dennis Browne, Mark Vinz, Thom Tammaro, Robert Cooperman, Kenneth Pabo, Phillip Dacey.

Unsolicited Manuscripts Received/
Published per Year: 1,000/100.
Payment: copies.
Reporting Time: 1-3 months after deadling (May 31; Dec. 31).
Copyright: Tom Heie.
1991: 2/yr; 500
$8/yr; $5/ea; 40%
60-75 pp; 8 x 5½
ISSN: 1059-2210

THE SIGNAL

Joan Silva, David Chorlton
P.O. Box 67
Emmett, ID 83617
(208) 365-5812

Poetry, fiction, criticism, essays, reviews, translation, interviews, photographs, graphics/artwork.

We would like to create a forum for inter-disciplinary work, bridging between literature, art, music; and ecological, socio/political concerns. We encourage submissions in the socio/scientific area; examples would be archeologic, rare travel experiences/philosophic essays on almost anything, but quality of thought and expression should be rigorous and must have literary merit.

Hans Raimund, Natalya Gorbanevskaga, Michele Zackheim, Maurice Kenny, Lloyd Van

Brunt, Olga Cabral, Clarissa
Pinkda Estes.
Unsolicited Manuscripts Received/
Published per Year: 300+/60+.
Payment: in copies.
Copyright held by magazine; reverts to author upon publication.
1987; 2/yr; 500
$10/yr; $6/ea; 40%
50+ pp; 8½ x 11
Ad Rates: $100/page (8½ x 11);
$65/½ page (8½ x 5½); $35/¼
page (4¼ x 2¾)

SILVERFISH REVIEW

Rodger Moody
P.O. Box 3541
Eugene, OR 97403
(503) 344-5060
Poetry, short short stories, reviews,
essays, translations, interviews,
photographs, annual poetry
chapbook contest.
The only criterion for selection of
material is quality. In future
issues SILVERFISH REVIEW
wants to showcase essays on
creative process and short short
stories. SILVERFISH RE-
VIEW also sponsors an annual
poetry chapbook contest.
Kevin Bowen, Lauren Mesa,
Floyd Skloot, Judith Skillman,
Robert Gregory.
Unsolicited Manuscripts Received/
Published per Year: 800/10-15.

Reading Period: year–round.
Payment: 2 copies plus a year subscription, and $5 per page
(when funding permits).
Reporting Time: 2–16 weeks.
Copyright held by author.
1979; 2/yr; 750
$12/3 issues ind, $15/3 issues inst;
$50 life subscription (individu-
als only); $4/ea plus $1.50 postage; 40%
48 pp; 5½ x 8½
Ad Rates: $100/page (4¼ x 7½);
$50/½ page (4¼ x 4)
ISSN: 0164-1085
Spring Church Book Company
(chapbooks only), Faxon, Ebsco, Boley, IPD

SING HEAVENLY MUSE!

P.O. Box 13320
Minneapolis, MN 55414
Fiction, creative prose, poetry.
A magazine to foster women's
writing and the writing of men
showing an awareness of wom-
en's consciousness, in fiction,
creative nonfiction and poetry.
Marihl Le Sugur, Chocolate Waters, Ann Ortit de Montellino,
etc.
Unsolicited Manuscripts Received/
Published per Year: 1,000/40.
Payment: an honorarium, depending on funding, plus contributor's copies.

Reporting Time: 2 months first reading, 6–9 months if it goes to second reading. Copyright by magazine, rights revert to authors. 1977; 1/yr; 400 $19/3 issues; $9/ea approx. 100 pp; 6 x 10 Olson, Ubiquity, Small Changes

SINISTER WISDOM

Ataila Onada-Sikwoia, Janet Wallace, Kyos Foather Zaneing
P.O. Box 3252
Berkeley, CA 94703

Poetry, fiction, criticism, essays, reviews, interviews, plays, photographs, graphics/artwork by lesbians.

A lesbian/feminist journal of art, literature and politics founded in 1976 by Harriet Desmoines and Catherine Nicholson, passed on in 1981 to Michelle Cliff and Adrienne Rich, in 1983 to Melanie Kaye/Kantrowitz and in 1986 to Elana Dykwomon, and in 1994 to the current editors. The primary commitment of the magazine is to publish creative work by lesbians from a broad range of racial, ethnic, cultural and class perspectives.
Sapphire, Gloria Anzaldva, Marilyn Frye, Adrienne Rich, Chrystos, Winn Gilmore, Judith Katz.

Unsolicited Manuscripts Received/ Published per Year: 300-500/60-90.
Payment: 2 copies.
Reporting Time: 6–9 months.
Copyright held by author.
1976; 3–4/yr; 3,000
$17/yr ind, $30/yr inst; $6/ea; 40%
144 pp; 5½ x 8½
Ad Rates: $200/page (5⅛ x 8¼); $100/½ page (5⅛ x 4); $75/⅓ page (5⅛ x 2⅝); $50/¼ page (2½ x 4); $35/2 x 2 or 2⅜ x 2⅜
ISSN: 0196-1853
Inland, Bookpeople

SIPAPU

Noel Peattie
23311 County Rd. 88
Winters, CA 95694
(916) 662-3364

Reviews, interviews, conference news.

Newsletter for librarians, editors, and collectors interested in dissent (feminist, Third World, pacifist, etc.) literature, together with small press poetry. Emphasis on peace and environmental concerns; all must have a print emphasis.
Karl Kempton, Loss P. Glazier, Mary Zeppa, John Daniel, Harry Polkinhorn.

Unsolicited Manuscripts Received/
Published per Year: 2/0.
Payment: 5¢/word.
Reporting Time: 5 months.
Copyright held by editor; reverts
to author upon publication.
1970; 450
$8/yr; $4/ea
36 pp; 8½ x 11
No ads
ISSN: 0037-5837
Ebsco, Faxon, Popular Subscrip-
tion Service, Turner

**SISTERSONG: Women Across
Cultures**
Valerie Staats
P.O. Box 7405
Pittsburgh, PA 15213
Essays, letters, fiction, poetry,
book reviews, b&w artwork and
photography.
A theme journal dedicated to exploring the conditions of contemporary women's lives
through letters and art. New
authors and works in translation
encouraged. Recent and upcoming themes: work; body;
memory; handwork; friendship;
identity; travel. Send SASE for
themes and guidelines.
Lynne Hugo deCourcy, Gisela
Notz, Ana María Rodas.
Unsolicited Manuscripts Received/
Published per Year: 250/60.

Payment: 3 copies.
Reporting Time: about 3 months.
Copyright: reverts to author on
publication.
1992; 3/yr; 1,000
$16/yr ind, $28/yr inst; $24/yr
overseas; $6/ea
80 pp; 6 x 9
ISSN: 1063-214X

THE SLATE
Rachel Fulkerson, Jessica Morris,
Philip Frank, Chris Dall
P.O. Box 581189
Minneapolis MN 55458-1189
(612) 879-8188
Fiction, poetry, essays, interviews
The Slate is dedicated to reviving
a cultural interest in the written
word and providing a forum for
new expressions. No restrictions
regarding subject or content.
Ron Wallace, Stephen Stark, Dan
Graves, Ericka Lutz.
Reading Period: year–round.
Payment: 2 copies
Reporting Time: 2 months.
Copyright held by the publisher
and reverts back to author 4
months after publication date.
1995; 3/yr; 1,500
4 issues for $18.00; $6/ea; 40%
100–120 pp; 6 x 9

Ad Rates: full page & half page price negotiable

ISSN: N/A

SLIPSTREAM

Dan Sicoli, Robert Borgatti, Livio Farallo

Box 2071

Niagara Falls, NY 14301

(716) 282-2616 after 5 p.m. E.S.T.

Poetry, short fiction, graphics.

We publish vital writings (poems & fiction) by many excellent writers whose work is often ignored or overlooked by mainstream or academic publishers.

Charles Bukowski, Denise Duhamel, Hal Sirowitz.

Unsolicited Manuscripts Received/ Published per Year: 2,000+/100–125.

Reading Period: year–round.

Payment: in copies.

Reporting Time: 2 weeks–2 months.

Copyright reverts to author upon publication.

1981; 1–2/yr; 300

$8.50/2 issues; $5/ea

128 pp; 7 x 8½

No ads

ISSN: 0749-0771

THE SMALL POND MAGAZINE, Inc.

Napoleon St. Cyr

P.O. Box 664

Stratford, CT 06497

(203) 378-4066

Poetry, fiction, essays, reviews, graphics/artwork.

Features contemporary poetry by new and established writers, but also uses short prose pieces of many genres, plus some art work—black and white only.

Marvin Solomon, Fritz Hamilton, Sid Harriet, Rika Lesser, Jane Somerville, H.R. Coursen.

Unsolicited Manuscripts Received/ Published per Year: 5,000/75.

Reading Period: year–round.

Payment: 2 copies.

Reporting Time: 10–30 days, longer in summer.

Copyright held by N. St. Cyr. Original mss. which are published become the property of the Beinecke Rare Books & Mss. Lib. at Yale.

1964; 3/yr; 300

$8/yr; $3/ea; random back issue/$2.50; inquire

40 pp; 5½ x 8½

Ad Rates: $40/page (4½ x 7½); $25/½ page (4½ x 3½); $15/¼ page (4½ x 2¼)

ISSN: 0037-721X

SMALL PRESS MAGAZINE

Martha Smith

Kymbolde Way

Wakefield, RI 02879

(401) 789-0074; Fax (401) 789-3793

Articles about independent publishing, book reviews, excerpts.

SMALL PRESS exists to serve small, independent publishers by printing articles for and about small presses, including reviews and excerpts of small press books and magazines.

Unsolicited Manuscripts Received/ Published per Year: 50/2.

Reading Period: year–round.

Payment: $50-200

Reporting Time: 1-2 months.

Copyright held by magazine.

1983; 4/yr; 7,500

$29/yr; $7.50/ea

100+pp; 8¼ x 11

Ad Rates: upon request

ISSN: 0000-0485

Eastern News

THE SNAIL'S PACE REVIEW

Darby Penney and Ken Denberg

RR#2 Box 403 Darwin Rd.

Cambridge, NY 12816

Poetry and poetry in translation.

THE SNAIL'S PACE REVIEW publishes contemporary poetry and poetry in translation. The editors especially welcome submissions from women, people of color, and members of ethnic and cultural minorities.

Maurice Kenny, Martha Collins, Ai.

Unsolicited Manuscripts Received/ Published per Year: 3,000/60.

Payment: 2 copies.

Reporting Time: 4 months.

Copyright reverts to author upon publication.

1991; 2/yr; 300

$7/yr; $4/ea; 40%

32–36 pp; 5½ x 8½

ISSN: 1054-1632

SNAKE NATION REVIEW

Roberta George, Sharmain van Bloomenstein, Nancy Phillips

110 #2 W. Force St.

Valdosta, GA 31601

(912) 249-8334

Poetry, fiction, essays, photographs, graphics/artwork.

SNAKE NATION REVIEW is a regional quarterly, founded in the fall of 1989. We encourage writing that addresses all areas of life. We look for good writing that encounters change and character; all subjects are acceptable if it meets our one requirement–well written.

Van K. Brock, D. Victor Miller, Judith Otiz Cofer.

Unsolicited Manuscripts Received/ Published per Year: 4,000/45.

Payment: Prize money (editors' choice); 2 copies/contribution.
Reporting Time: 6 months.
Copyright: Snake Nation Press.
1989; 2/yr; 1,000
$20/ yr ind, $30/yr inst; $6/ea; 40%
100 pp; 6 x 9
Ad Rates: $100/page; $50/½ page; $25/¼ page
ISSN: 1046-5006

Payment: copies. Annual contests in fiction, poetry and creative non-fiction. Send SASE for guidelines.
Reporting Time: 2–3 months, longer during summer.
Copyright reverts to author.
1980; 2/yr
$12/yr; $24/2 yrs; $6/ea
120 pp; 6 x 9

SONORA REVIEW

Department of English
University of Arizona
Tucson, AZ 85721
(602) 626-8383
Poetry, fiction, reviews, translation, interviews, criticism, essays.
We're looking for the liveliest new writing we can get our hands on, including experimental and non-conformist work. Most issues are general in nature, though recent special features have profiled "Crossing Borders: Writing from Alternative Traditions" and "Voices from the Southwestern Landscape." We welcome simultaneous submissions.
Jane Miller, David Foster Wallace, Rick Bass, Frances Sherwood, Antonya Nelson.
Unsolicited Manuscripts Received/ Published per Year: 2,000/24.

SOPHOMORE JINX

Anne-Marie Mooney, Anthony Rutella, Jr.
P.O. Box 770728
Woodside, NY 11377-0728 USA
(718) 507-8360
Poetry.
Quarterly poetry magazine geared towards beginning/unpublished poets.
Unsolicited Manuscripts Received/ Published per Year: 1,000/300.
Reading Period: year-round.
Payment: publication, we have 3 cash prizes per issue.
Reporting Time: 1–4 weeks.
Copyright held by writers and contributors.
1994; 4/yr; 1,000
$15/yr; $25/2 yrs; $5/ea
80+ pp; 5½ x 8½
Ad rates: $50/full page; $25/½ page; yearly discount available & we exchange ad space also.
SophomoreJinx

SOUNDINGS EAST

Rod Kessler, Claire Keyes
English Dept.
Salem State College
Salem, MA 01970
(508) 741- 6270

Original poetry, fiction, artwork.
SOUNDINGS EAST is a collection of original poetry, short fiction, and art work, published biannually by the students of Salem State College.
Debra Allbery, Robert Cooperman, Antonya Nelson.
Unsolicited Manuscripts Received/Published per Year: 400/60.
Reading Period: Sept.–Nov., Jan.–April.
Payment: 2 copies.
Reporting Time: 2 to 4 months.
Copyright reverts to author.
1978; 2/yr; 2,000
$6/yr; $3/ea
65 pp; 5½ x 8½

SOUTH CAROLINA REVIEW

Elizabeth Boleman-Herring
English Department
Clemson University
Clemson, SC 29634-1503
(803) 656-3457

Poetry, fiction, criticism, essays, reviews, translation, interviews.
Listed as one of the twenty most outstanding literary magazines in the United States by the *The New York Quarterly,* THE SOUTH CAROLINA REVIEW is now in its third decade of publication. Our primary goal is to continue to publish fiction, poetry, and criticism of the quality that has earned us several Pushcart nominations, as well as election to *The Best American Short Stories 1982* and *Prize Stories 1982: The O. Henry Awards.*
Stephen Dixon, Rosanne Coggeshall, Joyce Carol Oates, Cleanth Brooks, Leslie Fiedler.
Reading Period: Jan.–May, Sept.–Nov.
Payment: in issues.
Reporting Time: 6–9 months.
Copyright held by magazine.
1968; 1 double-issue per annum; 600
$7/yr ind; $5/ea; 33⅓%
200 pp; 9 x 6
Ad Rates: negotiable
ISSN: 0038-3163

SOUTH COAST POETRY JOURNAL

John J. Brugaletta
English Department
California State University Fullerton
Fullerton, CA 92634
(714) 773-3163

Poetry, graphics/artwork.

SOUTH COAST POETRY

JOURNAL avoids theorizing so
as to remain open to every kind
of excellence in poetry, no
matter what the style or
school. Our standards for
excellence, however, are
high.
Richard Eberhart, Rita Dove,
Marge Piercy, William
Stafford, John Hollander,
Denise Levertov, Mark
Strand.
Unsolicited Manuscripts Received/
Published per Year: 4,000
poems/80.
Reading Period: Sept.–May.
Payment: in single copies.
Copyright held by magazine; reverts to author upon publication.
1986; 2/yr; 450
$10/yr ind, $12/yr inst; $6/ea;
40%
60 pp; 5½ x 8½
Ads accepted
ISSN: 0887-2074

SOUTH DAKOTA REVIEW

John R. Milton
University of South Dakota
Vermillion, SD 57069
(605) 677-5229

Poetry, fiction, criticism, essays,
occasional translation and inter-
views.
When the material warrants, an
emphasis on the American
West; writers from the West;
Western places or subjects; fre-
quent issues with no geographical emphasis. Periodic special
issues on one theme, or one
place, or one writer, e.g., Ross
MacDonald (Spring 1986), Wallace Stegner (Winter 1985).
Max Evans, D. E. Steward, Bart
Paul, Diane Lefer.
Unsolicited Manuscripts Received/
Published per Year: 1,000/up to
100.
Reading Period: year–round.
Payment: in copies.
Reporting Time: 2 weeks–2
months, slowest in summer.
1963; 4/yr; 600
$15/yr, $25/2 yrs; $5/ea; 40%
150–190 pp; 6 x 9
ISSN: 0038-3368

THE SOUTHERN CALIFOR-NIA ANTHOLOGY

James Ragan Editor-in-Chief
Master of Professional Writing
Program
University of Southern California
WPH 404
Los Angeles, CA 90089-4034
(213) 740-3252

Poetry, fiction, interviews,
graphics/artwork (on cover).
Published through the Master of
Professional Writing Program at

the University of Southern California, **THE SOUTHERN CALIFORNIA ANTHOLOGY** is a literary journal of fiction, poetry, and interviews. Seventy percent of the pieces are solicited. Volume X (published Dec. 1992) includes works by: Amiri Baraka, Robert Bly, Vance Bourjaily, Donald Hall, John Hollander, David Madden, James Merrill, John Frederick Nims, Joyce Carol Oates, James Ragan, Hubert Selby, Jr., Mark Strand, Henry Taylor, John Updike, Peter Viereck, Richard Yates.
Unsolicited Manuscripts Received/ Published per Year: 1,000/10.
Reading Period: Sept. 1–Jan 1.
Payment: 3 copies.
Copyright held by the University of Southern California, Master of Professional Writing Program; reverts to author upon publication.
1983; 1/yr; 1,000
$9.95/yr; 40%
144 pp; 5½ x 8½
ISBN: 0-9615108-5-4
Blackwell North America, Ballen Booksellers, SPD

SOUTHERN EXPOSURE

Pat Arnow
P.O. Box 531
Durham, NC 27702
(919) 419-8311

Essays, reviews, interviews, photographs, graphics/artwork.
SOUTHERN EXPOSURE is a winner of the National Magazine Award and is widely respected as the voice of the progressive South. Investigative journalism and oral history are emphasized. Very little fiction and no poetry; mostly nonfiction articles on social issues.
Unsolicited Manuscripts Received/ Published per Year: 1,000/1-2.
Payment: up to $200.
Reporting Time: 6–8 weeks.
Copyright held by magazine.
1973; 4/yr; 4,000
$24/yr; $5/ea; 40%
Ad Rates: $400/page; $270/½ page
64 pp; 8½ x 11
ISSN: 0146-809X
Ingram

SOUTHERN HUMANITIES REVIEW

Dan R. Latimer, R.T. Smith, co-editors
9088 Haley Center
Auburn University, AL 36849
(205) 844-9088

Poetry, fiction, essays, reviews.
THE SOUTHERN HUMANITIES REVIEW publishes fiction, poetry and critical essays on the arts, literature, philoso-

phy, religion, and history. Essays, articles, or stories should, in general, range between 3,500 and 5,000 words. Poems should not exceed two pages in length. No multiple submissions.

Margaret Holley, Robert Morgan, Donald Hall, Peter Green, Yannis Ritsos, Reynolds Price.

Unsolicited Manuscripts Received/ Published per Year: 1,500-2,000/40-55.

Payment: copies.

Reporting Time: 1–3 months.

Copyright reverts to author upon publication.

1967; 4/yr; 700

$15/yr; $5/ea

100 pp; 4½ x 7½

Ad Rates: $100/page (4½ x 7½); only with adequate notice.

ISSN: 0038-4186

SOUTHERN POETRY REVIEW

Ken McLaurin
Department of English
University of North Carolina
Charlotte, NC 28223
(704) 547-4336

Poetry, reviews.

Poetry submissions accepted from established and previously unpublished poets. **SPR** is a natural outlet for poets writing in the South, but has no regional bias. Variety in style and content encouraged.

Susan Ludvigson, Linda Pastan, David Keller, Dave Smith, Marge Piercy.

Reading Period: Sept.—May.

Payment: in copies.

Copyright held by magazine; reverts to author upon request.

1958; 2/yr; 1,100

$8/yr; $4.50/ea; 40%

80 pp; 6 x 9

No ads

ISSN: 0038-447X

THE SOUTHERN QUARTERLY: A Journal of the Arts in the South

Stephen Flinn Young
University of Southern Mississippi
Southern Station Box 5078
Hattiesburg, MS 39406-5078
(601) 266-4370

Criticism, essays, reviews, interviews, photographs.

A non-profit scholarly journal, **THE SOUTHERN QUARTERLY** includes essays, articles, interviews and reviews on the arts and society—defined broadly—in the southern U.S. General and special issues include research on music, theatre, dance, literature, film, art, architecture, popular and folk arts.

Unsolicited Manuscripts Received/
Published per Year: 30/10.
Payment: 1 year subscription.
Reporting Time: 2–3 months.
Copyright held by University of
Southern Mississippi; reverts to
author upon publication.
1962; 4/yr; 750
$12/yr ind, $20/2 yrs ind, $30/yr
inst; $5/ea; 15%
180 pp; 7 x 10
Ad Rates: $100/page (4½ x 6¾);
$75/½ page (4½ x 3⅜)
ISSN: 0038-4496

THE SOUTHERN REVIEW

James Olney, Dave Smith
43 Allen Hall
Louisiana State University
Baton Rouge, LA 70803-5005
(504) 388-5108

Fiction, poetry, criticism, reviews,
interviews.

THE SOUTHERN REVIEW
publishes poetry, fiction, criticism, essays, reviews and excerpts from novels in progress,
with emphasis on contemporary
literature in the United States
and abroad, and with special
interest in Southern history and
culture.

Ernest J. Gaines, Reynolds Price,
Lee Smith, W. D. Snodgrass,
Jill McCorkle, Hayden Carruth,

A. R. Ammons, M. L.
Rosenthal.
Unsolicited Manuscripts Received/
Published per Year: 10,000/100.
Reading Period: Sept.–May.
Payment: $12/printed page for
prose; $20/printed page for po-
etry; 2 complimentary copies.
Reporting Time: 2 months.
Copyright held by LSU; reverts to
author upon publication.
1935 (original series), 1965 (new
series); 4/yr; 3,100
$20/yr, $36/2yr, $50/3yr, ind;
$40/yr; $65/2yr; $90/3yr; inst,
Foreign subscribers: add $4/yr
for postage
250 pp; 6¾ x 10
Ad Rates: $250/page (4½ x 7½);
$150/½ page (4½ x 3⅝);
$100/¼ page (4½ x 1⅔)
ISSN: 0038-4534
DeBoer, Fine Print

SOUTHWEST

Janine Kelley
3490 South Walkup Dr.
Flagstaff, AZ 86001
(602) 774-6159

Fiction, essays, interviews, poetry,
film/book reviews.

SOUTHWEST is an international
literary magazine celebrating the
cultural and artistic diversity of
the region publishing writers
with a range of light.

Simon Ortiz, James Cervantes,
Mary Sojourner, Ruth L.
Schwartz, Ann Walka, Ernesto
Carriazo-Osorio.
Unsolicited Manuscripts Received/
Published per Year: 500/17.
Reading Period: Mar. 1–June 1.
Payment: copies.
Reporting Time: 2–5 weeks.
Copyright reverts to the author
upon publication.
1993; 1/yr; 300–500
$5/yr; $5/ea
72 pp; 6 x 9
Ad Rates: $75/4 x 6
ISSN: 1065-0156
McGaugh's Newsstand

THE SOUTHWEST REVIEW

Willard Spiegelman, Editor-in-
Chief; Elizabeth Mills, Senior
Editor
307 Fondren Library West
Box 374
Southern Methodist University
Dallas, TX 75275
(214) 768-1037
Poetry, fiction, essays, interviews.
THE SOUTHWEST REVIEW is
a quarterly that serves the interests of its region but is not
bound by them. **SWR** has always striven to present the work
of writers and scholars from the
surrounding states and to offer
analyses of problems and

themes that are distinctly south-
western and, at the same time,
publishes the works of good
writers regardless of their lo-
cales.
Alice Adams, Albert Goldbarth,
Wayne Koestenbaum,Rosellen
Brown, Padgett Powell, Rey-
nolds Price, Adrienne Rich,
Harvey Sachs.
Unsolicited Manuscripts Received/
Published per Year: 3,600±/60.
Reading Period: Sept.–May 31.
Payment: varies.
Reporting Time: 1 month.
Copyright held by SMU; reverts to
author upon publication.
1915; 4/yr; 1,500
$20/yr ind, $25/yr inst; $5/ea;
40%
160 pp; 6 x 9
Ad Rates: $250/page (25 x 42½
picas); $150/½ page (25 x 21
picas)
ISSN: 0038-4712
Fine Print, Total

SOU'WESTER
Fred W. Robbins
School of Humanities,
Southern Illinois University
Edwardsville, IL 62026-1438
(618) 692-3190
Poetry, fiction.
Published twice a year, Fall and
Spring; **SOU'WESTER** is

somewhat selective and prefers
to publish new writers.
Robert Wexelblatt, Jared Carter,
Kathleen Thompson, Jeanne
Bryner.
Unsolicited Manuscripts Received/
Published per Year: 1,000/45.
Reading Period: year–round.
Payment: 2 free copies, 1 yr sub-
scription.
Reporting Time: 3–4 months.
Copyright: first serial rights; re-
leased upon request, with ac-
knowledgement.
1960; 3/yr; 300
$10/yr; $5/ea; 40%
84 pp; 6 x 9
Ad Rates: $80/page; $60/½ page;
$30/¼ page
ISSN 0098-499X
Literati & Co.

on subject matter or style. We
use B & W art to complement
poetry.
Single poem competition, Sept.
and Oct., with $500 prize and
publication; chapbook competition March and April, $500
prize and publication. SASE for
guidelines.
Alan Atkinson, Carole Bernstein,
Lois Harrod, Kerry Shawn
Keys, Susan Terris, Ioanna-
Veronika Warwick.
Unsolicited Manuscripts Received/
Published per Year: 3,000/150.
Payment: in copies.
Reporting Time: 3–6 months.
Copyright reverts to author.
1988; 4/yr; 500
$10/4 issues; $3.50/ea; 40%
32 pp; 8½ x 11

THE SOW'S EAR POETRY REVIEW

Larry Richman, Managing Editor;
Mary Calhoun, Graphics Editor
19535 Pleasant View Dr.
Abingdon, VA 24211-6827
(703) 628-2651
Poetry, reviews, interviews, graphics, photography.
Contemporary poetry exported
from and imported into Southern Appalachia. No nostalgia.
We publish both established and
new poets, with no restrictions

SPARROW POVERTY PAMPHLETS

Felix and Selma Stefanile
103 Waldron St.
West Lafayette, IN 47906
(317) 743-1991
Poetry.
The one-poet-an-issue magazine,
providing a forum for mature
poets. We are in the modernist
tradition, with its emphasis on
craft, shaped language, unity of
voice and vision.
Christopher Bursk, Geraldine C.

Little, Roger Finch, Gail White, Gray Burr, Ger Killeen.
Payment: $30, plus royalties of 20%.
Sparrow is in reorganization for 1991. For the time, no new manuscripts are being sought. Query with SASE late in 1991. Copyright reverts to author on request.
1954; 3/yr; 900
$9/yr; $2/ea for back copies; 35%
28–32 pp; 5½ x 8½
ISSN: 0038-6588
Spring Church (for our chapbooks), SPD

SPECTRUM
Robert H. Goepfert
Anna Maria College
Paxton, MA 01612-1198
(508) 849-3450
Non-fiction, fiction, poetry, art, photography.
An interdisciplinary national publication geared to the scholarly non-specialist.
Unsolicited Manuscripts Received/ Published per Year: 600/10.
Reading Period: year–round.
Payment: $20 honorarium and 2 free copies.
Reporting Time: 6 weeks.
Copyright First North American serial rights.
1985; 2/yr; 1,000

$7/yr; $4/ea
64 pp; 6 x 9
ISSN: 0895-8270

SPOON RIVER POETRY REVIEW
Lucia Getsi
English Department
Illinois State University 4240
Normal-Bloomington, IL 61790
(309) 438-7906
Poetry, translation, interviews, photographs, reviews.
SRPR wants poetry that is interesting and compelling. Our standards are high—the acceptance rate is about 2%. We publish emerging and established poets, and occasionally feature groups of poets working at the edges and margins of language and American poetics. $500 Editor's Prize entry deadline is April 15.
Tim Seibles, Diane Glancy, Roger Mitchell, Richard Jackson, Katherine Soniat, Frankie Paino, William Trowbridge.
Unsolicited Manuscripts Received/ Published per Year: 6-7,000/120.
Reading Period: Sept.–May 1.
Payment: one year subscription.
Reporting Time: 8 weeks.
Copyright reverts to author upon publication.

1976; 2/yr; 600
$12/yr ind, $16/yr inst; $6/ea;
40%
128 pp; 5½ x 8½
Ad Rates: $150/page (5 x 8);
$75/½ page
ISSN: 0738-8993
Ebsco, Ingram, Faxon, Ubiquity,
Fine Print

**SPRING: The Journal of the
E.E. Cummings Society**
Norman Friedman, David V. Forrest
33–54 164 St.
Flushing, NY 11358-1442
(718) 353-3631
Essays, poems, photographs, drawings, bibliographies, etc.
We publish material relating to and about E. E. Cummings. Since 1994 was the centennial of his birth, we feel the time is ripe for re-evaluating and honoring him.
Milton A. Cohen, Richard S. Kennedy, Linda Wagner-Martin.
Unsolicited Manuscripts Received/Published per Year: 20/10–12.
Reading Period: Oct.–Mar.
Payment: none.
Reporting Time: we publish once a year so far, so there's no hurry.
Copyright held The E. E. Cummings Society.

1992; 1/yr; 2–300
$15/yr; $15/ea
144 pp; 5½ x 8½

STAND MAGAZINE
Jon Silkin, Lorna Tracy, Rodney Pybus
179 Wingrove Road
Newcastle upon Tyne NE4 9DA, UK
Tel/Fax (091) 273 3280
STAND MAGAZINE is an independent quarterly of new writing. Politically left of centre, **STAND** has shown a strong awareness of social injustices and emphasizes the need for commitment between the writer and his or her community.
Unsolicited Manuscripts Received/Published per Year: 520–624 stories, 1,000–1,300 poems/10–12 stories, 30–40 poems depending on length.
Payment: £30.00 per poem/per thousand words.
Reporting Time: 4–6 weeks.
Copyright reverts to authors, but magazine reserves right of first publication.
1952; 4/yr; 4,500
84 pp; A5 landscape
Ad Rates: £220.00/page;
£110.00/½ page; £55.00/¼page
UK ISSN: 0038-9366

STET MAGAZINE
Cassandra L. Oxley
P.O. Box 75, Cambridge MA
   02238
(508) 264-4938
Poetry, short fiction, nonfiction,
   art.
We are a small literary magazine
   with a national following—we
   are presently seeking more essays & fiction though we love
   to present poetry. We hope to
   publish as a quarterly in '95.
Max Money, William J. Vernon,
   Estelle Gilson.
Unsolicited Manuscripts Received/
   Published per Year:
   300–500/60–80.
Reading Period: year–round.
Payment: 2 copies.
Reporting Time: 6 weeks—3
   months.
Copyright; 1st rights.
1994; 2/yr; 100+
$12/yr; $4/ea
44+ pp; 7 x 8½ or 8½ x 11
ISSN 1060-8028

STILETTO
Michael Annis
P.O. Box 27276
Denver, Colorado 80227-0276
Poetry, short stories, essays, excerpts from fiction, plays, "illustrated," experimental, (but
   accessible etc.); politics & social works given priority. Bold,
   uncompromising, often radical.
All genres, street poets to academia. Strong content. Large
   enough sections to clearly demonstrate the author's ability and
   vision. If you have a statement
   to make for posterity, make it
   here. Guidelines may be found
   in previous issues. No free
   samples—these are Cadillacs.
Antler, Wm. Burroughs, Andrei
   Codrescu, Diane DiPrima, William Heyen, David Ray,
   Nathaniel Tarn, Diane Wakoski,
   Anne Waldman, Jimmy Santiago Baca, Charles Bukowski.
Unsolicited Manuscripts Received/
   Published per Year: many/12.
Reading Period: year–round.
Payment: 20 contributor copies,
   1st Ed.
Mss. not selected for **STILETTO**
   may be considered for inclusion
   in a companion volume titled
   The BEAST.
Copyright reverts to author/artist.
1989; no schedule latest issue
   1992
$31.50 1st Ed. collectors hard-
   bound; $21.50 Commercial Ed.
   softcover; prices include postage.
   30%
250+ pp; 5 x 11¼
ISSN 1043-9501
Howling Dog Press

STORY

Lois Rosenthal
1507 Dana Ave.
Cincinnati, OH 45207
(513) 531-2222
Short fiction.
STORY is devoted to publishing fine short stories.
Bobbie Ann Mason, Joyce Carol Oates, Robert Ward, Madison Smartt Bell, Alice Adams, Tobias Wolff, Rick De Marinis, William Kotzwinkle.
Unsolicited Manuscripts Received/ Published per Year: 15,000/50.
Reading Period: year–round.
Payment: $600.
Reporting Time: 1 month.
Copyright: First North American serial rights.
1989; 4/yr; 35,000
$19/yr; $6.95/ea
128 pp; 6½ x 9¼
ISSN: 1045-0831
Ingram, Eastern News

STORY QUARTERLY

Anne Brashler, Diane Williams
P.O. Box 1416
Northbrook, IL 60065
(708) 564-8891
Fiction and interviews.
STORY QUARTERLY is looking for great fiction.
Unsolicited Manuscripts Received/ Published per Year: 2,500/20.

Reporting Time: 2 months.
Copyright held by magazine; reverts to author upon publication.
1974; 2/yr; 1,500
$12/4 issues; $5/ea; 40%
110 pp; 6 x 9
ISSN: 0361-0144
DeBoer, Ingram

THE STYLUS

Roger Reus
9412 Huron Avenue
Richmond, VA 23294
Fiction, essays
An eclectic literary journal devoted to the writings of John Fante, Charles Bukowski, Edgar A. Poe, Henry Miller, and others. Essays and original fiction.
Joyce Fante, Mark Rich, Don Herron, Peter Cannon, Sam Maio
Unsolicited Manuscripts Received/ Published per Year: 400/10.
Payment: in copies.
Copyright reverts to author upon publication.
1993; 1/yr; 300
$3/copy; $3/ea
38–56 pp; 5½ x 8½

SUB-TERRAIN MAGAZINE

Brian Kaufman, Dennis Bolen, Paul Pitre, Hilary Green, Bryan Wade, Dirk Beck, Ken Gilchrist, Andrea Shearer

P.O. Box 1575, Bentall Centre
Vancouver, B.C. V6G 2P7
CANADA
(604) 876-8710; Fax (604) 879-2667
Fiction, poetry, excerpts of novels, essays, art, photography.

SUB-TERRAIN has garnered substantial kudos for its unusual material, daring art, and contentious commentary. We continue to publish a new front line of writers and artists who might otherwise never get the exposure we strive to offer.
Mark Salerno, Tom Osborne, Libby Hart, Pat McKinnon, Simon Perchik, Don Austin, Jean Smith.
Unsolicited Manuscripts Received/Published per Year: 7–1,000/75–100.
Reading Period: Sept.–June.
Payment: in copies; payment for solicited material.
Reporting Time: 2–4 months.
Copyright: 1 time only, reverts to author.
1993; 4/yr; 3,000
$15/yr ind, $20/yr inst; $3.95/ea; 40%
40 pp; 7 x 10
Ad Rates: $300/back cover; $210/page; $120/½ page; $65/¼ page
ISSN: 0840-7533
Canada Magazine Publishers Assoc., US: Fine Print, Ubiquity, Desert Moon

SULFUR
Clayton Eshleman
210 Washtenaw Ave.
Ypsilanti, MI 48197
(313) 483-9787
Poetry, fiction, criticism, essays, reviews, translation, photographs, graphics/artwork.
Contemporary American poetry, translations, archival materials, book reviews, reproduction of art and photography.
Jerome Rothenberg, John Ashbery, Michael Palmer, William Carlos Williams, Aimé Césaire.
Unsolicited Manuscripts Received/Published per Year: 1,800/10.
Reading Period: year–round.
Payment: $40/contribution.
Reporting Time: 1–2 weeks.
Copyright held by magazine; reverts to author upon publication.
1981; 2/yr; 2,000
$14/yr ind, $20/yr inst; $9/ea; 40%
250 pp; 6 x 9
Ad Rates: $150/page (6 x 9); $85/½ page (6 x 3⅞)
ISSN: 0730-305X
Inland, SPD, DeBoer, Bookpeople, Armadillo, Small Change

SUN DOG: The Southeast Review
Michael Trammell, Ron Wiginton
406 Williams Building
Florida State University

Tallahassee, FL 32306
(904) 644-4230

Poetry, fiction, graphic art.
SUN DOG: The Southeast Review reads both fiction and poetry year-round. We are looking for striking images, incidents, and characters rather than particular styles or genres. We also publish the winner and runners-up of the World's Best Short Short Story Contest, as well as the winner and runners-up of the Richard Eberhart Prize in Poetry.

Janet Burroway, David Bottoms, Jesse Lee Kercheval, Leon Stokesbury, Rick Lott, Helen Norris, David Kirby.

Unsolicited Manuscripts Received/ Published per Year: 300-400/12- fiction; 20-poems.

Reading Period: year–round.

Payment: 2 copies.

Copyright held by magazine; reverts to author upon publication.

1979; 2/yr; 1,250

$4/ea; 40%

90 pp; 6 x 9

THE SUN MAGAZINE
Sy Safransky
107 N. Roberson St.
Chapel Hill, NC 27516
(919) 942-5282

Essays, poetry, fiction, interviews, photography.

A monthly magazine in its 21st year of publication, **THE SUN MAGAZINE** celebrates good writing—and the warmth of shared intimacies—in essays, fiction, interviews, and poetry. People write in the magazine of their struggle to understand their lives, often bearing themselves with remarkable candor.

Tim Melley, Jim Ralston, Sarajane Archdeacon.

Payment: $100–$300/nonfiction; $100/fiction; $25/poetry.

Reporting Time: 3–6 months.

Copyright held by magazine.

1974; 12/yr; 26,000

40 pp; 8½ x 11

ISSN: 0744-9666

Armadillo, Bear Family, Daybreak, Desert Moon, Olson, Doormouse, Ingram, Mercury, New Leaf, Serendipity, Small Changes, Stadler, Ubiquity, Wholistic Health.

SWIFT KICK
Robin Kay Willoughby
1711 Amherst St.
Buffalo, NY 14214
(716) 837-7778

Poetry, fiction, plays, translation, photographs, graphics/artwork. We specialize in unusual formats, genres and styles.

Jerry McGuire, Dennis Maloney,
Simon Perchik, Penny Kemp,
Maurice Kenny.

Payment: in copies.

Reporting Time: varies.

Copyright held by magazine; reverts to author upon publication.

1980; 4/yr; 200

$20/yr ind, $40/yr inst; $6 +
postage/sample (checks payable
to editor); 40%

ISSN: 0277-447X

SYCAMORE REVIEW

Michael Manley
Department of English
Purdue University
West Lafayette, IN 47907
(317) 494-3783

Fiction, poetry, essays, interviews,
translations, drama.

SYCAMORE REVIEW publishes new writers of contemporary fiction and poetry alongside
well-known, experienced writers.

Patricia Henley, H. E. Francis,
Louis Simpson, Lee Upton,
Brigit Kelly, Elaine Terranova,
Elizabeth Dodd, Julie Schumacher, Cruck Wachtel.

Unsolicited Manuscripts Received/
Published per Year:
1,000–1,200/40-45.

Reading Period: Sept.—May.

Payments: 2 copies.

Reporting Time: 4 months or
less—SASE must be included
for response.

Copyright: first serial rights.

1989; 2/yr; 800–1,000

$9/yr in US; $11/yr outside US;
$5/current issue each; $4/back
issues each. List available 1 &
2-yr. subscriptions only.

160 pp; 6 x 9

Ad swaps w/other magazines or
small presses. No contest ads.

ISSN: 1043-1497

T

TAKAHE

Sandra Arnold, Tony Scanlan, Bernadette Hall, Cassandra Fusco, Ray Mutton, Jim Norcliffe, Isa Moynihan

P.O. Box 13335
Christchurch, New Zealand

Quality shortfiction and poetry.

TAKAHE traverses the literary landscape to help young writers gain reputation and readership.

L. E. Scott, David Hill, Barbara Else, David Eggleton, P.N.W. Donnelly.

Unsolicited Manuscripts Received/Published per Year: hundreds600 approx./40 approx., ten per issue short fiction.

Reading Period: year-round.

Payments: $40 approx. dependenton continuation of QEII grant.

Reporting Time: 4–8 weeks

Copyright held by Takahe Publishing Collective, or direct approach to author.

1989; 4/yr; 300

$32/4 issues

58 pp

Ad Rates: $80/page; $40/½ page; $30/¼ page; $15/⅛ page.

ISSN: 0114-4138

Takahe Magazine Collective

TALISMAN: A Journal of Contemporary Poetry and Poetics

Edward Foster
Box 1117
Hoboken, NJ 07030
(201) 798-9093

Poetry, essays on poetry and poetics, interviews.

Each issue centers on the poetry and poetics of a major contemporary poet and includes a selection of new work by other important contemporary writers. Susan Howe, Charles Bernstein,

John Yau, Clark Coolidge, Robert Creeley, Rosmarie Waldrop, Ron Padgett, Alice Notley, Leslie Scalapino.
Unsolicited Manuscripts Received/ Published per Year: hundreds/20-25.
Reading Period: year—round.
Payments: copies.
Reporting Time: 2 months.
Copyright reverts to author upon publication.
1988; 2/yr; 1,200
$9/yr ind, $13/yr inst; $5/ea; 40%
224 pp; 5½ x 8½
Ad Rates: $100/page; $50/½ page
ISSN: 0898-8684
DeBoer, Anton J. Mikofsky, SPD, IN Book, Spectacular Diseases (UK)

TAMPA REVIEW

Richard B. Mathews, Ed., Andy Solomon, Fiction Ed., Kathryn Van Spanckeren & Don Morrill, Poetry Editors.
Box 19F
The University of Tampa
Tampa, FL 33606-1490
(813) 253-3333 ex. #6266

Poetry, fiction, essays, interviews, photographs, graphics and art.
TAMPA REVIEW is the faculty-edited literary journal of the University of Tampa. It publishes new poetry, fiction, translations, nonfiction and art in a variety of styles and voices. Each issue includes works from other countries, reflecting the international flavor of the city of Tampa and its ties to the international cultural community. Tom Disch, Eavan Boland, Shang Zhongmin, Dionisio Martínez, Peter Meinke, W. S. Merwin, Elizabeth Jolley, Denise Levertov, Stephen Dunn.
Unsolicited Manuscripts Received/ Published per Year: 1,200–2,000/60.
Reading Period: Sept.–Dec.
Payment: $10/page.
Reporting Time: up to 12 weeks after Dec. 31.
Copyright: first North American serial copyright held by Magazine then reverts to author.
2/yr
$10/yr; $5.95/ea
72 pp; 7½ x 10½
ISSN: 0896-064X

TAPROOT: A Journal of Older Writers

Philip W. Quigg, Enid Graf
Fine Arts Center 4290
University at Stony Brook,
Stony Brook, NY 11794-5410
(516) 632-6635

Poetry, fiction, graphics/artwork, reviews.

Publish the works of older writers; interested in "capturing the stories, poems and recountings of events related to and growing from tradition," as well as the realities of our elders' participation in community life. Publication open to members of Taproot Workshops only.
No Unsolicited Manuscripts Received/Published per Year: 15/0.
Payment: 1 copy.
Copyright held by magazine; reverts to author upon publication.
1974; 1/yr; 1,000
$6/ea; 40%
100 pp; 8½ x 11
Ad Rates: $500/page; $300/½ page; $175/¼ page
ISSN: 0887-9257

sentimental, flat statement verse. Though we often publish the work of established poets, we are open to the work of newcomers as well.
A.R. Ammons, Brendan Galvin, Sharon Bryan, Betty Adcock, Naomi Shihak Nye, Michael Mott, Peter Davison, Leslie Norris, Emily Grosholz.
Unsolicited Manuscripts Received/ Published per Year: 4,500/125.
Reading Period: Sept.–April.
Payment: none.
Reporting Time: 5–7 weeks.
Copyright reverts to author.
1965; 2/yr; 1,000
$10/1 yr, $18/2 yr; $5.50/sample; 40%
62 pp; 6 x 9

TAR RIVER POETRY

Peter Makuck
English Department
East Carolina University
Greenville, NC 27834
(919) 757-6041
Poetry, reviews, interviews, essays.
We are looking for poetry that shows skillful use of figurative language. Narrative poems, short image poems, poems in closed and open form are welcome. We are not interested in

THE TEXAS REVIEW

Paul Ruffin
English Department
Sam Houston State University
Huntsville, TX 77341
(409) 294-1429
Poetry, fiction, criticism, essays, reviews.
We are interested in the very best fiction and poetry available; our nonfiction may be literary, historical, or "familiar." We are interested principally in reviews of contemporary poetry and fiction.

Fred Chappell, Richard Eberhart, George Garrett, Donald Justice, William Stafford, Richard Wilbur.
Unsolicited Manuscripts Reveived/ Published per Year: 3,000/150.
Reading Period: Sept.–Apr.
Payment: in contributor's copies plus 1 year subscription to magazine.
Copyright held by magazine; reverts to author upon publication.
1979; 2/yr; 750–1,000
$10/yr (ind and inst); $5/ea; 40%
144 pp; 6 x 9
ISSN: 0885-2685

THEATER MAGAZINE
Erika Munk
Yale School of Drama
222 York St.
New Haven, CT 06520
(203) 432-1568/Fax (203) 432-8336
Playscripts, essays, articles, interviews,performance and book reviews.
The foremost journal on contemporary theater, **THEATER** publishes noted American and International critics, playwrights, and scholars. Each issue features a collection of essays, a new play, reports and reviews.
Jarold Bloom, Richard Gilman, Marie-Irene Fornes, Suzan-Lori Parks, Richard Foreman.

Unsolicited Manuscripts Received/ Published per Year: 250/3–5.
Reading Period: academic year, Sept.–May.
Payment: $100 plus issues.
Reporting Time: 4–6 weeks.
Copyright held by Theater Magazine.
1968; 3/yr; 2600/issue
$22/yr ind; $35/yr inst; $8/ea; 25%
120 pp; ½ x 10
Ad rates: $250/full page (5½ x 8½); $150/½ page (5½ x 4¼); $100/¼ page (2½ x 4¼)
ISSN: 0161-0775
Fine Print, DeBoer, Ubiquity, Inland

THEMA
Virginia Howard
Thema Literary Society
Box 74109
Metairie, LA 70033-4109
(504) 887-1263
Fiction, poetry.
Stories and poems must relate to premise specified for each issue. Upcoming themes: Laughter on the Steps, A Solitary Clue, Jogging on Ice, A Visit from the Imp, *I KOW WHO YOU ARE!*, and more to be announced.
Jewel Mogan, E. L. Wyrick, Helen Tzagoloff, Kaye Bache-Snyder.
Unsolicited Manuscripts Received/

Published per Year: 800/75.
Payment: $25 for short story, $10
for poems, $10 for short-shorts
and illustrations.
Reporting Time: dependent on
deadlines.
Copyright reverts to author.
1988; 3/yr; 300
$16/yr; $8/ea; 40%
200 pp; 5½ x 8½
ISSN: 1041-4851

13th MOON

Judith E. Johnson
English Department
SUNY
Albany, NY 12222

Poetry, fiction, criticism, essays,
reviews, translation, interviews,
photographs, graphics/artwork,
by women.
13th MOON is a feminist literary
magazine, placing primary emphasis on the quality of writing.
It is specifically interested in
work from feminist, lesbian,
third-world, and working-class
perspectives.
Joanna Russ, Cheryl Clarke, Ne-
lida Pinon, Marie Ponsot.
Unsolicited Manuscripts Received/
Published per Year: 1,000/30.
Reading Period: Sept.—May.
Payment: in copies.
Reporting Time: varies.
Copyright held by 13th Moon,

Inc.; reverts to author upon publication.
1973; 1/yr; 2,500
$10/ind, $20/inst; $10/ea; 40%
200 pp; 6 x 9
Ad Rates: inquire

THIS: A Serial Review

Robin Yale Bergstrom
6600 Clough Pike
Cincinnati, Ohio 45244
(513) 231-8020; (513) 231-2818
Fax

Poetry, fiction, essays, art, drama,
criticism.
We strive to publish new and es-
tablished artists regardless of
bias. We're committed to
stretching the literary magazine
genre by taking the risks neces-
sary to pull it in directions it
has yet to go.
Barry Spacks, James Bertolino,
David Shevin, Lynn Lifshin,
S.P. Elledge.
Unsolicited Manuscripts Received/
Published per Year: 2,000/130.
Reading Period: 12 months.
Payment: in copies, beginning
1996 cash payment.
Reporting Time: 6–8 weeks.
Copyright held by Pants Dance
Productions; reverts to author
upon publication.
1994; 3/yr; 500+
$24/yr, $9/ea; 20%

120 pp; 8 x 8
ISSN: 1075-2862
Fine Print

$360/¼ page (4½ x 7¼)
ISSN: 0275-1410
Ingram, Ubiquity

THE THREEPENNY REVIEW

Wendy Lesser
P.O. Box 9131
Berkeley, CA 94709
(510) 849-4545

Poetry, fiction, criticism, essays, reviews, memoirs, graphics/artwork.

THE THREEPENNY REVIEW is a quarterly journal publishing essays on literature, theater, film, television, dance, music, and the visual arts, as well as new poetry, original fiction, and socio-political articles. While based in California, it is aimed at a nationwide audience.

John Berger, Seamus Heaney, Elizabeth Hardwick, Thom Gunn, Amy Tan.

Unsolicited Manuscripts Received/Published per Year: 5,200/20.

Payment: $100–$200.

Reporting Time: 3 weeks–2 months.

Copyright held by magazine; reverts to author upon publication.

1980; 4/yr; 10,000
$16/yr; $6/ea; 30%–50%
40 pp; 11 x 17
Ad Rates: $900/page (10 x 14);
  $500/½ page (10 x 7½);

THUNDER & HONEY

Akbar Imhotep
P.O. Box 11386
Atlanta, GA 30310
(404) 688-3376

Poetry, fiction, interviews, photographs, graphics/artwork.

THUNDER & HONEY is primarily devoted to poetry and fiction. Future issues will have arts-related articles and some interviews.

Charlie Braxton, Nome Poem, R.F. Smith, Askia Toure, Jeanne Towns.

Payment: 15 copies.

Copyright held by magazine; reverts to author upon publication.

1984; 4/yr; 1,500
$2.50/yr; 75¢/ea
4 pp; 8½ x 11
Ad Rates: $210/page (10 x 16);
  $120/½ page (10 x 8); $60/¼ page (5 x 4)

TIGHTROPE

Ed Rayher
323 Pelham Rd.
Amherst, MA 01002

Poetry, fiction, translation, graphics/artwork. Not reading

short fiction until 1994. We stress excellence and accessibility to unpublished or little published authors. Our format is erratic, but we always emphasize form as well as content.
Steven Ruhl, Linda Burggraf, Gillian Conoley, Lance Liskus.
Unsolicited Manuscripts Received/ Published per Year: 500/25.
Payment: inquire.
Copyright held by magazine; reverts to author upon publication.
1977; 2/yr; 350
$10/yr; $6/ea; 40%
40 pp; size varies; Letterpress

TO: A Journal of Poetry, Prose and the Visual Arts
Seth Frechie, Andrew Mossin
Box 121
Narberth, PA 19072
Biannual.
Contemporary fiction, poetry, and poetics featuring new translation, archival material, essay and review. Each issue features work, in the visual arts with a special emphasis placed on work by contemporary american photographiers.
John Ashbery, Charles Bernstein, Leslie Scalapino, Jack Sturges.
Payment: in copies.
Reporting Time: 6 weeks.
Copyright reverts to author.

1992; 2/yr; 1,000
$15/yr ind, $30/yr inst; $8/ea; 40%
approx. 140 pp; 7 x 10 page
Ad Rates: $100/page; $50/½ page
SPD, DeBoer

TOMORROW MAGAZINE
Tim W. Brown
P.O. Box 148486
Chicago, IL 60614
(312) 984-6092
Poetry, fiction, essay, B&W Art.
TOMORROW is a magazine that tries not to discriminate against style or subject, although we tend to shy away from academically inclined work.
Hugh Fox, Richard Kostelanetz, Antler, Cheryl Townsend, Paul Weinman.
Unsolicited Manuscripts Received/ Published per Year: 500/75.
Reading Period: year-round.
Payment: in copies.
Reporting Time: 3 weeks to 3 months.
Copyright reverts to the author.
1982; 2/yr; 300
$13/3 issues; $5/ea
32 pp; 8½ x 11
ISSN: 1075-3796

TOOK: Modern Poetry in English Series
Edward Mycue
P.O. Box 640543
San Francisco, CA 94164-0543
Poetry, drama, prose, history, criticism, music, food, art, psychology, self-help, philosophy, film, vinyl/recordings, travel.
Laura Kennelly, Owen Hill, Lawrence Fixel, Martha King, Jules Mann, Betsy Ford, Judy Stedman, Elizabeth Hurst, Agnes McGaha, Helen Sventitsky, Jim Gove, Dan Bellm, William Talcott, Ann Erickson.
Payment: in copies.
Reporting Time: 1 month.
Copyright reverts to the contributors.
1988; occasional; 150
$5/ea
8 to 40 pp; 5½ x 4½
Ad Rates: $50/¼ page

TOP STORIES
Anne Turyn
228 Seventh Ave.
New York, NY 10011
Fiction, graphics/artwork.
TOP STORIES is a prose periodical; a chapbook series which (usually) features the work of one author/artist per issue.
Constance DeJong, Lynne Tillman,
Susan Daitch, Tama Janowitz, Richard Prince.
Payment: varies.
Reporting Time: 1 year.
Copyright held by author.
1979; 3/yr; 1,500
$13.50/yr ind, $14.50/yr inst; $3/ea single issue; $6/ea double issue; 40%
5¼ x 8¼
No ads

TOUCHSTONE: Literary Journal
William Laufer
P.O. Box 8308
Spring, TX 77387-8308
Poetry, criticism, essays, reviews, translation, interviews, graphics/artwork, fiction.
We publish fiction, nonfiction, poetry and graphics. We do not care for "Creative Writing Program" fiction. We welcome minority viewpoints, and look for imaginative, experimental trends. We also publish (poetry and fiction) chapbooks, no theme, no reading fee. Send SASE for submission guidelines.
Lyn Lifshin, Rebecca Gonzales, Ramona Weeks, Vassar Miller, Arthur Smith, Sheila Murphy, Walter McDonald, Annette Sanford.
Reading Period: Jan.–Oct.

Payment: 2 copies (magazine), or
10 copies (chapbooks).
Reporting Time: 6 weeks.
Copyright reverts to author .
1976; 1/yr; 1,000
$5/ea
52–60 pp; 5½ x 8, perfect bound
ISSN: 1715-1697
No ads

TRAFIKA INTERNATIONAL LITERARY REVIEW

Michael Lee, Alfredo Sanchez,
Jeffrey Young
Janovského 14, 170 00 Prague 7
CZECH REPUBLIC

Short fiction, essays, poetry.
TRAFIKA is a new international
literary review for the contemporary poetry, fiction, and essays
of established and emerging writers from throughout the world.
Don DeLillo, Arnošt Lustig, Miro-
slar Holub, Czeslaw Milosz,
Yang Lian, Denis Johnson.
Unsolicited Manuscripts Received/
Published per Year: 15,000/100
Payment: contributor's copies.
Reporting Time: 3 months.
Copyright reverts to author upon
publication.
1993; 4/yr; 5,000
$35/yr; $10/yr; $10/issue; 25%
224 pp; 6 x 9
Ad Rates: $500(US)/$300(US) for

nonprofit organizations/page
(5½ x 8¼)
SPD

TRANSLATION REVIEW

Rainer Schulte
Box 830688
University of Texas at Dallas
Richardson, TX 75083-0688

TRANSLATION REVIEW publishes articles on the art and
craft of translation, interviews
with well known translators,
criticisms of revent translations,
profiles of publishers.
Payment: no.
Reporting Time: 3 months.
Copyright held by magazine.
1978; 3/yr; 1,500
$30/yr ind, $125/yr inst; $35/yr
Colleges and Univ. Student
(US) $20; indivual (foreign)
$40; library (US) $35; library
(foreign) $45.
65 pp; 8½ x 11
Ads Rates: $200/page (7½ x 9)
$125/½ page (7½ x 4½ or
3½ x 9); $75/¼ page (2¼ x 3½)
ISSN: 0737-4836

TRIQUARTERLY

Reginald Gibbons
Susan Hahn
Northwestern University

2020 Ridge
Evanston, IL 60208
Fiction, poetry, essays, reviews, translation, interviews, photographs, graphics/artwork.
TRIQUARTERLY is especially dedicated to short fiction, although substantial amounts of poetry are also published regularly in every issue, including long poems. Brief book reviews and occasional essays round out the contents.
Stanley Elkin, Alice Fulton, Linda McCarriston, Sandra McPherson, Jim Powell, Alan Shapiro, Bruce Weigl.
Unsolicited Manuscripts Received/ Published per Year: 8,000/100
Reading Period: Oct.—Mar. 31
Payment: $20/printed page, prose; $1.50/line, poetry.
Reporting Time: 2–3 months.
Copyright reverts to author upon request.
1964; 3/yr; 4,000
$20/yr ind; $26/yr inst; $5/sample; varies
250 pp; 6 x 9¼
Ad Rates: $250/page (6 x 9¼); $150/½ page (6 x 4⅝)
ISSN: 0041-3097
Ingram, DeBoer, Bookpeople, Fine Print, Ubiquity

TRIVIA: A Journal of Ideas
Erin Rice, Kay Parkhurst
P.O. Box 606
North Amherst, MA 01059
(413) 367-0168
TRIVIA publishes the finest, most "lively and vicious" writing from radical, visionary women. Essays, reviews, translations, interviews, original art and experimental forms that combine rigorous thinking with uncompromising feminist vision. Articles on language and memory, aging, lesbian ethics, feminism's seduction by New Age philosophy.
Nicole Brossard, Michèle Causse, Christina Thürmer-Rohr, Barbara Mor, C. C. Sundance, Lee Maracle, Lou Robinson.
Unsolicited Manuscripts Received/ Published per Year: 50–60+/10+.
Reporting Time: 4–6 months.
Copyright reverts to author.
1982; 2/yr; 2,000
$16/3 issues ind; $20/3 issues inst; $5/ea
120 pp; 5½ x 8½
Ad Rates: inquire
ISSN: 0736-928X
Inland, Bookpeople, Small Changes, Fine Print, Spectacular Diseases (UK)

TUCUMCARI LITERARY REVIEW

Troxey Kemper
3108 W. Bellevue Ave.
Los Angeles, CA 90026
(213) 413-0789

Poetry, fiction, essays, nostalgia, memories, vignettes, humor.

TUCUMCARI LITERARY REVIEW is old fashioned and the preference is for types of writing in vogue in the 1930s to 1950s. Most of the poetry is rhyming, in "standard" forms, not disjointed phrases and odd-shaped lines of prose arranged like poetry. The emphasis is on writing that "says something."

Harvey Stanbrough, Marian Ford Park, William J. Middleton, Fontaine Falkoff, Patricia Higginbotham, Daniel Kaderli, Ken MacDonnell, Wilma Elizabeth McDaniel.

Unsolicited Manuscripts Received/ Published per Year: 1,500/400.

Payment: in copies upon publication.

Copyright held by author.

1988; 6/yr; 170

$12/yr ind & inst; $2/ea by mail; 40%

40 pp; 5½ x 8½

Ad Rates: free for readers

TURNSTILE

George Witte, Lindsey Crittenden
175 Fifth Avenue, Suite 2348
New York, NY 10010

Fiction, poetry, essays, interviews, photographs, artwork/graphics.

TURNSTILE publishes high-quality fiction, poetry, essays, interviews and artistic works. A passageway for variety and difference, **TURNSTILE** encourages new and emerging writers and artists.

Unsolicited Manuscripts Received/ Published per Year: 1,000+/20.

Payment: in copies.

Reporting Time: 10–12 weeks.

Copyright reverts to author upon publication.

1988; 2/yr; 1,200

$22/4 issues; $6.50/ea; 40–50%

128 pp; 6 x 9

$150/page; $100/½ page

ISSN: 0896-5951

Deboer, Inland, Ingram

U

THE UNDERGROUND FOREST—La Selva Subterranea

Joseph Richey, Ann Becker
1701 Bluebell Ave.
Boulder, CO 80302

Nonfiction, poetry, investigative articles, politics.

A bilingual (Spanish-English), hemispheric publication devoted to the dissemination of informed opinions and good writing.

Margaret Randall, Agnes Bushell, Gioconda Belli, Victor Hernandez Cruz.

Payment: 2 copies.
Reporting Time: as soon as we can.
Copyright reverts to author.
1986; 2/yr; 2,000
$12/yr; $3/sample; 40%
96 pp; 17 x 5¼
Ad Rates: Write for information
ISSN: 1045-3660
Maine Writers and Publishers Association, Ubiquity

UNMUZZLED OX

Michael Andre
105 Hudson St.
New York, NY 10013
(212) 226-7170

Poetry, political.

Library Journal called **OX** "Outrageous and outstanding" perhaps because I published Robert Mapplethorpe; given the current climate I'd settle for "lively." We do publish the dead—a forthcoming issue features baroque librettists; plus W. H. Auden, the late Andy Warhol, John Cage.

Robert Creeley, Dan Berrigan, Allen Ginsberg.

Unsolicited Manuscripts Received/Published per Year: 500/4.
Payment: confidential.

Reporting Time: varies.
Copyright held by Michael Andre.
1971; varies; 15,000
$20/yr; $3/ea; varies
150 pp; 5½ x 8½
Ad Rates: inquire.
ISSN: 0049-5557

URBANUS MAGAZINE

Peter Drizhal, Editor; Geoffrey
    Manson, Senior Editor
P.O. Box 192561
San Francisco, CA 94119-2561

Fiction, poetry, essays, graphics.
URBANUS is a magazine of con-
    temporary and post-modernist
    writing; our focus is urban cul-
    ture and its offsprings.
Yusef Komunyakaa, Louise
Rafkin, Clarence Major, Amy
Gerstler, Heather McHugh,
James Sallis.
Unsolicited Manuscripts Received/
    Published per Year: 3,000/20.
Reading Period: Dec.–Feb.,
    June–Aug.
Payment: prose: 1¢ per word and
    copies; Poetry: $5/page and
    copies.
Reporting Time: 2–10 weeks.
Copyright held by Urbanus Press
1988; 2/yr; 1000
$8/yr; $5/ea; 40%
64 pp; ½ x 8½
Ad rates: $100/page (5 x 8);
    $50/½ page (5 x 4).
ISSN: 1078-6686
Desert Moon

V

THE VINCENT BROTHERS REVIEW

Kimberly A. Willardson, Roger Willardson, Michelle Whitley-Turner, Valerie Benge
4566 Northern Circle
Riverside, OH 45424-5733

Fiction, nonfiction, poetry, reviews, essays, artwork, photos.

TVBR's purpose is to encourage, promote and support the work of artists, poets, and prose writers through the publication of 3 magazines per year.

Matthew Spireng, Doris Read, Susan Streeter Carpenter.

Unsolicited Manuscripts Received/Published per Year: 9,000/180.

Payment: $10 minimum for short stories and articles plus 2 copies of issue; 2 copies of issue to all other contributors.

Reporting Time: 2–3 months.

Copyright: all rights revert to artists/authors upon publication.

1988; 3/yr; 400
$12/yr; $5.00/ea
64–80 pp; 5½ x 8
Ad Rates: $75/page (7 x 4);
   $45/½ page (3¼ x 4);
   $25/business card (2 x 3½)
ISSN: 1044-615X

THE VINYL ELEPHANT

Matthew Duncan
700 Cotanche #1
Greenville, NC 27858

Poetry, Fiction, B/W Art/Photography.

Literary Journal of Experimental work often edged out due to "extravagances" in subtext matter, "contrivances" in voice or diction, and "inconveniences" of structure or layout.

Guy Beining, Thomas Zimmer-

man, Juliet Cook!, Richard
Levesque.

Unsolicited Manuscripts Received/
Published per Year: 1,500/100.

Payment: 1 copy.

Reporting Time: 4–6 weeks.

Copyright reverts to author.

1992; 3/yr; 125

$10/6 issues; $3/ea

44 pp; 8½ x 5½, digest

Ad Rates: $25/page; $15/½ page;
$10/¼ page: trade for equal

THE VIRGINIA QUARTERLY REVIEW

Staige D. Blackford
One West Range
Charlottesville, VA 22903
(804) 924-3124; (804) 924-1397
FAX

Poetry, fiction, essays, reviews.

One of the oldest and most distinguished literary journals in the
country; contains articles and
essays covering economics, art,
the sciences, politics, and literature. Publishes high-quality fiction and poetry by established
and newer authors. 75–100
brief, tightly-written book reviews per issue.

George Garrett, Jay Parini, Joyce
Carol Oates, Mary Lee Settle,
Ann Beattie, Robert Olin Butler.

Unsolicited Manuscripts Received/
Published per Year: 2,000+/12-
16.

Reader Period: year–round.

Payment: $10/page essays & fic-
tion; $1/line for poetry;
$50/essay reviews.

Copyright held by magazine/The
University of Virginia; reverts
to author upon publication.

1925; 4/yr; 4,200

$15/yr ind, $22/yr inst; $5/ea; 50%

188 pp; 5½ x 8

Ad Rates: $150/page (5½ x 8);
$75/½ page (5½ x 4 or
2⅜ x 8)

ISSN: 0042-675X

VISIONS–International, The World Journal of Illustrated Poetry

Bradley R. Strahan, Poetry Editor;
Shirley Sullivan, Associate Editor
1110 Seaton Lane
Falls Church, VA 22046
(703) 521-0142

Poetry, reviews, translations,
graphics/artwork.

We're international in scope and
content. We emphasize the in-
terplay between artwork, poem
and appearance of the magazine. We look for strong, well-
crafted work that has emotional
content (without sentimentality).
VISIONS also publishes issues
on special themes (usually once

a year). Many of these, including our specials on Scandinavian/ Nordic and Australia/New Zealand poetry, are still in print. We oppose the trend to publish facile word play instead of meaningful poetry. We are always interested in translations, especially from work that has not previously appeared in English and from less translated languages such as: Frisian, Basque, Telegu, Malayan, Gaelic, Macedonian, etc.
Allen Ginsberg, Ted Hughes, Marilyn Hacker, Louis Simpson, Lawrence Ferlingletti.
Unsolicited Manuscripts Received/ Published per Year: 5,000+/250.
Reading Period: year–round.
Payment: in copies or $5–$10 when we get a grant.
Read a sample copy ($3.50) before submitting work
Reporting Time: 1–3 weeks.
Copyright held by VIAS; reverts to author upon publication.
1979; 3/yr; 750
$14/yr; $4.50/ea; 30%–40%
56 pp; 5½ x 8½
ISSN: 0194-1690

VIVO

Carolyn Miller
1195 Green St.
San Francisco, CA 94109
(415) 885-5695
Art, photographs, cartoons, essays, fiction, poetry, humorous, and serious work.
VIVO is a lively little magazine of art, fiction, essays, and poetry that mixes humorous and serious work.
Carol Snow, Terry Ehret, Jeanne Lohmann, Gerald Fleming.
Unsolicited Manuscripts Received/ Published per Year: 250/8.
Payment: 2 copies of magazine.
Reporting Time: 6 weeks.
Copyright reverts to author on request.
1991; 1/yr; 700
$8/2 issues; $4/ea (postpaid); 40% bookstores, 50% newsstands
16 pp; tabloid 11 x 17
Ad Rates: $120/¼ page (4½ x 7½); $15/2 column inch.
ISSN 1056-3474
Fine Print, Inland, Armadillo

VOICES INTERNATIONAL

Clovita Rice
1115 Gillette Dr.
Little Rock, AR 72207
(501) 225-0166
Poetry, essays, photographs, graphics/artwork.
VOICES INTERNATIONAL focuses on high literary quality poetry, accepting for publication

poetry with strong visual imag- ery and haunting impact. We encourage the beginner and have no preference in subject matter (as long as in good taste) if it presents a fresh approach and special awareness.
Sarah Singer, Eunice de Chazeau, Frederick Zydek.
Unsolicited Manuscripts Received/ Published per Year: 160–180
Reading Period: year–round.
Payment: in copies.
Reporting Time: averages 6 weeks.
Copyright held by magazine.
1966; 4/yr; 325

$10/yr; $2.50/ea
32 pp; 6 x 9

VREMYA I MY (TIME AND WE)
Victor Perelman
409 Highwood Ave.
Leonia, NJ 07605
(201) 592-6155
Russian language literature and commentary. Fiction, essays, poetry, criticism, translation, graphics/artwork, interviews, photographs.
$59/yr ind, $86/yr inst; $19/ea; 40%

W

WASHINGTON REVIEW

Clarissa Wittenberg, Editor; Mary Swift, Managing Editor; Pat Kolmer, Jeff Richards, Joe Ross, Ross Taylor, Anne Pierce, Editorial Board
P.O. Box 50132
Washington, DC 20091-3066
(202) 638-0515

Poetry, fiction, essays, reviews, plays, interviews, photographs, graphics/artwork.

Bi-monthly tabloid-size journal of arts and literature including poetry, fiction, book and art reviews, essays on the arts, original art work. Emphasis on arts of Washington, D.C. One special issue on single topic each year.

Terence Winch, Doug Lang, Lee Fleming.

Unsolicited Manuscripts Received/Published per Year: 150 fiction, 150 poetry/5-6 fiction, 15-20 poetry.

Payment: $15–20/review, $50–100/article if available.

Reporting Time: 2 months.

Copyright held by magazine; reverts to author upon publication.

1975; 6/yr; 1,500

$12/yr ind, $20/2 yrs, $8.50/yr inst; $2/ea; 40%

Ad Rates: $250/page (16 x 11¼); $175/½ page (8 x 11¼); $135/⅓ page (7⅜ x 8)

ISSN: 0163-903X

WATERWAYS

Barbara Fisher, Richard Alan Spiegel
393 St. Pauls Ave.
Staten Island, NY 10304-2127
(718) 442-7429; (718) 442-4978 FAX

Poetry, graphics.

We publish poets of all ages and types provided we like their work and it pertains to our monthly themes. Our page size is small to encourage portability and accessibility.

Joanne Seltzer, Kit Knight, Arthur Winfield Knight, Albert Huffstickler, Ida Fasel.
Unsolicited Manuscripts Received/ Published per Year: 200/20.
Reading Period: year–round.
Payment: 1 copy.
Reporting Time: 1 month.
Copyright held by Ten Penny Players; reverts to author upon publication.
1977; 11/yr; 100–200
$20/yr; $2/ea; 40%–60%
48 pp; 7 x 4¼
ISSN: 0197-4777

WEBSTER REVIEW

Editors
Webster Review
Eng. Dept. SLCC–Meramec
11333 Big Bend Rd.
St. Louis, MO 63122
(314) 432-2657

Poetry, fiction, essays, translation, interviews.

WEBSTER REVIEW emphasizes translations of contemporary fiction, poetry and essays. We look for quality original work in those categories. We are particularly open at this time to nonfiction of a general literary nature.

William Stafford, Jared Carter, Barbara Lefcowitz, Charles Edward Easton, Etelvina Astrada.
Unsolicited Manuscripts Received/ Published per Year: 1,200/50.
Payment: in copies.
Copyright held by magazine; reverts to author upon publication.
1974; 1/yr; 1,100
$5/yr; $2.50/ea; 40%
128 pp; 5½ x 8½
ISSN: 0363-1230

WEST BRANCH

Karl Patten, Robert Taylor
Bucknell Hall
Bucknell University
Lewisburg, PA 17837
(717) 524-1853

Poetry, fiction, reviews.

A twice-yearly magazine of poetry, fiction, and reviews.

Denise Duhamel, Kathleen George, Harry Humes, Colette Inez, Charles Rafferty.
Unsolicited Manuscripts Received/ Published per Year: 900+/90.
Reading Period: year–round.
Payment: 2 copies and 1 year subscription.
Reporting Time: 6–8 weeks.
Copyright held by magazine; reverts to author upon publication.

1977; 2/yr; 500
$7/yr, $11/2 yrs; $4/ea
88–106 pp; 5½ x 8½
No ads
ISSN: 0149-6441

WEST HILLS REVIEW
William Fahey
246 Old Walt Whitman Rd.
Huntington Station, NY 11746
(516) 427-5240
Poetry, essays, photographs, graphics/artwork.
Good lyric poetry. Prose related to Walt Whitman.
John Ciardi, Dave Smith, Gay Wilson Allen, David Ignatow, Edmund Pennant.
Payment: none.
Reporting Time: 3 months.
Copyright held by magazine; reverts to author upon publication.
1979; 1/yr; 500
$5/yr; $5/ea; 50%
125 pp; 5 x 8

WESTERN HUMANITIES REVIEW
David Kranes, Richard Howard, Barry Weller
3500 UNCO/ University of Utah
Salt Lake City, UT 84112
(801) 581-6070
Poetry, fiction, criticism, essays,
reviews, nonfiction.
We print fiction, poetry, articles on the humanities (we prefer 2–3M words). Our standard is excellence; we publish work by established writers as well as new writers.
Mary Oliver, Charles Simic, Francine Prose, Sandra McPherson, Philip Levine, Joseph Brodsky.
Unsolicited Manuscripts Received/Published per Year: 4,000+/70+.
Reading Period: Oct.–June.
Payment: $50/poem, $150/story-criticism.
Copyright held by magazine.
1947; 4/yr; 1,100
$20/yr ind, $26/yr inst; $6/ea; 40%; 50% to distributors
96 pp; 6 x 9
No ads
ISSN: 0043-3845

WHETSTONE
Barrington Area Arts Council
Sandra Berris, Julie Fleenor, Marsha Portnoy, Jean Tolle
P.O. Box 1266
Barrington, IL 60011
(708) 382-5626
Poetry, short stories, novel excerpts, creative nonfiction.
Prefer to see 3–7 poems or up to 25 pages of fiction or nonfiction. Include SASE.
Reginald Gibbons, Rebecca Rule,

Bill Roorbach, Eleanore Divine, Tom Grimes, Alision Baker, John Jacob, Peyton Houston, Paulette Roeske, Lucia Getsi.
Unsolicited Manuscripts Received/ Published per Year: 1,000+/15-25.
Reading Period: year–round.
Payment: variable. Work accepted is eligible for annual Whetstone Prizes which are cash awards. 1994 prize—$500.
Reporting Time: 3 months.
Copyright reverts to author.
1983; 1/yr; 700
$6.25/ea postpaid; sample copies, including guidelines for The Whetstone Prize, $3.25 post paid; Trade disc.
100–120 pp; 5⅞ x 9
Will consider ads for 1995 issue.

WHISPERS
Stuart David Schiff
70 Highland Ave.
Binghamton, NY 13905
(607) 729-6020
Fiction, criticism, reviews, graphics/artwork.
WHISPERS is a literary magazine of fantasy and horror. The journal publishes original fiction and art as well as news and reviews.
Stephen King, William Nolan, Ray Bradbury, Harlan Ellison, Ray Russell.
Unsolicited Manuscripts Received/ Published per Year: 300/2.
Payment: varies.
Reporting Time: 1–3 months.
Copyright held by Stuart David Schiff; reverts to author upon publication.
1973; 2/yr; 3,000
No subscriptions; 40%
176 pp; 5½ x 8½
Ad Rates: $90/page (4⅜ x 8); $50/½ page (4¾ x 4½); $30/¼ page (4¾ x 2¼)

WHITE CLOUDS REVUE
Scott Preston
P.O. Box 462
Ketchum, ID 83340
Poetry, one prose piece in 4 issues so far.
WCR is a serially-issued journal specifically interested in delineating and suggesting trends in inter-mountain American West Poetics, divergent from those foisted on hapless readers & writers by the homogenized tyranny of regional MFA syndromes and syndicates.
Charles Potts, Ed Dorn, Rosalie Sorrels, Bruce Embree, Peter Boweb, Brooke Medicine Eagle.
Payment: several copies.

Reporting Time: 2 weeks–2
months.
Copyright reverts to author.
1987; 1½/yr; 200+
$12/4 issues; $3.50/ea; 30%
28–44 pp; 7 x 8½

WHOLE NOTES

Nancy Peters Hastings
P.O. Box 1374
Las Cruces, NM 88004
(505) 382-7446
Poetry.
WHOLE NOTES features work
by unknown or beginning writ-
ers as well as established poets.
We welcome writers whose
work is memorable, with fresh
images and authentic emotion.
William Stafford, Harold Witt, Ted
Kooser, and Carole Oles.
Unsolicited Manuscripts Received/
Published per Year: 800/40.
Reading Period: year–round.
Payment: in copies.
Reporting Time: 3 weeks.
Copyright held by Nancy Peters
Hastings.
1984; 2/yr; 400
$6/yr ind & inst; $3/ea; 40%
28 pp; 5½ x 8½
Ad Rates: Contact CLMP for in-
formation.

THE WILLIAM AND MARY REVIEW

Laura Sims
P.O. Box 8795
The College of William & Mary
Williamsburg, VA 23187-8795
(804) 221-3290
Poetry, fiction, criticism, interviews, photographs, graphics/
artwork.
**THE WILLIAM AND MARY
REVIEW** is an internationally-
distributed literary magazine
published by undergraduate stu-
dents of The College of William
and Mary, without faculty su-
pervision or censorship. It is the
express purpose of **THE WIL-
LIAM AND MARY REVIEW**
to publish the work of established writers as well as that
of—and with an emphasis
on—new, vital voices.
Amy Clampitt, Julie Agoos, Carole Glickfeld, David Ignatow,
Dana Gioia, Robert Hershon,
Elizabeth Alexander, W. D.
Snodgrass, Cornelius Eady.
Unsolicited Manuscripts Received/
Published per Year: 300/10.
Reading Period: Sept.–Apr.
Payment: in copies.
Copyright held by College of William and Mary and Editor; re-
verts to author upon publication.
1962; 1/yr; 3,500

$5.50/yr ind, $8/yr inst; $6/ea;
40%
120 pp; 6 x 9
ISSN: 0043-5600

WILLOW REVIEW
Paulette Roeske
19351 West Washington St.
Grayslake, IL 60030
(708) 223-6601 ext. 555
Poetry, short fiction, creative nonfiction.
WILLOW REVIEW is a flat-
spined annual which publishes
poetry, short fiction and creative
nonfiction (up to 4,000 words).
Its orientation is toward high
quality, literary work as opposed to genre fiction and light
verse.
Lisel Mueller, Garrett Hongo, Lu-
cien Stryk, Diane Ackerman,
David Ray, Gregory Orr, Gloria
Naylor.
Unsolicited Manuscripts Received/
Published per Year: 1,500/30-
35.
Reading Period: year-round, with
publication in April.
Payment: Awards of $100, $50,
and $25 in both prose and po-
etry each year for work deemed
best of issue; payment in copies.
Reporting Time: 1-2 months.

Copyright reverts to author upon
publication.
1969; 1/yr; 1,000
$13/3 years; $20/5 issues; $5/ea;
40%
84 pp; 6 x 9
ISSN: 1068-2546
Ad Rates: $125/page (4¼ x 7);
$75/½ page (4¼ x 3½); $50/¼
page (2⅛ x 3½).

WILLOW SPRINGS
Nance Van Winckel
MS-1 526 5th St.
Eastern Washington University
Cheney, WA 99004-2431
(509) 458-6429
Poetry, fiction, essays, reviews,
translation, interviews.
WILLOW SPRINGS is commit-
ted to the imagination and the
power of language fully en-
gaged in the act of telling. We
publish high quality poetry, fic-
tion, translation, essays, and art.
Russell Edson, Thomas Lux, Al-
berto Rios, Madeline DeFrees,
Olga Broumas, Jane Miller,
Donald Revell, Charlie Smith.
Unsolicited Manuscripts Received/
Published per Year: 1,000/50.
Reading Period: Sept. 15 – May
15.
Payment: small honorarium plus 2
copies on publication.
Reporting Time: 6 weeks.

Copyright reverts to author.
1977; 2/yr; 1,000
$7/yr; $4/ea; 40%
104 pp; 6 x 9
Ad Rates: $125/page (4¼ x 7);
$75/½ page (4¼ x 3½); $50/¼
page (2⅛ x 3½)
ISSN: 0739-1277
Pacific Pipeline, Small Changes

WIND

Steven R. Cope, Charlie G.
Hughes
P.O. Box 24548
Lexington, KY 40524
Poetry, fiction, essays, reviews of
small press publications.
Focus and emphasis are on the
writers who have something
special to say: nothing cold and
lifeless. WIND is highly eclec-
tic; any form, subject matter or
approach.
Peter Wild, Larry Rubin, T.M.
McNally, Richard E. Brown,
Carolyn Osborn.
Unsolicited Manuscripts Received/
Published per Year: 4,200/2%
Payment: in copies.
Reporting Time: 2–4 weeks.
Copyright held by author.
1971; 2/yr; 450
$10/yr ind, $12/yr inst, $15/yr for-
eign; $6.00/ea; $3.50/backissue
100 pp; 5½ x 8¼; perfect bound.
ISSN: 0361-2481

WINDFALL

Ron Ellis
Friends of Poetry
c/o Department of English
University of Wisconsin
Whitewater, WI 53190
(414) 472-1036
Poetry.
We are interested in short, intense,
highly-crafted poems in any
form. Longer poems occasion-
ally considered. No xerox or dot
matrix.
William Stafford, Ralph Mills,
Francine Sterle, Sheila Murphy,
Joanne Hart.
Unsolicited Manuscripts Received/
Published per Year: 400/30.
Payment: contributor's copies.
Reporting Time: 8 weeks.
Copyright held by Friends of Po-
etry; reverts to author upon pub-
lication.
1979; 2/yr; 400
$5/yr; $3/ea
40 pp; 5½ x 8½
ISSN: 0893-3375

THE WINDLESS ORCHARD

Robert Novak
English Department
Indiana University
2101 East Coliseum
Fort Wayne, IN 46805
(219) 483-6845
Poetry, criticism, review, photo-

graphs, graphics/artwork.
Our muse is interested only in the beautiful, the sacred, and the erotic. Excited, organic forms, with thinking and feeling done in imagery and epigram.
Ruth Moon Kempher, Elliot Richman, Mike Martone, Michael Emery.
Unsolicited Manuscripts Received/ Published per Year: 920/44.
Payment: 2 copies.
Reporting Time: 1 week and up.
Copyright reverts to author.
1970; irregular; 320
$10/yr; $4/ea
52 pp; 5½ x 8
No ads

WINDSOR REVIEW: A Journal of the Arts

Wanda Campbell
Department of English
University of Windsor
Windsor, Ontario, N9B 3P4
CANADA
(519) 253-4232 ext. 2332
Poetry, short stories.
Publishes poetry and short fiction. We subscribe to no particular school or "ism."
Walter McDonald, Lyn Lifshin, W.P. (Bill) Kinsella, Deborah Joy Cory.
Unsolicited Manuscripts Received/ Published per Year: 10/stories, 52/poems in a volume year (2 issues).
Payment: $50/story; $15/poem.
Reporting Time: 6–8 weeks.
Copyright reverts to author.
1965; 2/yr; 450
$12/yr; $6/ea; Canada: indiv: $21.35; inst: $32.05, USA and others: indiv: $19.95; inst:$29.95.
100 pp; 6 x 9
ISSN: 0042-0352

WITHOUT HALOS

Frank Finale, Lora Dunetz, Barbara Finale, H.G. Stacy, Donna Sharp.
P.O. Box 1342
Pt. Pleasant Beach, NJ 08742
Poetry, graphics/artwork.
We consider all types of poetry—mainstream, avant-garde, haiku, light verse, etc. We judge each poem not on a poet's name but on the passion it displays, the honesty of its roots.
Harold Witt, Ted Weiss, Gale Elen Harvey, Margaret Diorio, Robert Cooperman, Philip Murray.
Unsolicited Manuscripts Received/ Published per Year: 1,000/80.
Reading Period: Jan.–June 30.
Payment: 1 copy.
Reporting Time: 3–4 months.
Copyright held by author.

1983; 1/yr; 1,000
$6.25/ea
112 pp; 8½ x 5½
No ads
ISSN: 1052-3162

1987; 2/yr
192 pp; 6 x 9
Ad Rates: $100/page (5 x 7);
$60/½ page (5 x 3½)
ISSN: 0891-1371
DeBoer, Ingram, Fine Print

WITNESS

Peter Stine
Oakland Community College
27055 Orchard Lake Rd.
Farmington Hills, MI 48334
(313) 471-7740
Fiction, essays, poetry, interviews, photographs, graphics/artwork.
WITNESS presents nationally known writers, as well as new talent, and highlights the role of the modern writer as witness. The magazine features a diverse selection of writings—fiction, poetry, essays, journalism, interviews—and regularly devotes every other issue to illuminating a single subject of wide concern.
Gordon Lish, Joyce Carol Oates, Robert Coover, Lynn Sharon Schwartz, Madison Smartt Bell.
Unsolicited Manuscripts Received/ Published per Year: 1,000/20.
Reading Period: year–round.
Payment: $6/page for prose, $10/page for poetry.
Reporting Time: 2–3 months.
Copyright held by magazine; reverts to author upon publication.

WOMAN POET

Elaine Dallman
P.O. Box 60550
Reno, NV 89506
(702) 972-1671
Poetry, criticism, photos, interviews.
The West, the East, and the Midwest.
Marilyn Hacker, Lisel Mueller, Judith Minty, Rosalie Moore.
Unsolicited Manuscripts Received/ Published per Year: 150/varies.
$12.95/ea paperback; $19.95/ea hardcover. Resale discount varies.

WOMEN & PERFORMANCE: A JOURNAL OF FEMINIST THEORY

Editorial Board; Judy Burns, Jennifer Fink, Judy Rosenthal, Leslie Satin, Jill Lane, Amanda Barrett
721 Broadway, 6th Fl.
New York, NY 10003
(212) 998-1625
Essays, criticism, plays, reviews,

interviews, translation.
Hélène Cixous, Marianne Gold-
berg, Sue-Ellen Case, Jill
Dolan, Lila Abu Lugnod, E.
Ann Kaplan, Peggy Phelan,
Lucy Fischer.
Number of Unsolicited Manu-
scripts Received/Published per
Year: 50/1-2
Reading Period: Sept.–June.
$14/yr ind, $25/yr inst; $7/ea;
$9/back issue; 40%

THE WOMEN'S REVIEW OF BOOKS

Linda Gardiner
Wellesley College Center for Re-
search on Women
Wellesley, MA 02181
(617) 283-2087
Reviews, poetry.
In-depth reviews of books by and
about women, in all areas, both
academic and general-interest;
feminist in orientation but not
committed to any one brand of
feminism or any specific politi-
cal position.
June Jordan, Diane Wakoski,
Gerda Lerner, Michelle Cliff,
Jane Marcus.
Unsolicited Manuscripts Received/
Published per Year: 60/2.
Payment: varies, $75 minimum.
Reporting Time: 1 month–6
weeks.

Copyright held by magazine; reverts to author upon publication.
1983; 11/yr; 15,000
$18/yr ind, $30/yr inst: $2/ea; 40%
32 pp; 10 x 15
Ad Rates: $1,520 (page/10 x 15);
$840/½ page (10 x 7½);
$435/¼ page (4¾ x 7½)
ISSN: 0738-1433

WOMEN'S WORDS: A JOURNAL OF CAROLINA WRITING

Lisa Granered, Editor; Elaine
Selden, Designer
128 E. Hargett St., Suite 10
Raleigh, NC 27601
(919) 829-3711
Poetry, some fiction and essay,
graphics.
WOMEN'S WORDS is a journal
seeking to promote women writ-
ers in North Carolina.
Jaki Shelton-Green, Tara Allan,
Laura Bolger.
Payment: none.
Copyright held by the Women's
Center, reverts to author upon
publication.
1992; 1/yr; 1,000
$11/yr; $11/ea; 40%
100 pp; 8½ x7
ISSN: 1069-4609

WOMEN'S WORK

Andrea Damm
606 Ave. A

Snohomish, WA 98290

(206) 568-5914

Articles, interviews, biography, fiction & poetry.

Publishes previously unpublished and emerging writers, writers of diverse cultural and economic backgrounds; explores traditional and modern definitions and expressions of "Women's Work."

Carole Bellacera, Sue Pace, Sibyl James.

Unsolicited Manuscripts Received/ Published per Year: 750/50–60.

Reading Period: year–round.

Payment: currently in copies and subscription.

Reporting Time: 2–6 months.

Copyright: first serial rights.

1991; 6/yr; 6,000

$12/yr; $4/ea; 40%

32–48 pp; 8½ x 11

Ad Rates: write or call for quote

ISSN: 1058-4870

THE WORCESTER REVIEW

Rodger Martin

6 Chatham St.

Worcester, MA 01609

(508) 797-4770 or (603) 924-7342

Poetry, fiction, criticism, essays, graphics/artwork, photographs.

We look for quality poetry and fiction, and also articles and essays about poetry that have a New England connection.

Stephen Dunn, Walter McDonald, William Stafford, Kathleen Spivack, Stanley Kunitz.

Payment: 2 copies plus honorarium dependant upon grants.

Reporting Time: 4–5 months.

Copyright held by Worcester Review of the Worcester County Poetry Assoc.; reverts to author upon publication.

1973; 1/yr; 1,000

$10/yr; $6/ea; $5 sample; 40%

150 pp; 6 x 9

Ad Rates: $195/page; $100/½ page; $55/¼ page

ISSN: 8756-5277

THE WORLD

Editor

c/o St. Mark's Church

10th St. & 2nd Ave.

New York, NY 10003

(212) 674-0910

Poetry, fiction.

A magazine of experimental writing.

Lorenzo Thomas, Chris Tysh, Ron Padgett.

Payment: none.

Reporting Time: 3 weeks.

Copyright held by author.

1966; 3/yr; 500

$20/4 issues; $5/ea

122 pp; 6 x 9

ISSN: 0043-8154

SPD

WORLD LETTER

Jon Cone
2726 E. Court St.
Iowa City, IA 52245
(319) 337-6022
E-mail: jcone@ins.infonet.net
Poetry, short prose, translations.
An international literary review.
Do not send unsolicited manuscripts. Query first.
Cesar Vallejo, Charles Bukowski, Edouard Roditi, Cid Corman.
Unsolicited Manuscripts Received/ Published per Year: 200/1.
Payment: in copies.
Reporting Time: 1 week or as soon as possible.
Copyright reverts to author upon publication.
1991; 1/yr; 200–300
$6/yr; $6/ea; 40%
48 pp; 6½ x 10
ISSN: 1054-8823
Water Row Books, Longhouse Books, Anton Mikofsky, Alyscamp Press

THE WORMWOOD REVIEW

Marvin Malone
P.O. Box 4698
Stockton, CA 95204-0698
(209) 466-8231
Poetry, reviews, translation, graphics/artwork.
Poetry and prose-poems reflecting the temper and depth of the present time. All types and schools from traditional-economic through concrete, dada and extreme avant-garde. Special fondness for prose poems and fables. Each issue has a special section devoted to one poet or topic. One chapbook per year.
Charles Bukowski, Lyn Lifshin, Ronald Koertge, Gerald Locklin, Judson Crews.
Unsolicited Manuscripts Received/ Published per Year: 6,000+/350+.
Payment: 3–6 copies of magazine or cash equivalent.
Copyright held by Wormwood Books & Magazines; reverts to author upon request.
1959; 4/yr; 700
$12/yr ind, $12/yr inst; $4/ea;
48 pp; 5½ x 8½
ISSN: 0043-9401

THE WRITERS' BAR-B-Q

Editorial Board: Timothy Osburn, Becky Bradway, Gary Smith, Marcia Womack, and Myra Epping
924 Bryn Mawr Blvd.
Springfield, IL 62703
(217) 525-6987
Fiction, photographs, graphics/artwork.
THE WRITERS' BAR-B-Q publishes stories and novel ex-

cerpts. Our preference is for realistic work that has strong characterization and story. We are looking for excellent, spirited, daring writing from all genres. We encourage work by gays and lesbians, people of color, and other writers who may have trouble fitting into the usual venues. Our idea is to publish good stories, and to have fun doing it. **THE WRITERS' BAR-B-Q** is a potluck of styles, subjects and characters. Almost all stories are fully illustrated.

Lowry Pei, Sharon Sloan Fiffer, Michael C. White, Martha M.

Vertreace, Shannon Keith Kelley, Nolan Porterfield, Deborah Insel, Paul Lisicky.

Payment: 3 copies, upon publication.

Copyright held by Sangamon Writers, Inc.; reverts to author upon publication.

1987; 1–2/yr; 1,000.

$10/yr; $5/ea

100 pp; 8½ x 11

Ad Rates: $75/½ page (4½ x 7½); inquire.

DeBoer

WRITERS FORUM

Alex Blackburn, Editor; Craig Lesley, Bret Lott, Fiction Editors; Victoria McCabe, Poetry Editor; Robert Dassanovsky–Harris, Managing Editor; Paul Scott Malone, Corresponding Editor

University of Colorado at Colorado Springs

Colorado Springs, CO 80933-7150

(719) 599-4023

Poetry, fiction.

We want the finest in contemporary short story and poetry, with some focus and emphasis on the trans-Mississippi West with its varieties of place and experience.

Gladys Swan, Ron Carlson, Frank Waters, Robert Olen Butler, Yusef Komunyakaa.

Unsolicited Manuscripts Received/ Published per Year: 600/35.

Payment: none.

Reporting Time: 3–6 weeks.

Copyright held by UCCS; reverts to author upon publication.

1974; 1/yr; 1,000

Note: Our prices now include cost of postage.

$10/yr ind, $8.20/yr inst; $10/ea

200 pp; 8½ x 5½

WRITER'S JOURNAL

Valerie Hockert

3585 N. Lexington Ave.

Suite 328

Arden Hills, MN 55112

(612) 486-7818

Essays, poetry, reviews, criticism, interviews, commentaries, writing techniques.

Provides writers and poets with practical advice and guidance, motivation and authorative instruction in the craft of writing. Includes book reviews, software reviews, poetry, advice and references.

Anthony Vasquez, Betty Ulrich, Ester M. Leiper, Cheryl Kempf.

Unsolicited Manuscripts Received/ Published per Year: 600/36.

Payment: variable.

Reporting Time: 2–6 weeks.

Copyright held by Minnesota Ink, Inc., reverts to author upon publication.

1980; 6/yr; 49,000

$14/yr; $4/ea; 50%

48 pp; 8 x 10½

Ad Rates: $845/page (6¾ x 8½); $465/½ page (6¾ x 4¼ or 3⅛ x 8 ½)

ISSN: 0891-9759

Ingram, Armadillo, IPD, Fine Print, ADS

X

XANADU

Mildred M. Jeffrey, Weslea Sidon,
Lois V. Walker, SueKain
Box 773
Huntington, NY 11743
(516) 691-2376

Poetry, essays.

XANADU publishes contemporary
poetry and articles on poetry.

Karen Swenson, David Ignatow,
Edmund Pennant, William
Stafford.

Unsolicited Manuscripts Received/
Published per Year: 500/30.

Reading Period: Sept.–June.

Payment: 1 copy per contributor.

Reporting Time: 3 months.

Copyright reverts to author upon
publication.

1975; 1/yr; 300

$5/ea 20%–40%

64–76 pp; 5½ x 8½

ISSN: 0146-0463

XAVIER REVIEW

Thomas Bonner, Jr., Editor;
Robert E. Skinner, Managing Ediitor
Box 110C, Xavier University
New Orleans, LA 70125
(504) 483-7304 (504) 486-7411

Poetry, fiction, criticism, essays,
reviews, translation, interviews.

XAVIER REVIEW is interested
in the usual genres of literature
and articles in the area of Black
literature, Southern literature,
religion and literature and Latin
American literature (although
not exclusively).

Alex Haley, Andrew Salkey, Fred
Chappell, John Keller, Gordon
Osing, James Baldwin, Andre
Dubus, Ernest J. Gaines, Patty
Friedmann.

Unsolicited Manuscripts Received/
Published per Year: 300/35.

Payment: none.

Reporting Time: 2 months.

Copyright held by magazine.
1980; 2/yr; 500
$10/year ind, $15/year inst;
  $5/each; 40%
70-75 pp; 6 x 9
ISSN: 0887-6681

xib
Tolek
P.O. Box 262112,
San Diego, Ca 92126
(619) 298-4927
Poems, drawings, photos, Fiction.
Writing and visual. Gritty, tight,
  slick, lean, tasty. Visual and
  writing.

Gerald Locklin, Richard Kostelan-
  etz, Oberc.
Unsolicited Manuscripts Received/
  Published per Year: 2,000/4%.
Reading Period: year–round.
Payment: 1 copy.
Reporting Time: 2½ weeks.
Copyright: Yes—First time author
  rights.
1990; 2/yr; 500
$10/year; $5/ea; 35%
54 pp; 8½ x 7
Ad Rates: varies, inquire
ISSN: 1058-420x

Y

YARROW

Harry Humes, Editor; Arnold
 Newman, Associate Editor
English Department
Kutztown University
Kutztown, PA 19530
(215) 683-4353

Poetry, interviews.

A journal of poetry.

William Pitt Root, Gerald Stern,
 John Engels, Gibbons Ruark,
 Lola Haskins, Fleda Brown
 Jackson, Sally Jo Sorenson.

Unsolicited Manuscripts Received/
 Published per Year:
 400–500/50-95.

Reading Period: year–round.

Payment: in copies.

Reporting Time: 1 month.

1981; 2/yr; 350

$5/2 yrs; $1.50/ea

36 pp; 6 x 9

YELLOW SILK: Journal of Erotic Arts

Lily Pond
P.O. Box 6374
Albany, CA 94706
(510) 644-4188

Fiction, poetry, essays, reviews,
 translations, photography,
 graphics/artwork, fine arts, science fiction, humor.

**YELLOW SILK: Journal of
 Erotic Arts:** Stunning sophisti-
 cated stories and poems meet
 explicit photographs and paintings in what may be the world's
 only fine literary magazine that
 is unabashedly erotic.

Marilyn Hacker, Galway Kinnell,
 Sharon Olds, Mary Oliver,
 Louise Erdrich.

Payment: 3 copies, 1 year subscription, and varying cash payments.

Reporting Time: approximately 3 months.

Copyright reverts to author after one year following publication; the magazine keeps non-exclusive reprint, electronic, and anthology rights.

1981; 4/yr; 16,000

$30/yr ind, $38/yr inst; $7.50/ea; 40%

60 pp; 8½ x 11

ISSN: 0736-9212

Bookpeople, Inland, Ingram, Ubiquity

YET ANOTHER SMALL MAGAZINE

Candace Catlin Hall

Box 14353

Hartford, CT 06114

(203) 549-6723

Poetry.

YASM publishes short, imagistic poems—special interest in lesser known poets— started broadside inclusion highlighting a single poem.

Lyn Lifshin, Charles Darling, Pat Bridges, Sister Mary Ann Henn, Neil Grill.

Reading Period: Aug. 1–Oct. 31.

Payment: in copies.

Reporting Time: November.

Copyright reverts to author.

1981; 1/yr; 300

$1.98/ea

8–12 pp; 11 x 17

ISSN: 0278-9442

Z

ZEBRA, a journal of literature & opinion
Mario Gortwin
P.O. Box 421584
San Francisco, CA 94142
(415) 753-4600
Poetry, fiction, nonfiction. No romance per se.
Leonard Sanazaro, Phyllis Stowell.
Unsolicited Manuscripts Received/
Published per Year: 1,100/200.
Payment: copies.
Reporting Time: 6–8 weeks.
Copyright reverts on publication.
1990; 2/yr; 200
$10/yr; $6/ea; 40%
56–80 pp; 5½ x 8½
Ad Rates: query
ISSN 1052-4967

ZUKUNFT
Prof. Yonia Fain, Joseph Mlotek, Matis Olitzki, Morris Steingart
25 East 21st St.
New York, NY 10010
Poetry, fiction, criticism, essays, reviews.
The **ZUKUNFT** is an independent literary publication. It serves as a vehicle for writers from many countries and is concerned with problems of Jewish life throught the world. In 1992 the **ZUKUNFT**, the oldest continously published Yiddish journal in the world, is celebrating its centennial. It has served to stimulate literary creativity for generations throughout Yiddish speaking communities.
Unsolicited Manuscripts Received/
Published per Year: 60/7.
Reading Period (Yiddish mss.): year–round.
Copyright held by Congress for Jewish Culture; reverts to author upon publication.

1892; 6/yr; 2,500
$25/yr ind; $3/ea; 20%
44 pp; 7½ x 10½
Ad Rates: $100/page; $50/½ page;
$25/¼ page

**ZUZU'S PETALS QUAR-
TERLY**

T. Dunn, Editor-in-Chief, D. Du-
Cap, Associate Editor
P.O. Box 4476
Allentown, PA 18105-4476
(610) 821-1324

Literary fiction, essays, poetry,
articles, book reviews, chapbook
reviews.

Our magazine is a celebration of
all aspects of the human experience, and is named after Jimmy
Stewart's daughter in the film
classic "It's A Wonderful Life".
Library Journal describes it as,
"an exciting new little." (November 1993, *LJ*)

Max Greenberg, Gayle Elen Harvey, Mark Soifer, Laura Telford.
Unsolicited Manuscripts Received/
Published per Year: approx.
2,000/100.

Payment: 1 contributor's copy.
Reporting Time: 2 weeks–2
months
1991; 4/yr; 350

$17/yr; $5/ea; $3/yr discount
50 pp; 8½ x 11
No ads
ISSN 1060-9571

ZYZZYVA

Howard Junker
41 Sutter St., Suite 1400
San Francisco, CA 94104
(415) 255-1282

Fiction, essays, plays, poetry,
translations, photographs, prints,
drawings.

West Coast writers, artists, and
publishers.

Sherman Alexie, Dorothy Allison,
Kate Braverman, Ethan Canin,
Greg Sarnis, William T. Voll-
mann.

Unsolicited Manuscripts Received/
Published per Year: 4,000/40.

Payment: $50–$250.
Reporting Time: prompt.
Copyright held by magazine; re-
verts to author upon publication.
1985; 4/yr; 4,800
$28/yr ind, $36/yr inst; $9/ea
160 pp; 6 x 9
Ad Rates: $500/page (5 x 7¾);
$300/½ page (5 x 3¹³⁄₁₆);
$200/¼ page (2⁷⁄₁₆ x 3¹³⁄₁₆)
ISSN: 8756-5633
Bookpeople, Ingram, SPD

INDEX BY STATE

NORTH CAROLINA